PARIS

TOP SIGHTS, AUTHENTIC EXPERIENCES

Catherine Le Nevez,
Christopher Pitts, Nicola Williams,
Damian Harper

Contents

Plan Your Trip
This Year in Paris

2019

Paris

Art fairs, music festivals, open-air cinema and epicurean events are just some of the highlights of Paris' calendar in 2019, with many more in the works: check www.parisinfo.com for updates.

Clockwise from above: Bastille Day parade (p12); Paris Plages (p12); French Open (p10)

artre &
rn Paris

artre's en-
g hilly streets
he red-light
district, home
Moulin Rouge.
249)

lique du
é-Cœur

re & Les Halles
et streets fan out
nd the mighty
re and the
g-edge Centre
oidou.
p250)

Centre Pompidou ⓐ

Musée National Picasso ⓐ

ainte-
apelle ⓞ

ⓞ
Notre Dame

Jardin des Plantes ⓞ

ⓡ Gare de Lyon

ⓡ Gare d'Austerlitz

tin Quarter
ome to beautiful
tanic gardens and
cked with vibrant
udent haunts.
Map p252)

ⓝ 0   2 km
0   1 mile

Le Marais, Ménilmontant & Belleville
Hip boutiques, bars
and restaurants,
and a celebrity-filled
cemetery. (Map p254)

◉ Cimetière du Père Lachaise

The Islands
Notre Dame domi-
nates the larger Île
de la Cité, while little
Île St-Louis is graced
with elegant build-
ings. (Map p254)

Bastille & Eastern Paris
The Parisians' Paris,
with fabulous markets,
intimate gourmet
bistros and lively
drinking and dancing
venues. (Map p254)

Welcome to Paris

Paris' seemingly timeless monument-lined boulevards, magnificent museums, classical bistros and chic boutiques are being enhanced by a new wave of multimedia galleries, cocktail bars, design shops and tech start-ups.

The French capital is awash with landmarks – the Eiffel Tower, Arc de Triomphe and Notre Dame among them – along with a trove of specialist museums and galleries. Creamy-stone, grey-metal-roofed apartment buildings, lamp-lit bridges and geometrically laid-out formal parks are equally integral to the city's fabric.

Contrary to its magnificently preserved cityscapes, however, *la Ville Lumière* (the City of Light; a moniker Paris acquired due to its leading role in the Age of Enlightenment) has never stood still, but has constantly evolved, spearheading industrial, artistic, scientific and architectural endeavours. This innovative spirit continues today, with pioneering green transport initiatives and dazzling new architectural projects that include skyscraping towers along the periphery and re-energised urban spaces, many as part of the city's ambitious Grand Paris (Greater Paris) expansion. Creativity is evident everywhere, from neobistro kitchens and cutting-edge bars to fashion ateliers and vibrant street art, plus a new digital art museum in a former foundry and the 1920s former railway depot housing Station F, the world's largest start-up hub.

la Ville Lumière has never stood still, but has constantly evolved...

Statue on the Pont Alexandre III over the Seine
AERIAL-MOTION/SHUTTERSTOCK ©

★ PARIS ★

St-Germain & Les Invalides
Literature lovers and fashionistas flock to this fabled cafe- and boutique-filled Left Bank neighbourhood. *(Map p246)*

Montm Northe
Montm chanti adjoin Pigalle to the *(Map*

Bas Sac

Arc de Triomphe ⊚

Champs-Élysées ⊚

Champs-Élysées & Grands Boulevards
Paris' grandest avenue, with art nouveau department stores and a 19th-century opera house. *(Map p246)*

Gare St-Lazare

Palais Garnier ⊚

Lou
Mar arou Lou cutt Pom *(Ma*

Jardin des Tuileries ❶

Seine

Eiffel Tower ⊚

Hôtel des Invalides ❶

Musée Rodin 🏛

Musée d'Orsay 🏛

Louvre 🏛

S C

Monnaie de Paris

Eiffel Tower & Western Paris
Stately boulevards flank the city's signature spire and major museums. *(Map p246)*

Jardin du Luxembourg ❶

Gare Montparnasse

Les Catacombes ⊚

Montparnasse & Southern Paris
Brasseries from the mid-20th-century and re-energised back-streets buzz with local life. *(Map p246)*

L
H b p s *(*

2019

EVER/SHUTTERSTOCK ©

JIMMIE48 PHOTOGRAPHY/SHUTTERSTOCK ©

★ Top Festivals & Events
Paris Plages, July (p12)
Bastille Day, July (p12)
Paris Cocktail Week, January (p6)
French Open, May (p10)
Nuit Blanche, October (p15)

Plan Your Trip
This Year in Paris

January

The frosty first month of the year isn't the most festive in Paris, but cocktails – as well as the winter soldes (sales) – brighten the mood.

✱ Epiphany   6 Jan
On this Christian feast day (aka Three Kings' Day), patisseries bake frangipane-filled puff-pastry *galettes des rois* (kings' cakes), which conceal a *fève* (small trinket). Whoever finds the *fève* is crowned 'king' for the day and wears the cardboard crown that comes with the cake.

✱ Louis XVI Commemorative Mass   20 Jan
On the Sunday closest to 21 January, royalists and right-wingers attend a mass at the Chapelle Expiatoire (www.monuments-nationaux.fr) marking the execution by guillotine of King Louis XVI in 1793.

♟ Paris Cocktail Week   Late Jan
Each of the 75-plus cocktail bars all over the city that take part in Paris Cocktail Week (https://pariscocktailweek.fr) creates two signature cocktails for the

✱ Outdoor Ice Skating
Each winter, ice-skating rinks pop up all over the city, including in some truly picturesque spots, such as beneath or within the Eiffel Tower. Skating is usually free but you'll need to pay for skate hire. Venues and dates change annually.

event. There are also workshops, guest bartenders, masterclasses and food pairings. Sign up for a free pass for cut-price cocktails.

Top: *Galette des rois* (kings' cake) for Epiphany;
Bottom: Ice skating outside the Hôtel de Ville

February

Festivities still aren't in full swing in February, but couples descend on France's romantic capital for Valentine's Day, when virtually all restaurants offer special menus.

☆ Chinese New Year   5 Feb

Paris' largest lantern-lit festivities and dragon parades for Chinese New Year take place in the city's main Chinatown in the 13e. Parades are also held in Belleville and Le Marais.

◉ Rétromobile   6–10 Feb

Some 600 vintage cars are displayed over five days in early February at the Parc des Expositions at Porte de Versailles, 15e during this motor enthusiasts' showcase (www.retromobile.com).

◉ Michael Jackson: On the Wall   Until 17 Feb

The influence of the King of Pop on artists such as Andy Warhol is explored at this exhibition inside Paris' art nouveau Grand Palais (www.grandpalais.fr).

✗ Salon International de l'Agriculture   23 Feb–3 Mar

At this appetising nine-day international agricultural fair (www.salon-agriculture. com) from late February to early March, produce and animals from all over France are turned into delectable fare at the Parc des Expositions at Porte de Versailles, 15e.

Above: Chinese New Year parade

Plan Your Trip
This Year in Paris

OLGA BESNARD/SHUTTERSTOCK ©

March

Blooms appear in Paris' parks and gardens, leaves start greening the city's avenues and festivities begin to flourish. And days get longer – the last Sunday morning of the month ushers in daylight-saving time.

✼ Livre Paris   15–18 Mar
France's largest international book fair (www.livreparis.com) takes place over four days in mid-March at the Parc des Expositions at Porte de Versailles, 15e.

☆ Printemps du Cinéma   Mid-Mar
Selected cinemas across Paris offer filmgoers a unique entry fee of €4 per session over three days sometime around the middle of March (www.printempsdu cinema.com).

⚑ La Verticale
de la Tour Eiffel   Mid-Mar
Elite athletes and amateur runners, drawn from a lottery, scale the stairs of the Eiffel Tower during this vertical race (www. verticaletoureiffel.fr) in mid-March.

🛅 Foire de Chatou   Mid-Mar
Some 500 antique and secondhand dealers, jewellers and art galleries set up at this 10-day fair (www.foiredechatou.com)

held in mid-March on the île des Impressionnistes, a 10-minute journey by RER A to Rueil-Malmaison with a free shuttle from the station.

☆ Banlieues
Bleues   Mid-Mar–Mid-Apr
Big-name acts perform during the Suburban Blues (www.banlieuesbleues.org) jazz, blues and R&B festival from mid-March to mid-April at venues in Paris' northern suburbs.

☆ Cinéma
du Réel   Late Mar–Early Apr
Dozens of French and international documentary films screen both in and out of competition at this prestigious 10-day festival (www.cinemadureel.org), which takes place at venues including the Centre Pompidou from late March to early April.

Above: Book stall, Livre Paris

April

Sinatra sang about April in Paris, and the month sees the city's 'charm of spring' in full swing, with chestnuts blossoming and cafe terraces coming into their own.

🏃 Salon du Running   Early Apr

In the run-up to the Marathon International de Paris, early April's three-day Salon du Running (www.salondurunning.fr) draws over 80,000 visitors (including competitors picking up their bibs) and 200-plus professional exhibitors at the Parc des Expositions, Porte de Versailles, 15e.

🏃 Marathon International de Paris   14 Apr

On your marks...the Paris International Marathon (www.schneiderelectricparis marathon.com), usually held on the second Sunday of April, starts on the av des Champs-Élysées, 8e, and finishes on av Foch, 16e, attracting 57,000 runners from 144 countries at last count.

🎡 Foire du Trône   Mid-Apr–Early Jun

Dating back over a millennium, from 957 AD, this huge funfair is held on the Pelouse de Reuilly of the Bois de Vincennes from around Easter to early June.

🎡 Foire de Paris   Late Apr–Early May

Gadgets, widgets, food and wine feature at this huge contemporary-living fair (www.foiredeparis.fr), held from late April to early May at the Parc des Expositions at Porte de Versailles, 15e.

Above: Rides, Foire du Trône

Plan Your Trip

This Year in Paris

May

The temperate month of May has more public holidays than any other in France. Watch out for widespread closures, particularly on May Day (1 May).

👁 La Nuit Européenne des Musées 18 May
Key museums across Paris stay open late for the European Museums Night (http://nuitdesmusees.culturecommunication.gouv.fr). Most offer free entry.

🍴 Taste Paris Mid-May
A highlight on foodies' calendars, mid-May's four-day gourmet festival Taste Paris (https://paris.tastefestivals.com) incorporates tastings, cooking classes and demonstrations by some of Paris' most acclaimed chefs.

👁 Portes Ouvertes des Ateliers d'Artistes de Belleville Late May
More than 200 painters, sculptors and other artists at over 120 Belleville studios open their doors to visitors over four days (Friday to Monday) in late May (http://ateliers-artistes-belleville.fr).

🏃 French Open Late May–Early Jun
The glitzy Internationaux de France de Tennis Grand Slam (www.rolandgarros.com) hits up from late May to early June at Stade Roland Garros at the Bois de Boulogne.

👁 Art St-Germain des Prés Late May–Early Jun
Dozens of galleries in St-Germain des Prés come together over two weeks from late May to early June to showcase their top artists (www.artsaintgermaindespres.com).

Top: Photography exhibition, Art St-Germain des Prés; Bottom: Crowds at the French Open

NEIL ANTON DUMAS/SHUTTERSTOCK ©

06

June

Paris is positively jumping in June, thanks to warm temperatures, a host of outdoor events and long daylight hours, with twilight lingering until nearly 11pm.

🍷 Paris Beer Week   Early Jun

Craft beer's popularity in Paris peaks during Paris Beer Week (www.laparisbeerweek.com), held, despite the name, over 10 days in early June, when events take place across the city's bars, pubs, breweries, specialist beer shops and other venues.

☆ Paris Jazz Festival   Mid-Jun–Jul

Jazz concerts swing every Saturday and Sunday afternoon in the second half of June and throughout July in the Parc Floral de Paris during the Paris Jazz Festival (www.parisjazzfestival.fr).

☆ Fête de la Musique   21 Jun

This national music festival (http://fetedelamusique.culturecommunication.gouv.fr) welcomes in summer on the solstice (21 June) with fabulous staged and impromptu live performances of jazz, reggae, classical and more all over the city.

🏳️‍🌈 Marche des Fiertés (Pride)   Late Jun

Late June's colourful Saturday-afternoon Marche des Fiertés (www.gaypride.fr) celebrates Gay Pride with a march incorporating over-the-top floats and outrageous costumes that crosses Paris via Le Marais.

☆ La Goutte d'Or en Fête   Late Jun–Early Jul

Raï, reggae and rap feature at this three-day world-music festival (https://gouttedorenfete.wordpress.com) on square Léon in the 18e's Goutte d'Or neighbourhood in late June/early July.

Above: Marche des Fiertés

This Year in Paris

DREAMSLAMSTUDIO/SHUTTERSTOCK ©

July

During the Parisian summer, 'beaches' – complete with sunbeds, umbrellas, atomisers, lounge chairs and palm trees – line the banks of the Seine, while shoppers hit the summer* soldes *(sales).

Bals des Pompiers 13 & 14 Jul

Bookending the city's Bastille Day celebrations, traditional Bals des Pompiers (Firemen's Balls) see dancing at many Parisian fire stations from 9pm to 4am on 13 and 14 July.

Bastille Day 14 Jul

The capital celebrates France's national day on 14 July with a morning military parade along the av des Champs-Élysées and fly-past of fighter aircraft and helicopters. *Feux d'artifice* (fireworks) light up the sky above the Champ de Mars by night.

Tour de France Late Jul

The last of the 21 stages of this legendary, 3500km-long cycling event (www.letour.com) finishes with a dash up the av des Champs-Élysées on the third or fourth Sunday of July.

Paris Plages Mid-Jul–Mid-Aug

From at least mid-July to mid-August, 'Paris Beaches' set up along Paris' riverbanks in two main zones, the Right Bank's Parc Rives de Seine, and the Bassin de la Villette (with swimming pools in the canal).

TOMMY LAREY/SHUTTERSTOCK ©

Cinéma au Clair de Lune Late Jul–Early Aug

Film screenings take place under the stars around town during Paris' free 'moonlight cinema', organised by the Forum des Images (www.forumdesimages.fr).

Top: Bastille Day parade;
Bottom: Swimming pool, Bassin de la Villette

CHRISTIAN BERTRAND/SHUTTERSTOCK ©

August

Parisians desert the city in droves during the summer swelter when, despite an influx of tourists, many restaurants and shops shut. It's a prime time to cycle, with far less traffic on the roads.

☆ **Classique au Vert**   Aug–Mid-Sep
In the Bois de Vincennes, the Parc Floral de Paris hosts classical-music concerts amid the greenery on weekends during August and the first half of September.

☆ **Rock en Seine**   Late Aug
Headlining acts rock the Domaine National de St-Cloud, on the city's southwestern edge, at this popular three-day, late-August music festival (www.rockenseine.com).

☆ **Silhouette**   Late Aug–Early Sep
Out-of-the-box short films by independent film-makers screen in competition alongside open-air concerts and workshops during this nine-day film festival (www.association-silhouette.com).

Above: Rock en Seine

This Year in Paris

September

Tourists leave and Parisians come home: la rentrée *marks residents' return to work and study after the summer break. Cultural life shifts into top gear and the weather is often at its blue-skied best.*

☆ Jazz à La Villette   Early Sep
This two-week jazz festival (www.jazzala villette.com) in the first half of September has sessions in Parc de la Villette, at the Cité de la Musique and at surrounding venues.

☆ Festival d'Automne   Mid-Sep–Early Jan
The long-running Autumn Festival of arts (www.festival-automne.com), from mid-September to early January, incorporates painting, music, dance and theatre at venues throughout the city.

☆ Techno Parade   Mid-Sep
On one Saturday in mid-September, floats carrying musicians and DJs pump up the volume as they travel through the city's streets during the Techno Parade (www. technoparade.fr).

◉ Journées Européennes du Patrimoine   15–16 Sep
The third weekend in September sees Paris open the doors of otherwise off-limits buildings – embassies, government ministries and so forth – during European Heritage Days (https://journeesdupatrimoine. culturecommunication.gouv.fr).

✕ Fête de la Gastronomie   Late Sep
Food markets, cookery workshops and demonstrations, and tasting sessions as well as events from aperitifs to dinners make up late September's three-day gastronomic festival (www.economie. gouv.fr/fete-gastronomie), held at venues Paris-wide.

Above: Techno Parade

ALL CANADA PHOTOS/ALAMY STOCK PHOTO ©

October

October heralds an autumnal kaleidoscope in the city's parks and gardens, along with bright, crisp days, cool, clear nights and excellent cultural offerings. Daylight saving ends on the last Sunday morning of the month.

⚑ Journée Sans Voiture   6 Oct
Pedestrians and cyclists reclaim Paris' streets from mid-morning to early evening on the first Sunday of October on this annual car-free day.

⚑ Fête des Vendanges de Montmartre   Mid-Oct
This five-day festival (www.fetedesven dangesdemontmartre.com) taking in the second weekend in October celebrates Montmartre's grape harvest with costumes, concerts, food events and a parade.

❂ Foire Internationale d'Art Contemporain   Mid-Oct
Scores of galleries are represented at the Foire Internationale d'Art Contemporain (FIAC) contemporary-art fair (www.fiac. com), held over four days in mid-October.

☆ Pitchfork Music Festival Paris   Late Oct
The Grande Halle de la Villette at the Parc de la Villette is the venue for this three-day fest (https://pitchfork musicfestival.fr) of pop, rock, indie and electro music in late October..

DAVID WOLFF · PATRICK/GETTY IMAGES ©

⚑ Nuit Blanche   5–6 Oct
From sundown until sunrise on the first Saturday and Sunday of October, museums stay open, along with bars and clubs, for one 'White Night' (ie 'All-Nighter').

Top: In costume for Fête des Vendanges de Montmartre; Bottom: Pitchfork Music Festival

Plan Your Trip
This Year in Paris

November

Dark, chilly days and long, cold nights see Parisians take refuge indoors: the opera and ballet seasons are going strong and there are plenty of cosy bistros and bars.

✗ Salon du Chocolat
Late Oct–Early Nov
Chocaholics won't want to miss this five-day chocolate festival's tastings, workshops, demonstrations and more at Paris Expo Porte de Versailles, 15e (www.salonduchocolat.fr), held from late October to early November. There are special activities for kids.

☆ Africolor
Mid-Nov–Late Dec
From mid-November to late December, this six-week-long African-music festival (www.africolor.com) is primarily held in outer suburbs, such as St-Denis, St-Ouen and Montreuil.

✻ Illuminations de Noël
Mid-Nov–Early Jan
From mid-November to early January, festive lights sparkle along the av des Champs-Élysées, rue du Faubourg Saint-Honoré and av Montaigne, all in the 8e, and others, while window displays enchant kids and adults alike at department stores including Galeries Lafayette and Le Printemps.

♟ Beaujolais Nouveau
21 Nov
At midnight on the third Thursday (ie Wednesday night) in November – as soon as French law permits – the opening of the first bottles of cherry-bright, six-week-old Beaujolais Nouveau is celebrated in Paris wine bars, with more celebrations on the Thursday itself.

Above: Christmas window display, Le Printemps (p150)

NOVIKOV ALEKSEY/SHUTTERSTOCK ©

December

Twinkling fairy lights, brightly decorated Christmas trees and shop windows, and outdoor ice-skating rinks make December a magical month to be in the City of Light.

🏇 Salon du Cheval de Paris   Late Nov–Early Dec

Sporting events and competitions including show jumping and dressage, plus a horseback parade through Paris, are part of the nine-day Paris Horse Fair (www.salon-cheval.com) from late November to early December.

🎡 Le Festival du Merveilleux   Late Dec–Early Jan

The magical private museum Musée des Arts Forains (www.arts-forains.com), filled with fairground attractions of yesteryear, opens from late December to early January, with enchanting rides, attractions and festive shows.

🎄 Christmas Eve Mass   24 Dec

Mass is celebrated at midnight on Christmas Eve at many Paris churches, including Notre Dame – arrive early to find a place.

🎄 New Year's Eve   31 Dec

Bd St-Michel, 5e, place de la Bastille, 11e, the Eiffel Tower, 7e, and especially the av des Champs-Élysées, 8e, are the Parisian hotspots for welcoming in the New Year.

Above: The Champs-Élysées on New Year's Eve

Plan Your Trip
Need to Know

Daily Costs

Budget:
Less than €100

- Dorm bed: €25–50

- Espresso/glass of wine/*demi* (half-pint of beer)/cocktail from: €2/3.50/3.50/9

- Metro ticket: €1.90

- Baguette sandwich: €4.50–6.50

- Frequent free concerts and events

Midrange:
€100–250

- Double room: €130–250

- Two-course meal: €20–40

- Museums: free–€15

- Admission to clubs: free–€20

Top end:
More than €250

- Historic luxury hotel double from €250

- Gastronomic restaurant menu from €40

- Private two-hour city tour from €150

- Premium opera/ballet tickets from €160

Advance Planning

Two months before Book accommodation, organise opera, ballet or cabaret tickets, check events calendars to find out what festivals will be on, and make reservations for high-end/popular restaurants.

Two weeks before Sign up for a local-led tour and start narrowing down your choice of museums, prepurchasing tickets online where possible to minimise ticket queues.

Two days before Pack your comfiest shoes to walk Paris' streets.

Useful Websites

Lonely Planet (www.lonely planet.com/paris) Destination information, hotel bookings, traveller forum and more.

Paris Info (www.parisinfo. com) Comprehensive tourist-authority website.

Sortiraparis (www.sortira paris.com) Up-to-date calendar listing what's on around town.

Bonjour Paris (www.bonjour paris.com) New openings, old favourites and upcoming events.

Secrets of Paris (www. secretsofparis.com) Loads of resources and reviews.

HiP Paris (www.hipparis. com) Not only vacation rentals ('Haven in Paris') but articles and reviews by expat locals too.

Currency

Euro (€)

Language

French

Visas

There are generally no restrictions for EU citizens. Usually not required for most other nationalities for stays of up to 90 days.

Money

ATMs are widely available. Visa and Master-Card accepted in most hotels, shops and restaurants; fewer accept American Express.

Mobile Phones

Check with your provider before you leave home about roaming costs and/or ensuring your phone is unlocked to use a French SIM card (available cheaply in Paris).

Time

Central European Time (GMT/UTC plus one hour).

Tourist Information

The main branch of the Paris Convention & Visitors Bureau (p233) sells tickets for tours, several attractions, museum and transport passes.

For more, see the **Survival Guide** (p230)

When to Go

Spring and autumn are ideal. Summer is the main tourist season but many places (restaurants, shops etc) close during August. Sights are quieter during winter.

Paris

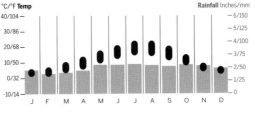

Arriving in Paris

Charles de Gaulle Airport Trains (RER), buses and night buses to the city centre €6 to €17; taxi €50 to €55, 15% higher evenings and Sundays.

Orly Airport Trains (Orlyval then RER), buses and night buses to the city centre €8.70 to €13.25; T7 tram to Ville-juif-Louis Aragon then metro to centre (€3.80); taxi €30 to €35, 15% higher evenings and Sundays.

Beauvais Airport Buses (€17) to Porte Maillot then metro (€1.90); taxi during the day/night around €170/210 (probably more than the cost of your flight!).

Gare du Nord train station Within central Paris; served by metro (€1.90).

Getting Around

Walking is a pleasure in Paris, and the city also has one of the most efficient and inexpensive public-transport systems in the world, making getting around a breeze.

Metro & RER The fastest way to get around. Metros run from about 5.30am and finish around 1.15am (to around 2.15am on Friday and Saturday nights), depending on the line. RER commuter trains operate from around 5.30am to 1.20am daily.

Bicycle Virtually free pick-up, drop-off Vélib' bikes have docking stations across the city; electric bikes are also available.

Bus Good for parents with prams/strollers and people with limited mobility.

Boat The Batobus is a handy hop-on, hop-off service stopping at nine key destinations along the Seine.

Arrondissements

Within the *périphérique* (ring road), Paris is divided into 20 *arrondissements* (city districts; see map p237), which spiral clockwise like a snail shell from the centre. *Arrondissement* numbers (1er, 2e etc) form an integral part of all Parisian addresses. Each *arrondissement* has its own personality, but it's the *quartiers* (quarters, ie neighbourhoods), which often overlap *arrondissement* boundaries, that give Paris its village atmosphere.

Sleeping

Paris has a range of accommodation for all budgets, but it's often *complet* (full) well in advance. Reservations are recommended year-round and essential during the warmer months (April to October) and all public and school holidays. See p211 for info on where to stay.

Plan Your Trip
Top Days in Paris

LUMIKK555/SHUTTERSTOCK ©

Central Right Bank

The central Right Bank is the ideal place to kick off your Parisian trip. As well as the ancient art and artefacts in Paris' mightiest museum, the Louvre, you'll also see ground-breaking modern and contemporary art inside the striking Centre Pompidou.

❶ Jardin des Tuileries (p90)

Start your day with a stroll through the elegant Jardin des Tuileries, stopping to view Monet's enormous *Waterlilies* at the Musée de l'Orangerie and/or photography exhibits at the Jeu de Paume.

➲ Jardin des Tuileries to Musée du Louvre

🚶 Stroll through the gardens to the Louvre.

❷ Musée du Louvre (p52)

Visiting the world's largest museum could easily consume a full day, but bear in mind that tickets are valid all day, so you can come and go as you please. Various tours (guided and self-guided) help you maximise your time.

➲ Musée du Louvre to Chez La Vieille

🚶 From the Louvre's Cour Carée, walk east via rue de Rivoli.

Day

01

MAZIARZ/SHUTTERSTOCK ©

❸ Lunch at Chez La Vieille (p124)

Dine on updated versions of timeless bistro dishes at Chez La Vieille.

➲ Chez La Vieille to Jardin du Palais Royal

🚶 Walk northwest via rue St-Honoré to place du Palais Royal.

❹ Jardin du Palais Royal (p101)

Browse the colonnaded arcades of the exquisite Jardin du Palais Royal.

➲ Jardin du Palais Royal to Église St-Eustache

🚶 Head back down rue St-Honoré, turn north into rue du Louvre and east on rue Coquillière.

❺ Église St-Eustache (p77)

One of Paris' most beautiful churches, Église St-Eustache has a magnificent organ – catch a classical concert here if you can.

➲ Église St-Eustache to Centre Pompidou

🚶 Continue east on rue Rambuteau to place Georges-Pompidou.

❻ Centre Pompidou (p74)

Head to the late-opening Centre Pompidou for amazing modern and contemporary art.

➲ Centre Pompidou to Brasserie Bofinger

Ⓜ Take Line 1 from Hôtel de Ville to Bastille; Brasserie Bofinger is just northwest.

❼ Dinner at Brasserie Bofinger (p131)

Dine beneath the stained-glass cupola on classic brasserie fare.

➲ Brasserie Bofinger to PasDeLoup

Ⓜ Line 8 from Bastille to Filles du Calvaire.

❽ Drinks at PasDeLoup (p177)

Le Marais really comes into its own at night, with a cornucopia of hip clubs and top-notch cocktail bars such as PasDeLoup.

From left: Jardin des Tuileries; Église St-Eustache

Plan Your Trip
Top Days in Paris

Western & Southern Paris

It's a day of Parisian icons today – from the triumphal span of the Arc de Triomphe to the world-famous avenue, the Champs-Élysées, and, of course, the city's stunning art nouveau Eiffel Tower, with some surprises, too, such as floating nightclubs.

❶ Arc de Triomphe (p42)

Climb the mighty Arc de Triomphe for a pinch-yourself Parisian panorama. Back down on ground level, take the time to check out the intricate sculptures and historic bronze plaques, and pay your respects to the Tomb of the Unknown Soldier.

⊙ Arc de Triomphe to Champs-Élysées

🚶 Walk downhill along the Champs-Élysées.

❷ Champs-Élysées (p150)

Promenade along Paris' most glamorous avenue, the Champs-Élysées, taking in the luxury display windows of high-end boutiques – and perhaps give your credit card a workout in the adjacent Triangle d'Or (Golden Triangle), home to flagship *haute couture* (high fashion) houses.

⊙ Champs-Élysées to Musée du Quai Branly

Ⓜ Line 9 from Franklin D Roosevelt to Alma Marceau.

Day
02

JHVEPHOTO/SHUTTERSTOCK ©

❸ Musée du Quai Branly (p40)

From Alma Marceau metro station, cross the Pont d'Alma and turn right along quai Branly to check out indigenous art as well as the awesome architecture of the Musée du Quai Branly. For lunch, drop by the museum's Café Branly or head to its elegant restaurant, Les Ombres (named 'the Shadows' for the webbed patterns cast by the adjacent Eiffel Tower).

➲ Musée du Quai Branly to Palais de Tokyo

🚶 Cross the Passerelle Debilly. Walk uphill along rue de la Manutention, turning east on av du Président Wilson.

❹ Palais de Tokyo (p41)

This stunning building takes on major temporary cutting-edge exhibits – the rooftop, for example, has been the setting for attention-getting projects such as the transient Hotel Everland and the see-through restaurant Nomiya.

➲ Palais de Tokyo to Eiffel Tower

Ⓜ Line 9 from Iéna to Trocadéro.

❺ Eiffel Tower (p36)

Exiting the Trocadéro metro station, walk east through the Jardins du Trocadéro for the ultimate Eiffel Tower snapshot, and cross Pont d'Iéna to the tower itself. Sunset is the best time to ascend the Eiffel Tower, to experience both the dazzling views during daylight and then the twinkling *Ville Lumière* (City of Light) by night. (Pre-purchase your tickets to minimise queuing.)

➲ Eiffel Tower to Le Cassenoix

🚶 Walk southeast through Parc du Champ de Mars, turn southwest on av Joseph Bouvard then rue Desaix to Le Cassenoix.

❻ Dinner & Drinks

Dining inside the Eiffel Tower (p39) is unforgettable. Alternatively, book ahead for modern French cuisine at Le Cassenoix (p143). Take metro line 6 to party aboard floating nightclubs such as Le Batofar (p185).

From left: View over the Champs-Élysées from the Arc de Triomphe; The Champs-Élysées

Top Days in Paris

ALBERTO ZAMORANO/SHUTTERSTOCK ©

The Islands & Left Bank

Begin the day in the heart of Paris at the city's colossal cathedral, then venture across to Paris' elegant Left Bank to see impressionist masterpieces in the Musée d'Orsay, and to visit the city's oldest church and its loveliest gardens.

❶ Notre Dame (p46)

Starting your day at the Notre Dame gives you the best chance of beating the crowds. In addition to viewing its stained-glass interior, allow an hour to climb to the top for exceptional views, and another to descend below ground to explore the crypt.

➲ Notre Dame to Sainte-Chapelle

🏃 Follow the Seine northwest to bd du Palais.

❷ Sainte-Chapelle (p92)

Don't miss the exquisite chapel Sainte-Chapelle. Consecrated in 1248, its stained glass forms a curtain of glazing on the 1st floor.

➲ Sainte-Chapelle to Musée d'Orsay

Ⓜ RER C from St-Michel–Notre Dame to Gare Musée d'Orsay.

Day

03

PREMIER PHOTO/SHUTTERSTOCK ©

❸ Musée d'Orsay (p62)

Set inside a magnificent art nouveau former railway station, the Musée d'Orsay is filled with impressionist tours de force by masters including Renoir, Monet, Van Gogh, Degas and dozens more. It's also an ideal place to dine at casual Café Campana or the ornate Restaurant Musée d'Orsay.

⭕ Musée d'Orsay to Église St-Germain des Prés

Ⓜ Solférino to Sèvres-Babylone (line 12), then change for Mabillon (line 10).

❹ Église St-Germain des Prés (p89)

Paris' oldest church sits in the heart of the buzzing St-Germain des Prés district, with chic boutiques and historic literary cafes, including Les Deux Magots, just opposite.

⭕ Église St-Germain des Prés to Jardin du Luxembourg

🏃 Head south on rue Bonaparte to place St-Sulpice and continue on to rue Vaugirard.

❺ Jardin du Luxembourg (p68)

Enter this lovely garden from rue Vaugirard and stroll among its chestnut groves, paths and statues.

⭕ Jardin du Luxembourg to Bouillon Racine

🏃 From rue Vaugirard, take rue Monsieur-le-Prince northwest to rue Racine.

❻ Dinner at Bouillon Racine (p138)

Feast on French classics in this art nouveau jewel. Afterwards, head to Shakespeare & Company for late-night book shopping.

From left: Notre Dame; Jardin du Luxembourg

Top Days in Paris

Northern & Eastern Paris

Montmartre's slinking streets and steep staircases lined with crooked ivy-clad buildings are especially enchanting to meander in the early morning when there are fewer tourists. Afterwards, explore charming Canal St-Martin and futuristic Parc de la Villette before drinking, dining and dancing in lively Bastille.

Day 04

❶ Musée de Montmartre (p61)

Brush up on the area's fascinating history at the local museum, the Musée de Montmartre. Not only was Montmartre home to seminal artists, but Renoir and Utrillo are among those who lived in this very building.

➲ Musée de Montmartre to Sacré-Cœur

🚶 Walk east to Sacré-Cœur along rue Cortot, rue du Mont Cenis then rue Azais.

❷ Sacré-Cœur (p58)

Head to the hilltop Sacré-Cœur basilica and, for an even more extraordinary panorama over Paris, climb up into the basilica's main dome. Regular metro tickets are valid on the funicular that shuttles up and down the steep Butte de Montmartre.

➲ Sacré-Cœur to Le Bistrot de la Galette

🚶 Head west, past place du Tertre, along rue Norvins and turn left onto rue Lepic.

CATHERINE LE NEVEZ/LONELY PLANET ©

❸ Lunch at Le Bistrot de la Galette (p128)

Below historic Montmartre windmill Moulin de la Galette, Le Bistrot de la Galette serves house-speciality *feuilletés* (pastry puffs) made from locally hand-milled flour.

➲ Le Bistrot de la Galette to Canal St-Martin

Ⓜ Line 2 Blanche to Jaurès.

❹ Canal St-Martin (p159)

A postcard-perfect vision of iron footbridges, swing bridges and shaded tow paths, Canal St-Martin's banks (and the surrounding streets) are lined with a steadily growing number of hip cafes and boutiques. Also here is cultural centre Point Éphemère, whose restaurant, Animal Kitchen, combines gourmet cuisine with music from Animal Records.

➲ Canal St-Martin to Parc de la Villette

Ⓜ Line 5 Jacques Bonsergent to Porte de Pantin.

❺ Parc de la Villette (p201)

In addition to its striking geometric gardens, innovative Parc de la Villette has a slew of attractions, including the kid-friendly Cité des Sciences museum and the Cité de la Musique – Philharmonie de Paris complex.

➲ Parc de la Villette to Le Bistrot Paul Bert

Ⓜ Porte de Pantin to République (line 5), changing for Faidherbe-Chaligny (line 8).

❻ Dinner at Le Bistrot Paul Bert (p134)

After a pre-dinner *apéro* (aperitif) at the classic, cherry-red Le Pure Café, head around the corner to enjoy exceptional bistro classics at Le Bistrot Paul Bert. After dinner head west to the Bastille neighbourhood's buzzing bars; there's a great concentration on rue de Lappe.

From left: Funicular carrying passengers to Sacré-Cœur; Le Bistrot de la Galette

Plan Your Trip
Hotspots For...

ACTIVE OUTDOORS

⊙ **Jardin du Luxembourg** Paris' most popular park, pictured above, is perfect for a stroll, run, sports or kids' activities. (p68)

⊙ **Eiffel Tower** Get up-close tower views while scaling 720 steps to the 2nd floor. (p36)

⚡ **Paris à Vélo, C'est Sympa!** Explore Paris on a bike tour. (p203)

⚡ **Piscine Joséphine Baker** Swim in this striking pool floating on the Seine. (p200)

⚡ **Bois de Boulogne** Explore Paris' western woods by rowing boat or bicycle. (p202)

ART NOUVEAU BUFFS

⊙ **Musée d'Orsay** Impressionist art is matched only by the magnificent art nouveau train station housing it. (p62)

⊙ **Musée Maxim's** Some 550 art nouveau artworks, objets d'art and furniture above the famed belle époque–era restaurant. (p91)

✘ **Bouillon Racine** With mirrored walls, floral motifs and ceramic tiling, this 1906 brasserie is a listed monument. (p138)

🛍 **Belle du Jour** Browse perfume bottles from the belle époque. (p152)

☆ **Le Carreau du Temple** This beautiful wrought-iron covered market is now a vibrant cultural centre. (p193)

EPICUREANS

⊙ **Musée du Louvre** Follow the Louvre's 'Art of Eating' thematic trail. (p52)

☞ **Le Cordon Bleu** Take a cooking class at one of the world's foremost culinary institutions. (p96)

🛍 **La Grande Épicerie de Paris** Stock up on luxury food items at Le Bon Marché's spectacular food hall. (p160)

✕ **Bustronome** Dine on gourmet cuisine aboard a glass-roofed bus cruising Paris' boulevards. (Map p246; www.bustronome.com)

✕ **Marché d'Aligre** Shop for fresh produce and delectable specialities at this outstanding Parisian market. (p83)

FASHION FANS

⊙ **Musée Yves Saint Laurent Paris** See sketches and couture creations by avant-garde designer YSL. (p105)

⊙ **Le Grand Musée du Parfum** Once Christian Lacroix' fashion house, now a fragrant perfume museum. (p91)

🕴 **Galeries Lafayette** Attend free fashion shows at this resplendent department store, pictured above. (p150)

🛍 **Triangle d'Or** Flit between flagships such as Chanel in Paris' Golden Triangle. (p153)

✕ **Lasserre** Style icon Audrey Hepburn was a patron of this Michelin-starred restaurant. (p123)

ART LOVERS

⊙ **Maison et Jardins de Claude Monet** Take a trip to Monet's house and gardens, pictured above. (p98)

⊙ **Musée National Picasso** An exceptional collection of Picasso's works. (p114)

🍷 **La Belle Hortense** Art and literary events take place at this wine bar. (p178)

🍷 **La Palette** Braque was among the artists who frequented this cafe; today it's popular with art dealers. (p185)

🛍 **Magasin Sennelier** Former clients of this 1887-founded art-supply shop include Cézanne and Picasso. (p160)

What's New

Contemporary Art

Spring 2019 sees the high-profile opening of the private Collection Pinault inside Paris' circular former grain market and stock exchange the Bourse de Commerce (p77), with a restaurant by triple-Michelin-starred chef Michel Bras.

Digital Art

A former foundry forms the blank canvas for the dazzling digital art projections at the city's first museum dedicated to the genre, 2018-opened L'Atelier des Lumières (p79).

Multidisciplinary Space

Experimental art, design and fashion works are explored and exhibited at Lafayette Anticipations (p150), opened in 2018 by the corporate foundation of French retailer Galeries Lafayette in a stunning Rem Koolhaas–designed space.

Avant-garde Fashion

Yves Saint Laurent's sketches through to his catwalk creations are displayed inside the iconic designer's *haute couture* studios now containing the Musée Yves Saint Laurent Paris (p105).

Department Store Debuts

Galeries Lafayette will open its Champs-Élysées premises in 2019; the same year sees the long-awaited (re-)opening of Seine-side art nouveau department store La Samaritaine (p151).

Above: Bourse de Commerce

Plan Your Trip
For Free

Free Museums

If you can, time your trip to be here on the first Sunday of the month, when you can visit national museums and a handful of monuments for free (some during certain months only). European citizens under 26 get free entry to national museums and monuments. At any time you can visit the permanent collections of Paris' musées municipaux (www.paris.fr/musees) for free (some only when temporary exhibitions aren't taking place).

Free Churches & Cemeteries

Some of the city's most magnificent buildings are its churches and other places of worship; entry to general areas is usually free. Paris' cemeteries, with elaborate tombs and numerous celebrity 'residents' are also free.

Free Music

Concerts, DJ sets and recitals regularly take place for free (or for the cost of a drink) at venues throughout the city. Busking musicians and performers entertain crowds on Paris' streets, squares and aboard the metro.

Free Literary Events

This literary-minded city is an inspired place to catch a reading, author signing or writing workshop. English-language bookshops such as Shakespeare & Company (p159) host literary events throughout the year.

Free Festivals & Events

Loads of Paris' festivals and events are free, such as the summertime Paris Plages riverside beaches.

Plan Your Trip
Family Travel

NIKOMAF/SHUTTERSTOCK ©

Sights & Activities

In addition to classic playgrounds, Paris' parks also have a host of children's activities.

○ The toy boats, *marionettes* (puppets), pony rides and carousel of the Jardin du Luxembourg (p68).

○ The new millennium playgrounds of Parc de la Villette (p201).

○ The fabulous interactive science museum **Cité des Sciences** (☏01 40 05 80 00; www.cite-sciences.fr; 30 av Corentin Cariou, Parc de la Villette, 19e; per attraction adult/child €12/9; ☺10am-6pm Tue-Sat, to 7pm Sun, La Géode 10.30am-8.30pm Tue-Sun; Ⓜ Porte de la Villette).

○ The Bois de Boulogne's **Jardin d'Acclimatation** (☏01 40 67 90 85; http://jardind acclimatation.fr; av du Mahatma Gandhi; admission €3.50, per attraction €2.90; ☺11am-6pm Mon-Fri, 10am-6pm Sat & Sun; Ⓜ Les Sablons) amusement park.

○ Animal-mad kids will love the lions, cougars, white rhinos and a gaggle of other creatures at the Bois de Vincennes' state-of-the-art Parc Zoologique de Paris (p202); the kid-friendly Muséum National d'Histoire Naturelle (p107); and the shark tank at **Cinéaqua** (Map p246; ☏01 40 69 23 23; www. cineaqua.com; av des Nations Unies, 16e; adult/child €20.50/13; ☺10am-7pm; Ⓜ Trocadéro).

○ A trip to the Louvre (p52) can be a treat, particularly following thematic trails such as hunting for lions or galloping horses.

○ Every kid, big and small, loves a voyage down the Seine with Bateaux-Mouches (p73) or Bateaux Parisiens (p73). But there's something extra special about the one-hour 'Paris Mystery' tours designed especially for children by Vedettes de Paris (p72).

○ Further afield, theme parks within day-trip distance include Disneyland Paris (www.disneylandparis.com) and Parc Astérix (www.parcasterix.fr).

Eating Out with Kids

Many restaurants accept little diners (confirm ahead), but they're expected to behave. Children's menus are common, although most restaurants don't have high chairs. A wave of gourmet pizza, pasta, bagel and burger restaurants throughout the city offer kid-friendly fare. In fine weather, good options include picking up sandwiches and crêpes from a street stall or packing a market-fresh picnic and heading to parks and gardens where kids can play to their hearts' content.

Getting Around with Kids

Paris' narrow streets and metro stairways are a trial if you have a stroller (pram or pushchair) in tow; buses offer an easier, scenic alternative. Children under four years of age travel free on public transport and generally receive free admission to sights. For older kids, discounts vary from place to place – anything from a euro off for over-fours to free entry up to the age of 18.

★ Best Parks & Playgrounds

Jardin du Luxembourg (p68)

Parc de la Villette (p201)

Parc Montsouris (p201)

Bois de Boulogne (p202)

Bois de Vincennes (p202)

Need to Know

Babysitting *L'Officiel des Spectacles* (www.offi. fr) lists *gardes d'enfants* (babysitters); some hotels will organise sitters for guests.

Equipment Rent strollers, scooters, car seats, travel beds and more while in Paris from companies such as Kidelio (www.kidelio.com).

Paris Mômes (www.parismomes.fr) Outstanding bimonthly magazine on Parisian kid culture (up to 12 years); print off playful kids' guides for major art exhibitions before leaving home.

From left: Toy boats on the Grand Bassin (p70), Jardin du Luxembourg; Miniature railway, Jardin d'Acclimatation

TOP
EXPERIENCES

The very best to see & do

Parc du Champ de Mars (p40) and the Eiffel Tower

Eiffel Tower

*Paris today is unimaginable
without its signature spire.
Originally only constructed as
a temporary 1889 Exposition
Universelle exhibit, it went on to
become the defining fixture of the
city's skyline.*

Great For...

ⓘ Need to Know

Map p246; ☎08 92 70 12 39; www.toureiffel.
paris; Champ de Mars, 5 av Anatole France,
7e; adult/child lift to top €25/6.30, lift to 2nd
fl €16/4, stairs to 2nd fl €10/2.50; ⊙lifts
& stairs 9am-12.45am mid-Jun–Aug, lifts
9.30am-11.45pm, stairs 9.30am-6.30pm
Sep–mid-Jun; Ⓜ Bir Hakeim or RER Champ de
Mars–Tour Eiffel

★ Top Tip
Head here at dusk for the best daytime vistas and glittering night-time city views.

Named after its designer, Gustave Eiffel, the Tour Eiffel was built for the 1889 Exposition Universelle (World Fair). It took 300 workers, 2.5 million rivets and two years of nonstop labour to assemble. Upon completion the tower became the tallest human-made structure in the world (324m or 1063ft) – a record held until the completion of the Chrysler Building in New York (1930). A symbol of the modern age, it faced massive opposition from Paris' artistic and literary elite, and the 'metal asparagus', as some Parisians derided it, was originally slated to be torn down in 1909. It was spared only because it proved an ideal platform for the transmitting antennas needed for the newfangled science of radio-telegraphy.

Tickets & Queues

Ascend as far as the 2nd floor (either on foot or by lift), from where it is lift-only to the top floor. Pushchairs must be folded in lifts and you are not allowed to take bags or backpacks larger than aeroplane-cabin size.

Buying tickets in advance online usually means you avoid the monumental queues at the ticket offices. Print your ticket or show it on a smartphone screen. If you can't reserve your tickets ahead of time, expect waits of well over an hour in high season.

Stair tickets can't be reserved online. They are sold at the south pillar, where the staircase can also be accessed: the climb consists of 360 steps to the 1st floor and another 360 steps to the 2nd floor.

Spring flowers beneath the Eiffel Tower

If you have reservations for either restaurant, you are granted direct access to the lifts.

1st Floor

Of the tower's three floors, the 1st (57m) has the most space, but the least impressive views. The glass-enclosed **Pavillon Ferrié** houses an immersion film along with a small cafe and souvenir shop, while the outer walkway features a discovery circuit to help visitors learn more about the tower's ingenious design. Check out the sections of glass flooring that proffer a dizzying view of the ant-like people walking on the ground far below.

☑ Don't Miss

Views of the tower from the Jardins du Trocadéro outside Palais de Chaillot.

TRAVELMAMA/BUDGET TRAVEL ©

This level also hosts restaurant **58 Tour Eiffel** (Map p246; ☎01 76 70 04 86; www.restaurants-toureiffel.com; menus lunch €37.20, dinner €93.70-113.70; ⏰11.30am-4.30pm & 6.30-11pm;).

Not all lifts stop at the 1st floor (check before ascending), but it's an easy walk down from the 2nd floor should you accidentally end up one floor too high.

2nd Floor

Views from the 2nd floor (115m) are the best – impressively high, but still close enough to see the details of the city below. Telescopes and panoramic maps placed around the tower pinpoint locations in Paris and beyond. Story windows give an overview of the lifts' mechanics, and the vision well allows you to gaze through glass panels to the ground. Also up here are toilets, a macaron bar and Michelin-starred restaurant Le Jules Verne (p122).

Top Floor

Views from the wind-buffeted top floor (276m) stretch up to 60km on a clear day, though at this height the panoramas are more sweeping than detailed. Celebrate your ascent with a glass of bubbly (€12 to €21) from the Champagne bar (open noon to 10pm). Afterwards peep into Gustave Eiffel's restored top-level office where life-like wax models of Eiffel and his daughter Claire greet Thomas Edison.

To access the top floor, take a separate lift on the 2nd floor (closed during heavy winds).

Nightly Sparkles

Every hour on the hour, the entire tower sparkles for five minutes with 20,000 6-watt lights. They were first installed for Paris' millennium celebration in 2000 – it

✕ Take a Break

At the tower's two restaurants, snack bars, macaron bar or top-floor Champagne bar.

took 25 mountain climbers five months to install the current bulbs and 40km of electrical cords. For the best view of the light show, head across the Seine to the Jardins du Trocadéro.

What's Nearby?

Parc du Champ de Mars   Park

(Map p246; Champ de Mars, 7e; Ⓜ École Militaire or RER Champ de Mars–Tour Eiffel) Running southeast from the Eiffel Tower, the grassy Champ de Mars – an ideal summer picnic spot – was originally used as a parade ground for the cadets of the 18th-century **École Militaire**, the vast French-classical building at the southeastern end of the park, which counts Napoléon Bonaparte among its graduates. The steel-and-etched-glass **Wall for Peace Memorial** (Map p246; http://wallforpeace.org), erected in 2000, is by Clara Halter.

Musée du Quai Branly   Museum

(Map p246; ☎ 01 56 61 70 00; www.quaibranly. fr; 37 quai Branly, 7e; adult/child €10/free; ⊙ 11am-7pm Tue, Wed & Sun, 11am-9pm Thu-Sat; Ⓜ Alma Marceau or RER Pont de l'Alma) A tribute to the diversity of human culture, Musée du Quai Branly's highly inspiring overview of indigenous and folk art spans four main sections – Oceania, Asia, Africa and the Americas. An impressive array of masks, carvings, weapons, jewellery and more make up the body of the rich collection, displayed in a refreshingly unique interior without rooms or high walls. Look out for excellent temporary exhibitions and performances.

Palais de Chaillot   Historic Building

(Map p246; place du Trocadéro et du 11 Novembre, 16e; Ⓜ Trocadéro) The two curved, colonnaded wings of this building (built for the 1937 International Expo) and central terrace afford an exceptional panorama of the **Jardins du Trocadéro**, Seine and Eiffel Tower. The eastern wing houses the standout **Cité de l'Architecture et du Patrimoine** (Map p246; www.citechaillot.fr; 1 place du Trocadéro et du 11 Novembre, 16e; adult/child €8/free; ⊙ 11am-7pm Wed & Fri-Sun, to 9pm Thu), devoted to French

architecture and heritage, as well as the **Théâtre National de Chaillot** (Map p246; ☎ 01 53 65 30 00; http://theatre-chaillot.fr; 1 place du Trocadéro, 16e), staging dance and theatre. The western wing houses the **Musée de la Marine** (Map p246; Maritime Museum; ☎ 01 53 65 69 69; www.musee-marine.fr; 17 place du Trocadéro et du 11 Novembre, 16e), which is closed for renovations until 2021, and the **Musée de l'Homme** (Map p246; Museum of Humankind; ☎ 01 44 05 72 72; www.museedelhomme.fr; 17 place Trocadéro et du 11 Novembre, 16e; adult/child €10/free; ⊙ 10am-6pm Wed-Mon).

Musée Guimet des Arts Asiatiques   Gallery

(Map p246; ☎ 01 56 52 53 00; www.guimet. fr; 6 place d'Iéna, 16e; adult/child €8.50/free; ⊙ 10am-6pm Wed-Mon; Ⓜ Iéna) Connoisseurs of Japanese ink paintings and Tibetan

Musée du Quai Branly

thangkas won't want to miss the Musée Guimet, the largest Asian art museum in France. Observe the gradual transmission of both Buddhism and artistic styles along the Silk Road in pieces ranging from 1st-century Gandhara Buddhas from Afghanistan and Pakistan to later Central Asian, Chinese and Japanese Buddhist sculptures and art.

Palais de Tokyo   Gallery
(Map p246; ☎01 81 97 35 88; www.palaisde tokyo.com; 13 av du Président Wilson, 16e; adult/ child €12/free; ☺noon-midnight Wed-Mon; Ⓜléna) The Tokyo Palace, created for the 1937 Exposition Internationale des Arts et Techniques dans la Vie Moderne (International Exposition of Art and Technology in Modern Life), has no permanent collection. Instead, its shell-like interior of concrete

and steel is a stark backdrop to interactive contemporary-art exhibitions and installations. Its bookshop is fabulous for art and design magazines, and its eating and drinking options are magic.

★ **Did You Know?**
Slapping a fresh coat of paint on the tower is no easy feat. It takes a 25-person team 18 months to complete the 60-tonnes-of-paint task, redone every seven years.

★ **Man on a Wire**
In 1989 tightrope artist Philippe Petit walked up an inclined 700m cable across the Seine, from Palais Chaillot to the Eiffel Tower's 2nd floor. The act, performed before an audience of 250,000 people, was held to commemorate the French Republic's bicentennial.

Arc de Triomphe

If anything rivals the Eiffel Tower as the symbol of Paris, it's this magnificent 1836-built triumphal arch commemorating Napoléon's 1805 victory at Austerlitz, which he commissioned the following year.

Great For...

ℹ Need to Know

Map p246; www.paris-arc-de-triomphe.fr; place Charles de Gaulle, 8e; viewing platform adult/child €12/free; ⊙10am-11pm Apr-Sep, to 10.30pm Oct-Mar; Ⓜ Charles de Gaulle–Étoile

★ Top Tip

Don't risk getting skittled by traffic by taking photos while crossing the Champs-Élysées.

History

Napoléon's armies never did march through the Arc de Triomphe showered in honour. At the time it was commissioned, his victory at Austerlitz seemed like a watershed moment that confirmed the tactical supremacy of the French army, but a mere decade later, Napoléon had already fallen from power and his empire had crumbled.

The Arc de Triomphe was never fully abandoned – simply laying the foundations had taken an entire two years – and in 1836, after a series of starts and stops under the restored monarchy, the project was finally completed. In 1840 Napoléon's remains were returned to France and passed under the arch before being interred at Invalides.

Accessing the Arch

Don't try to cross the traffic-choked roundabout above ground! Stairs on the Champs Élysées' northeastern side lead beneath the Étoile to pedestrian tunnels that bring you out safely beneath the arch.

There is a lift/elevator at the arch, but it's only for visitors with limited mobility or those travelling with young children, and there are still 46 unavoidable steps.

Beneath the Arch

Beneath the arch at ground level lies the **Tomb of the Unknown Soldier**. Honouring the 1.3 million French soldiers who lost their lives in WWI, the Unknown Soldier was laid to rest in 1921, beneath an eternal flame that is rekindled daily at 6.30pm.

Tomb of the Unknown Soldier

Also here are a number of bronze plaques laid into the ground. Take the time to try and decipher some: these mark significant moments in modern French history, such as the proclamation of the Third French Republic (4 September 1870) and the return of Alsace and Lorraine to French rule (11 November 1918). The most notable plaque is the text from Charles de Gaulle's famous London broadcast on 18 June 1940, which sparked the French Resistance to life: 'Believe me, I who am speaking to you with full knowledge of the facts, and telling you that nothing is lost for France. The same means that overcame us can bring us victory one day. For France is not alone! She is not alone!'

☑ Don't Miss

Some of the best vistas in Paris from the top of the arch.

FOTO3593/SHUTTERSTOCK ©

Sculptures

The arch is adorned with four main sculptures, six panels in relief, and a frieze running beneath the top. Each was designed by a different artist; the most famous sculpture is the one to the right as you approach from the Champs-Élysées: *La Marseillaise* (Departure of the Volunteers of 1792). Sculpted by François Rude, it depicts soldiers of all ages gathering beneath the wings of victory, en route to drive back the invading armies of Prussia and Austria. The higher panels depict a series of important victories for the Revolutionary and imperial French armies, from Egypt to Austerlitz, while the detailed frieze is divided into two sections: the *Departure of the Armies* and the *Return of the Armies*. Don't miss the multimedia section beneath the viewing platform, which provides more detail and historical background for each of the sculptures.

Viewing Platform

Climb the 284 steps to the viewing platform at the top of the 50m-high arch and you'll be suitably rewarded with magnificent panoramas over western Paris. From here, a dozen broad avenues – many of them named after Napoléonic victories and illustrious generals – radiate towards every compass point. The Arc de Triomphe is the highest point in the line of monuments known as the *axe historique* (historic axis, also called the grand axis); it offers views that sweep east down the Champs-Élysées to the gold-tipped obelisk at place de la Concorde (and beyond to the Louvre's glass pyramid), and west to the skyscraper district of La Défense, where the colossal **Grande Arche** (☏01 40 90 52 20; www. lagrandearche.fr; 1 Parvis de la Défense; adult/child €15/7; ⊙10am-7pm; Ⓜ La Défense) marks the western terminus of the *axe*.

✕ Take a Break

Pair an evening visit with a traditional French dinner at Le Hide (p123).

Rose window, Notre Dame

Notre Dame

A vision of stained-glass rose windows, flying buttresses and frightening gargoyles, Paris' glorious cathedral, on the larger of the two inner-city islands, is the city's geographic and spiritual heart.

Great For...

☑ **Don't Miss**

Climbing the bell towers, which brings you face to face with the cathedral's ghoulish gargoyles.

When you enter the cathedral its grand dimensions are immediately evident: the interior alone is 127m long, 48m wide and 35m high, and can accommodate some 6000 worshippers.

Architecture

Built on a site occupied by earlier churches and, a millennium prior, a Gallo-Roman temple, Notre Dame was begun in 1163 and largely completed by the early 14th century. The cathedral was badly damaged during the Revolution, prompting architect Eugène Emmanuel Viollet-le-Duc to oversee extensive renovations between 1845 and 1864. Enter the magnificent forest of ornate flying buttresses that encircle the cathedral chancel and support its walls and roof.

Notre Dame is known for its sublime balance, though if you look closely you'll see

ℹ Need to Know

Map p250; 📞01 42 34 56 10, towers 01 53 10 07 00; www.notredamedeparis.fr; 6 Parvis Notre Dame – place Jean-Paul-II, 4e; cathedral free, adult/child towers €10/free, treasury €5/3; ⊙cathedral 7.45am-6.45pm Mon-Fri, to 7.15pm Sat & Sun, towers 10am-6.30pm Sun-Thu, 10am-11pm Fri & Sat Jul & Aug, 10am-6.30pm Apr-Jun & Sep, 10am-5.30pm Oct-Mar, treasury 9.45am-5.30pm; MCité

✕ Take a Break

On hidden place Dauphine, Le Caveau du Palais (p136) serves contemporary French fare.

★ Top Tip

Invariably huge queues get longer throughout the day – arrive as early as possible.

all sorts of minor asymmetrical elements introduced to avoid monotony, in accordance with standard Gothic practice. These include the slightly different shapes of each of the three main portals, the statues of which were once brightly coloured to make them more effective as a *Biblia pauperum* – a 'Bible of the poor' to help the illiterate faithful understand Old Testament stories, the Passion of the Christ and the lives of the saints.

Rose Windows & Pipe Organ

A cathedral highlight, the three rose windows colouring its vast interior are its most spectacular feature. Admire a 10m-wide window over the western façade above the organ – one of the largest in the world, with 7800 pipes (900 of which have historical classification), 111 stops, five 56-key manuals and a 32-key pedalboard – and

the window on the northern side of the transept (virtually unchanged since the 13th century).

Towers

A constant queue marks the entrance to the **Tours de Notre Dame**, the cathedral's bell towers. Climb the 400-odd spiralling steps to the top of the western façade of the North Tower, where you'll find yourself on the rooftop **Galerie des Chimères** (Gargoyles Gallery), face to face with frightening gargoyles. These grotesque statues divert rainwater from the roof to prevent masonry damage, with the water exiting through the elongated, open mouth; they also, purportedly, ward off evil spirits. Although they appear medieval, they were installed by Eugène Viollet-le-Duc in the 19th century. From the rooftop there's a spectacular view over Paris.

In the South Tower hangs Emmanuel, the cathedral's original 13-tonne bourdon bell (all of the cathedral's bells are named). During the night of 24 August 1944, when the Île de la Cité was retaken by French, Allied and Resistance troops, the tolling of the Emmanuel announced Paris' approaching liberation.

Nine new bells were installed in 2013, replicating the original medieval chimes.

Treasury

In the southeastern transept, the *trésor* (treasury) contains artwork, liturgical objects and first-class relics; pay a small fee to enter. Among its religious jewels and gems is the **Ste-Couronne** (Holy Crown), purportedly the wreath of thorns placed on Jesus' head before he was crucified. It is exhibited between 3pm and 4pm on the first Friday of each month, 3pm to 4pm every Friday during Lent, and 10am to 5pm on Good Friday.

Easier to admire is the treasury's wonderful collection, **Les Camées des Papes** (Papal cameos). Sculpted with incredible finesse in shell and framed in silver, the 268-piece collection depicts every pope in miniature from St Pierre to Pope Benoit XVI. Note the different posture, hand gestures and clothes of each pope.

The Mays

Walk past the choir, with its carved wooden stalls and statues representing the Passion of the Christ, to admire the cathedral's wonderful collection of paintings in its nave side chapels. From 1449 onwards, city goldsmiths offered to the cathedral each year on 1 May a tree strung with devotional ribbons and banners to honour the Virgin

Statues inside Notre Dame

Christus apparet ij apostolis

Mary – to whom Notre Dame (Our Lady) is dedicated. Fifty years later the goldsmiths' annual gift, known as a May, had become a tabernacle decorated with scenes from the Old Testament, and, from 1630, a large canvas – 3m tall – commemorating one of the Acts of the Apostles, accompanied by a poem or literary explanation. By the early 18th century, when the brotherhood of goldsmiths was dissolved, the cathedral had received 76 such monumental paintings – just 13 can be admired today.

Crypt

Under the square in front of Notre Dame lies the **Crypte Archéologique** (Map p250; Archaeological Crypt; ☑01 55 42 50 10; www.crypte. paris.fr; 7 Parvis Notre Dame – place Jean-Paul II, 4e; adult/child €8/free; ☺10am-6pm Tue-Sun; Ⓜ Cité), a 117m-long and 28m-wide area displaying in situ the remains of structures built on this site during the Gallo-Roman period, a 4th-century enclosure wall, the foundations of the medieval foundlings hospice and a few of the original sewers sunk by Haussmann.

Audioguides & Tours

Pick up an audioguide (€5, including treasury admission) from Notre Dame's information desk, just inside the entrance.

Free 45-minute English-language tours take place at 2pm Wednesday to Friday, and at 2.30pm Monday, Tuesday and Saturday.

Landmark Occasions

Historic events that have taken place at Notre Dame include Henry VI of England's 1431 coronation as King of France, the 1558 marriage of Mary, Queen of Scots, to the Dauphin Francis (later Francis II of France), the 1804 coronation of Napoléon I by Pope Pius VII and the 1909 beatification and 1920 canonisation of Joan of Arc.

Music at Notre Dame

Music has been a sacred part of Notre Dame's soul since birth. Experience its musical heritage on Sundays at a Gregorian or polyphonic Mass (10am and 6.30pm respectively) or a free organ recital (4.30pm).

> ### ★ The Heart of Paris
> Notre Dame is very much the heart of Paris – so much so that distances from Paris to every part of metropolitan France are measured from the vast square in front of the cathedral. A bronze star across the street from the cathedral's main entrance marks the exact location of **Point Zéro des Routes de France** (Map p250; Parvis Notre Dame – place Jan-Paul II, 4e; Ⓜ Cité).

apparet r apostolis et Chomæ

STEVE LOVEGROVE/SHUTTERSTOCK ©

> ### ★ Square Jean XXIII
> One of the best views of the cathedral's flying buttresses is from square Jean XXIII, the little park behind the cathedral.

Notre Dame

TIMELINE

1160 Maurice de Sully becomes bishop of Paris. Mission: to grace growing Paris with a lofty new cathedral.

1182–90 The ❶ **choir with double ambulatory** is finished and work starts on the nave and side chapels.

1200–50 The ❷ **west façade**, with rose window, three portals and two soaring towers, goes up. Everyone is stunned.

1345 Some 180 years after the foundation stone was laid, the Cathédrale de Notre Dame is complete. It is dedicated to notre dame (our lady), the Virgin Mary.

1789 Revolutionaries smash the original ❸ **Gallery of Kings**, pillage the cathedral and melt all its bells except the great bell Emmanuel. The cathedral becomes a Temple of Reason then a warehouse.

1831 Victor Hugo's novel *The Hunchback of Notre Dame* inspires new interest in the half-ruined Gothic cathedral.

1845–64 Architect Viollet-le-Duc undertakes its restoration. Twenty-eight new kings are sculpted for the west façade. The heavily decorated ❹ **portals** and ❺ **spire** are reconstructed. The neo-Gothic ❻ **treasury** is built.

1860 The area in front of Notre Dame is cleared to create the parvis, an al fresco classroom where Parisians can learn a catechism illustrated on sculpted stone portals.

1935 A rooster bearing part of the relics of the Crown of Thorns, St Denis and Ste Geneviève is put on top of the cathedral spire to protect those who pray inside.

1991 The architectural masterpiece of Notre Dame and its Seine-side riverbanks become a Unesco World Heritage Site.

2013 Notre Dame celebrates 850 years since construction began with a bevy of new bells and restoration works.

PAL TERAVAGIMOV PHOTOGRAPHY / GETTY IMAGES ©

Virgin & Child
Spot all 37 artworks representing the Virgin Mary. Pilgrims have revered the pearly cream sculpture of her in the sanctuary since the 14th century. Light a devotional candle and write some words to the *Livre de Vie* (Book of Life).

North Rose Window
See prophets, judges, kings and priests venerate Mary in vivid blue and violet glass, one of three beautiful rose blooms (1225–70), each almost 10m in diameter.

Flying Buttresses

DIGITAL/IMAGINATION / GETTY IMAGES ©

Choir Screen
No part of the cathedral weaves biblical tales more evocatively than these ornate wooden panels, carved in the 14th century after the Black Death killed half the country's population. The faintly gaudy colours were restored in the 1960s.

Treasury

This was the cash reserve of French kings, who ordered chalices, crucifixes, baptism fonts and other sacred gems to be melted down in the Mint during times of financial strife – war, famine and so on.

BRIAN A JACKSON / SHUTTERSTOCK ©

SYAOCHKA / SHUTTERSTOCK ©

Great Bell

The peal of Emmanuel, the cathedral's great bell, is so pure thanks to precious gems and jewels Parisian women threw into the pot when it was recast from copper and bronze in 1631. Admire its original siblings in Square Jean XXII.

Chimera Gallery

Scale the north tower for a Paris panorama admired by birds, dragons, grimacing gargoyles and grotesque chimera. Nod to celebrity chimera Stryga, who has wings, horns, a human body and sticking-out tongue. This bestial lot wards off demons.

5 Spire

6

North Tower

South Tower

Great Gallery

West Rose Window

2

3

4

Transept

North Tower Staircase

The 'Mays'

On 1 May 1630, city goldsmiths offered a 3m-high painting to the cathedral – a tradition they continued every 1 May until 1707 when the bankrupt guild folded. View 13 of these huge artworks in the side chapels.

Three Portals

Play I spy (Greed, Cowardice et al) beneath these sculpted doorways, which illustrate the seasons, life and the 12 vices and virtues alongside the Bible.

Portal of the Virgin (Exit)

Portal of the Last Judgement

Portal of St-Anne (Entrance)

Parvis Notre Dame

Cour Napoléon, Musée du Louvre

Musée du Louvre

The Mona Lisa *and the* Venus de Milo *are just two of the priceless treasures resplendently housed inside the fortress turned royal palace turned France's first national museum.*

Few art galleries are as prized or as daunting as the Musée du Louvre – one of the world's largest and most diverse museums. Showcasing 35,000 works of art, it would take nine months to glance at every piece, rendering advance planning essential.

Works of art from Europe form the permanent exhibition, alongside priceless collections of Mesopotamian, Egyptian, Greek, Roman and Islamic art and antiquities – a fascinating presentation of the evolution of Western art up through the mid-19th century.

Visiting

You need to queue twice to get in: once for security and then again to buy tickets. The longest queues are outside the Grande Pyramide; use the Carrousel du Louvre

Great For...

☑ Don't Miss

The museum's thematic trails – from the 'Art of Eating' to 'Love in the Louvre'.

❶ Need to Know

Map p250; ☎01 40 20 53 17; www.louvre.fr; rue de Rivoli & quai des Tuileries, 1er; adult/child €15/free; ⏰9am-6pm Mon, Thu, Sat & Sun, to 9.45pm Wed & Fri; Ⓜ Palais Royal–Musée du Louvre

✕ Take a Break

The Hall Napoléon sells sandwiches; ideal for a Jardin des Tuileries (p90) picnic.

★ Top Tip

Tickets are valid for the whole day, meaning you can come and go.

entrance (99 rue de Rivoli or direct from the metro).

A Paris Museum Pass or Paris City Passport gives you priority; buying tickets in advance (on the Louvre website) will also help expedite the process.

Self-guided thematic trails range from Louvre masterpieces and the art of eating to family-friendly topics. Download trail brochures in advance from the website.

Another good option is to rent a Nintendo 3DS multimedia guide (€5; ID required). More formal, English-language **guided tours** (☎01 40 20 52 63; adult/child €12/9; ⏰11am & 2pm except 1st Sun of month) depart from the Hall Napoléon. Reserve a spot up to 14 days in advance or sign up on arrival at the museum.

In late 2014, the Louvre embarked on a 30-year renovation plan, with the aim of modernising the museum to make it more accessible. Phase 1 increased the number of main entrances in order to reduce security wait times. It also revamped the central Hall Napoléon to vastly improve what was previously bewildering chaos. Important changes to come include increasing the number of English-language signs and artwork texts to aid navigation.

Palais du Louvre

The Louvre today rambles over four floors and through three wings: the **Sully Wing** creates the four sides of the Cour Carrée (literally 'Square Courtyard') at the eastern end of the complex; the **Denon Wing** stretches 800m along the Seine to the south; and the northern **Richelieu Wing** skirts rue de Rivoli. The building started life as a fortress built by Philippe-Auguste in the 12th century – medieval remnants are still visible on the Lower Ground Floor (Sully). In the 16th century it became a royal residence, and after the Revolution, in 1793, it was turned into a national museum. At the time, its booty was no more than 2500 paintings and objets d'art.

Over the centuries French governments amassed the paintings, sculptures and artefacts displayed today. The 'Grand Louvre' project, inaugurated by the late President Mitterrand in 1989, doubled the museum's exhibition space, and both new and renovated galleries have since opened, including the state-of-the-art **Islamic art galleries** (Lower Ground Floor, Denon) in the stunningly restored Cour Visconti.

Priceless Antiquities

Whatever your plans are, don't rush by the Louvre's astonishing cache of treasures from antiquity: both Mesopotamia (ground floor, Richelieu) and Egypt (ground and 1st floors, Sully) are well represented, as seen in the *Code of Hammurabi* (Room 3, ground floor, Richelieu) and the *Seated Scribe* (Room 22, 1st floor, Sully). Room 12 (ground floor, Sackler Wing) holds impressive friezes and an enormous two-headed-bull column from the Darius Palace in ancient Iran, while an enormous seated statue of Pharaoh Ramesses II highlights the temple room (Room 12, Sully).

Also worth a look are the mosaics and figurines from the Byzantine empire (lower ground floor, Denon), and the Greek statuary collection, culminating with the world's most famous armless duo, the *Venus de Milo* (Room 16, ground floor, Sully) and the *Winged Victory of Samothrace* (top of Daru staircase, 1st floor, Denon).

Statues in the Cour Puget, Richelieu Wing, Musée du Louvre

French & Italian Masterpieces

The 1st floor of the Denon Wing, where the *Mona Lisa* is found, is easily the most popular part of the Louvre – and with good reason. Rooms 75 through 77 are hung with monumental French paintings, many iconic: look for the *Consecration of the Emperor Napoléon I* (David), *The Raft of the Medusa* (Géricault) and *Grande Odalisque* (Ingres).

Rooms 1, 3, 5 and 8 are also must-visits. Filled with classic works by Renaissance masters (Raphael, Titian, Uccello, Botticini), this area culminates with the crowds around the *Mona Lisa*. But you'll find plenty else to contemplate, from Botticelli's graceful frescoes (Room 1) to the superbly detailed *Wedding Feast at Cana* (Room 6).

Mona Lisa

Easily the Louvre's most admired work (and the world's most famous painting) is Leonardo da Vinci's *La Joconde* (in French; *La Gioconda* in Italian), the lady with that enigmatic smile known as *Mona Lisa* (Room 6, 1st floor, Denon).

Mona (*monna* in Italian) is a contraction of *madonna*, and Gioconda is the feminine form of the surname Giocondo. Canadian scientists used infrared technology to peer through paint layers and confirm *Mona Lisa's* identity as Lisa Gherardini (1479–1542?), wife of Florentine merchant Francesco de Giocondo. Scientists also discovered that her dress was covered in a transparent gauze veil typically worn in early 16th-century Italy by pregnant women or new mothers; it's surmised that the work was painted to commemorate the birth of her second son around 1503, when she was aged about 24.

★ Italian Sculptures

On the ground floor of the Denon Wing, take time for the Italian sculptures, including Michelangelo's *The Dying Slave* and Canova's *Psyche and Cupid* (Room 4).

AN/IOR LIGHT/SHUTTERSTOCK ©

The Pyramid Inside & Out

Almost as stunning as the masterpieces inside is the 21m-high glass pyramid designed by Chinese-born American architect IM Pei that bedecks the main entrance to the Louvre in a dazzling crown. Beneath Pei's Grande Pyramide is the **Hall Napoléon**, the main entrance area, comprising an information booth, temporary exhibition hall, bookshop, souvenir store, cafe and auditoriums.

★ Louis XV's Crown

French kings wore their crowns only once – at their coronation. Lined with embroidered satin and topped with openwork arches and a fleur-de-lis, Louis XV's 1722-crafted crown (Room 66, 1st floor, Denon) was originally adorned with pearls, sapphires, rubies, topazes, emeralds and diamonds.

The Louvre

A HALF-DAY TOUR

Successfully visiting the Louvre is a fine art. Its complex labyrinth of galleries and staircases spiralling three wings and four floors renders discovery a snakes-and-ladders experience. Initiate yourself with this three-hour itinerary – a playful mix of *Mona Lisa*–obvious and up-to-the-minute unexpected.

Arriving in the newly renovated ❶ **Hall Napoléon** beneath IM Pei's glass pyramid, pick up colour-coded floor plans at an information stand, then ride the escalator up to the Sully Wing and swap passport or credit card for a multimedia guide (there are limited descriptions in the galleries) at the wing entrance.

The Louvre is as much about spectacular architecture as masterful art. To appreciate this, zip up and down Sully's Escalier Henri II to admire ❷ **Venus de Milo**, then up parallel Escalier Henri IV to the palatial displays in ❸ **Cour Khorsabad**. Cross Room 1 to find the escalator up to the 1st floor and the opulent ❹ **Napoleon III apartments**. Next traverse 25 consecutive galleries (thank you, floor plan!) to flip conventional contemplation on its head with Cy Twombly's ❺ **The Ceiling**, and the hypnotic ❻ **Winged Victory of Samothrace** sculpture, which brazenly insists on being admired from all angles. End with the impossibly famous ❼ **The Raft of the Medusa**, ❽ **Mona Lisa** and ❾ **Virgin & Child**.

BRIAN KINNEY / SHUTTERSTOCK ©

Napoleon III Apartments
1st Floor, Richelieu
Napoleon III's gorgeous gilt apartments were built from 1854 to 1861, featuring an over-the-top decor of gold leaf, stucco and crystal chandeliers that reaches a dizzying climax in the Grand Salon and State Dining Room.

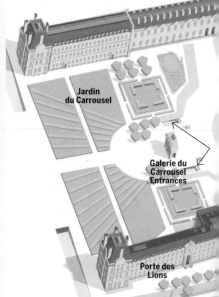

Jardin du Carrousel

Galerie du Carrousel Entrances

Porte des Lions

TOP TIPS

➡ Don't even consider entering the Louvre's maze of galleries without a floor plan, free from the information desk in the Hall Napoléon.

➡ The Denon Wing is always packed; visit on late nights (Wednesday or Friday) or trade Denon in for the notably quieter Richelieu Wing.

➡ Tickets to the Louvre are valid for the whole day, meaning that you can nip out for lunch.

LOUVRE AUDITORIUM

Classical-music concerts are staged several times a week at the Louvre Auditorium (off the main entrance hall). Don't miss the Thursday lunchtime concerts featuring emerging composers and musicians. The season runs from September to April or May, depending on the concert series.

Mona Lisa
Room 6, 1st Floor, Denon
No smile is as enigmatic or bewitching as hers. Da Vinci's diminutive *La Joconde* hangs opposite the largest painting in the Louvre – sumptuous, fellow Italian Renaissance artwork *The Wedding at Cana*.

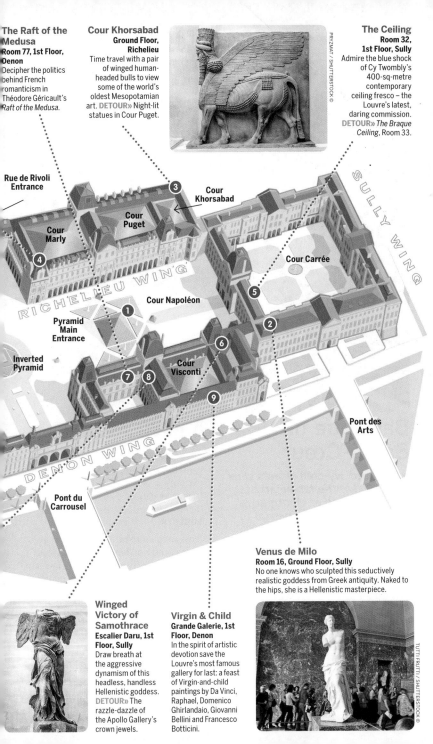

The Raft of the Medusa
Room 77, 1st Floor, Denon
Decipher the politics behind French romanticism in Théodore Géricault's *Raft of the Medusa*.

Cour Khorsabad
Ground Floor, Richelieu
Time travel with a pair of winged human-headed bulls to view some of the world's oldest Mesopotamian art. DETOUR» Night-lit statues in Cour Puget.

PRYZMAT / SHUTTERSTOCK ©

The Ceiling
Room 32, 1st Floor, Sully
Admire the blue shock of Cy Twombly's 400-sq-metre contemporary ceiling fresco – the Louvre's latest, daring commission. DETOUR» *The Braque Ceiling*, Room 33.

Rue de Rivoli Entrance

Cour Khorsabad

③

Cour Puget

Cour Marly

④

RICHELIEU WING

SULLY WING

Cour Carrée

⑤

Cour Napoléon

①

Pyramid Main Entrance

②

Inverted Pyramid

⑥

Cour Visconti

⑦ ⑧

⑨

DENON WING

Pont des Arts

Pont du Carrousel

Venus de Milo
Room 16, Ground Floor, Sully
No one knows who sculpted this seductively realistic goddess from Greek antiquity. Naked to the hips, she is a Hellenistic masterpiece.

Winged Victory of Samothrace
Escalier Daru, 1st Floor, Sully
Draw breath at the aggressive dynamism of this headless, handless Hellenistic goddess. DETOUR» The razzle-dazzle of the Apollo Gallery's crown jewels.

Virgin & Child
Grande Galerie, 1st Floor, Denon
In the spirit of artistic devotion save the Louvre's most famous gallery for last: a feast of Virgin-and-child paintings by Da Vinci, Raphael, Domenico Ghirlandaio, Giovanni Bellini and Francesco Botticini.

TUTTI FRUTTI / SHUTTERSTOCK ©

NATTEE CHALERMTIRAGOOL/SHUTTERSTOCK ©

Basilique du Sacré-Cœur

Staircased, ivy-clad streets slink up the hill of the fabled artists' neighbourhood of Montmartre to a funicular that glides up to the dove-white domes of Paris' landmark basilica, Sacré-Cœur.

Great For...

☑ Don't Miss

Dizzying vistas across Paris, especially from up inside the basilica's main dome.

More than just a basilica, Sacré-Cœur is a veritable experience, from the musicians performing on the steps to the groups of friends picnicking on the hillside park.

History

It may appear to be a place of peacefulness and worship today, but in truth Sacré-Cœur's foundations were laid amid bloodshed and controversy. Its construction began in 1875, in the wake of France's humiliating defeat by Prussia and the subsequent chaos of the Paris Commune. Following Napoléon III's surrender to von Bismarck in September 1870, angry Parisians, with the help of the National Guard, continued to hold out against Prussian forces – a harrowing siege that lasted four long winter months. By the time a ceasefire was negotiated in early 1871, the split be-

❶ Need to Know

Map p249; ☎01 53 41 89 00; www.
sacre-coeur-montmartre.com; Parvis du
Sacré-Cœur; basilica free, dome adult/child
€6/4, cash only; ⏱basilica 6am-10.30pm,
dome 8.30am-8pm May-Sep, 9am-5pm Oct-
Apr; Ⓜ Anvers, Abbesses

✕ Take a Break

Head to the terrace of **L'Été en Pente
Douce** (Map p249; ☎01 42 64 02 67;
http://lete-en-pente-douce.business.site;
8 rue Paul Albert, 18e; mains €10.50-17;
⏱noon-midnight; Ⓜ Château Rouge) for
French classics.

★ Top Tip

To skip walking up the hill, use a regular
metro ticket aboard the funicular.

tween the radical working-class Parisians
(supported by the National Guard) and the
conservative national government (supported by the French army) had become
insurmountable.

Over the next several months, the
rebels, known as Communards, managed
to overthrow the reactionary government
and take over the city. It was a particularly
chaotic and bloody moment in Parisian
history, with mass executions on both
sides and a wave of rampant destruction
that spread throughout Paris. Montmartre
was a key Communard stronghold – it was
on the future site of Sacré-Cœur that the
rebels won their first victory – and it was
consequently the first neighbourhood to be
targeted when the French army returned
in full force in May 1871. Ultimately, many
Communards were buried alive in the gypsum mines beneath the Butte.

The Basilica

Within the historical context, the construction of an enormous basilica to expiate the
city's sins seemed like a gesture of peace
and forgiveness – indeed, the seven million
French francs needed to construct the
church's foundations came solely from the
contributions of local Catholics. However,
the Montmartre location was certainly no
coincidence: the conservative old guard
desperately wanted to assert its power in
what was then a hotbed of revolution. The
battle between the two camps – Catholic
versus secular, royalist versus republican –
raged on and in 1882 the construction of
the basilica was even voted down by the
city council on the grounds that it would

continue to fan the flames of civil war. It was overturned in the end by a technicality.

The Romano-Byzantine–style basilica's travertine stone exudes calcite, ensuring it remains white despite weathering and pollution. Six successive architects oversaw construction of the basilica, and it wasn't until 1919 that Sacré-Cœur was finally consecrated, contrasting the surrounding area's bohemian lifestyle.

While criticism of its design and white travertine stone has continued throughout the decades (one poet called it a giant baby's bottle for angels), the interior is enlivened by the glittering apse mosaic *Christ in Majesty*, designed by Luc-Olivier Merson in 1922 and one of the largest in the world.

On Sundays, you can catch the organ being played during Mass and Vespers.

The Dome

Outside, to the west of the main entrance, 300 spiralling steps lead you to the basilica's dome, which affords one of Paris' most spectacular panoramas; it's said you can see for 30km on a clear day. Weighing in at 19 tonnes, the bell called La Savoyarde in the tower above is the largest in France.

What's Nearby?

Place du Tertre Square

(Map p249; 18e; M Abbesses) Today filled with visitors, buskers and portrait artists, place du Tertre was originally the main square of the village of Montmartre before it was incorporated into the city proper.

Espace Dalí Gallery

(Map p249; 01 42 64 40 21; www.daliparis.com; 11 rue Poulbot, 18e; adult/child €12/9; 10am-

Place du Tertre

6pm Sep-Jun, to 8pm Jul & Aug; M Abbesses)
More than 300 works by Salvador Dalí
(1904–89), the flamboyant Catalan
surrealist printmaker, painter, sculptor and
self-promoter, are on display at this basement museum located just west of place
du Tertre. The collection includes Dalí's
strange sculptures, lithographs, and many
of his illustrations and furniture, including
the famous Mae West Lips Sofa.

Clos Montmartre · Vineyard

(Map p249; 18 rue des Saules, 18e; M Lamarck–
Caulaincourt) Epitomising Montmartre's
enchanting village-like atmosphere, the
quartier has its own small vineyard. Planted
in 1933, its 2000 vines produce an average
of 800 bottles of wine a year. Each October
the grapes are pressed, fermented and bottled in Montmartre's town hall, then sold by
auction to raise funds for local community
projects. It's closed to the public except for
a handful of special events.

Musée de Montmartre · Museum

(Map p249; ☎ 01 49 25 89 39; http://museede
montmartre.fr; 12 rue Cortot, 18e; adult/child
€9.50/5.50, garden only €4; ☺ 10am-7pm Apr-Sep,
to 6pm Oct-Mar; M Lamarck–Caulaincourt) This
delightful 'village' museum showcases paintings, lithographs and documents illustrating
Montmartre's bohemian, artistic and he-
donistic past – one room is dedicated to the
French cancan. It's housed in a 17th-century
manor where several artists, including Renoir
and Raoul Dufy, had their studios in the 19th
century. You can also visit the studio of painter Suzanne Valadon, who lived and worked
here with her son Maurice Utrillo and partner
André Utter between 1912 and 1926.

Moulin Blute Fin · Windmill

(Map p249; Moulin de la Galette; rue Lepic, 18e;
M Abbesses) Sister windmill to surviving
Moulin Radet (Map p249; 83 rue Lepic,
18e) on the same street, this abandoned
18th-century windmill ground flour on
its hillock perch above rue Lepic. It later
became known as Moulin de la Galette after
the *guinguette* (dance hall) – immortalised
in Renoir's painting, *Bal du Moulin de la Galette* (1876), now in the Musée d'Orsay – that
sprang up around its base in the 1930s.

★ Top Tip

Allow ample time to stroll the Musée
de Montmartre gardens, named after
Renoir, who painted his masterpieces
Bal du Moulin de la Galette and *Jardin de
la rue Cortot* while working in his studio
here from 1875 to 1877.

Musée d'Orsay

The grand former railway station in which the Musée d'Orsay is located is an art nouveau marvel, but the masterpieces from 1848 to 1914 are the stars of the show.

Great For...

ℹ Need to Know

Map p246; ☎01 40 49 48 14; www.musee-orsay.fr; 1 rue de la Légion d'Honneur, 7e; adult/child €12/free; ⏱9.30am-6pm Tue, Wed & Fri-Sun, to 9.45pm Thu; MAssemblée Nationale, RER Musée d'Orsay

The Four Parts of the World Holding the Celestial Sphere by Jean-Baptiste Carpeaux, Musée d'Orsay

★ **Top Tip**

Musée d'Orsay admission drops to €9 after 4.30pm (after 6pm on Thursday).

History

The Gare d'Orsay railway station was designed by competition-winning architect Victor Laloux. Even on its completion, just in time for the 1900 Exposition Universelle, painter Edouard Detaille declared that the new station looked like a Palais des Beaux Arts. But although it had its own hotel and all the mod-cons of the day – including luggage lifts and passenger elevators – by 1939 the increasing electrification of the rail network meant the platforms were too short for mainline trains, and within a few years all rail services ceased.

The station was used as a mailing centre during WWII, and in 1962 Orson Welles filmed Kafka's *The Trial* in the then-abandoned building. Fortunately, it was saved from being demolished and replaced with a hotel complex by a Historical Monument listing in 1973, before the government set about establishing the palatial museum.

Transforming the languishing building into the country's premier showcase for art from 1848 to 1914 was the grand project of President Valéry Giscard d'Estaing, who signed off on it in 1977. The museum opened its doors in 1986.

Far from resting on its laurels, major renovations at the Musée d'Orsay between 2008 and 2011 incorporated a re-energised layout and increased exhibition space. World-renowned paintings now gleam from richly coloured walls that create an intimate, stately-home-like atmosphere, with high-tech illumination literally casting the masterpieces in a new light.

Le Restaurant, Musée d'Orsay

Paintings

Most visitors make a beeline for the world's largest collection of impressionist and post-impressionist art, the highlights of which include Manet's *On the Beach* and *Woman with Fans;* Monet's gardens at Giverny and *Rue Montorgueil, Paris, Celebration of June 30, 1878;* Cézanne's card players, *Green Apples* and *Blue Vase;* Renoir's *Ball at the Moulin de la Galette* and *Young Girls at the Piano;* Degas' ballerinas; Toulouse-Lautrec's cabaret dancers; Pissarro's *The Seine and the Louvre;* Sisley's *View of the Canal St-Martin;* and Van Gogh's self-portraits,

> ### ☑ Don't Miss
>
> The cavernous former station is a magnificent setting for sculptures, including works by Degas, Gauguin, Camille Claudel, Renoir and Rodin.

CHRISTIAN MUELLER/SHUTTERSTOCK ©

Bedroom in Arles and *Starry Night over the Rhône*. Less high-profile but classified a National Treasure is James Tissot's 1868 painting *The Circle of the Rue Royale.*

Decorative & Graphic Arts

Household items such as hat and coat stands, candlesticks, desks, chairs, bookcases, vases, pot-plant holders, freestanding screens, wall mirrors, water pitchers, plates, goblets and bowls become works of art in the hands of their creators from the era, incorporating exquisite design elements.

Drawings, pastels and sketches from major artists are another of the d'Orsay's lesser-known highlights. Look for Georges Seurat's *The Black Bow* (c 1882), which uses crayon on paper to define forms by contrasting between black and white, and Paul Gauguin's poignant self-portrait (c 1902–03), drawn near the end of his life.

Visiting

Combined tickets are available with the Musée de l'Orangerie (p90; €16) and the Musée Rodin (p67; €18); both combination tickets are valid for a single visit to the museums within three months.

The museum is busiest Tuesday and Sunday, followed by Thursday and Saturday. Save time by buying tickets online and head directly to entrance C.

For a thorough introduction to the museum, 90-minute 'Masterpieces of the Musée d'Orsay' guided tours (€6) in English run at 11.30am and 2.30pm on Tuesday and 11.30am from Wednesday to Saturday. Kids under 13 aren't permitted on adult tours (family tours are available). An audioguide costs €5.

✗ Take a Break

Time has scarcely changed the museum's – originally the station's – **Le Restaurant** (Map p246; ☎ 01 45 49 47 03; 2-course lunch menu €22.50, mains €18-27; ⏱ 11.45am-5.30pm Tue, Wed & Fri-Sun, 11.45am-2.45pm & 7-9.30pm Thu; ♿; Ⓜ Assemblée Nationale, RER Musée d'Orsay).

Gardens of the Musée Rodin

GIMAS/SHUTTERSTOCK ©

Musée Rodin

Paris' most romantic museum displays Auguste Rodin's sculptural masterpieces in his former workshop and showroom, the 1730-built, beautifully restored Hôtel Biron, as well as in its rambling rose gardens.

Sculptor, painter, sketcher, engraver and collector Auguste Rodin donated his entire collection to the French state in 1908 on the proviso they dedicate his former workshop and showroom to displaying his works. They're now installed not only in the mansion itself, but also in its rose-filled garden – one of the most peaceful places in central Paris.

Sculptures

The first large-scale cast of Rodin's famous sculpture **The Thinker** (*Le Penseur*), made in 1902, resides in the garden – the perfect place to contemplate this heroic naked figure conceived by Rodin to represent intellect and poetry (it was originally titled *The Poet*).

   The Gates of Hell (*La Porte de l'Enfer*) was commissioned in 1880 as the entrance

Great For...

☑ Don't Miss

Rodin's collection of works by artists including Van Gogh, Renoir and Camille Claudel.

The Gates of Hell by Rodin

ALARICO/SHUTTERSTOCK ©

❶ Need to Know

Map p246; ☎ 01 44 18 61 10; www.musee-rodin.fr; 79 rue de Varenne, 7e; adult/child €10/free, garden only €4/free; ⊙ 10am-5.45pm Tue-Sun; Ⓜ Varenne or Invalides

✕ Take a Break

Paris' oldest restaurant, **À la Petite Chaise** (Map p246; ☎ 01 42 22 13 35; www.alapetitechaise.fr; 36 rue de Grenelle, 6e; 2-/3-course lunch menu €25/33, 3-course dinner menu €26, mains €21; ⊙ noon-2pm & 7-11pm; Ⓜ Sèvres-Babylone), **still serves excellent traditional fare.**

★ Top Tip

Cheaper garden-only entry is available.

for a never-built museum, and Rodin worked on his sculptural masterwork up until his death in 1917. Standing 6m high by 4m wide, its 180 figures comprise an intricate scene from Dante's *Inferno*.

Marble monument to love **The Kiss** (*Le Baiser*) was originally part of *The Gates of Hell*. The sculpture's entwined lovers caused controversy on its completion due to Rodin's then-radical approach of depicting women as equal partners in ardour.

The museum also features many sculptures by Camille Claudel, Rodin's protégé and muse.

Rodin at the Hôtel Biron

Extensive renovations to the museum between 2012 and 2015 – the first since Rodin worked here until his death in 1917 – included the creation of Biron Grey, a new colour of paint by British company Farrow & Ball. It now provides a backdrop to sculptures within the mansion.

The 'Rodin at the Hôtel Biron' room incorporates original furniture to recreate the space as it was when he lived and worked here.

Visiting

Prepurchase tickets online to avoid queuing. Audioguides cost €6. A combined ticket with the Musée d'Orsay costs €18; combination tickets are valid for a single visit to each of the museums within three months.

What's Nearby?

Hôtel Matignon   Landmark

(Map p246; 57 rue de Varenne, 7e; Ⓜ Solférino) Hôtel Matignon has been the official residence of the French prime minister since the start of the Fifth Republic (1958). It's closed to the public.

Jardin du Luxembourg

The city's most beautiful park, the Jardin du Luxembourg, is an inner-city oasis encompassing 23 gracefully laid-out hectares of formal terraces, chestnut groves and lush lawns.

Great For...

ℹ Need to Know

Map p252; www.senat.fr/visite/jardin; ⊙hours vary; Ⓜ Mabillon, St-Sulpice, Rennes, Notre Dame des Champs, RER Luxembourg

Toy boats on the Grand Bassin (p70), outside the Palais du Luxembourg (p71)

★ **Top Tip**

For a quick snack or drink, kiosks and cafes are dotted throughout the park.

The Jardin du Luxembourg has a special place in Parisians' hearts. Napoléon dedicated the gardens to the children of Paris, and many residents spent their childhood prodding little wooden sailboats with long sticks on the octagonal pond, watching puppet shows, and riding the carousel or ponies.

All those activities are still here today, as are modern playgrounds and sporting and games venues.

History

The Jardin du Luxembourg's history stretches further back than Napoléon's dedication. The gardens are a backdrop to the Palais du Luxembourg, built in the 1620s for Marie de Médici, Henri IV's consort, to assuage her longing for the Pitti Palace in Florence. The Palais is now home to the French Senate, which, in addition to parliamentary-assembly activities like voting on legislation, is charged with promoting the palace and its gardens.

Numerous overhauls over the centuries have given the Jardin du Luxembourg a blend of traditional French- and English-style gardens that is unique in Paris.

Grand Bassin

All ages love the octagonal Grand Bassin, a serene ornamental pond where adults can lounge and kids can play with 1920s **toy sailboats** (Map p252; sailboat rental per 30min €4; ☺11am-6pm Apr-Oct; Ⓜ Notre Dame des Champs, RER Luxembourg). Nearby, littlies can take **pony rides** (Map p252; 🖉06 07 32 53 95; www.animaponey.com; 600m/900m pony ride €6/8.50; ☺3-6pm Wed, Sat, Sun & school holidays) or romp around the **playgrounds** (Map p252; adult/child €1.50/2.50; ☺hours

Jardin du Luxembourg

vary) – the green half is for kids aged seven to 12 years, the blue half for under-sevens.

Puppet Shows

You don't have to be a kid or speak French to be delighted by marionette shows, which have entertained audiences in France since the Middle Ages. The lively puppets perform in the little **Théâtre du Luxembourg** (Map p252; 01 43 29 50 97; www.marionnettesduluxembourg.fr; tickets €6.40; Wed, Sat & Sun, daily during school holidays; Notre Dame des Champs). Show times can vary; check the program online and arrive half an hour ahead.

☑ Don't Miss

Discovering the park's many sculptures, which include statues of Stendhal, Chopin, Baudelaire and Delacroix.

Orchards

Dozens of apple varieties grow in the **orchards** (Map p252; Notre Dame des Champs or RER Luxembourg) in the gardens' south. Bees have produced honey in the nearby apiary, the **Rucher du Luxembourg** (Map p252), since the 19th century. The annual Fête du Miel (Honey Festival) offers two days of tasting and buying its sweet harvest around late September in the ornate **Pavillon Davioud** (Map p252; 55bis rue d'Assas, 6e).

Palais du Luxembourg

The **Palais du Luxembourg** (Map p252; www. senat.fr; rue de Vaugirard, 6e; Mabillon, RER Luxembourg) was built in the 1620s and has been home to the Sénat (French Senate) since 1958. It's occasionally open for visits by guided tour. East of the palace is the ornate, Italianate **Fontaine des Médici** (Map p252), built in 1630. During Baron Haussmann's 19th-century reshaping of the roads, the fountain was moved 30m, and the pond and dramatic statues of the giant bronze Polyphemus discovering the white-marble lovers Acis and Galatea were added.

Musée du Luxembourg

Prestigious temporary art exhibitions, such as *Cézanne et Paris*, take place in the beautiful **Musée du Luxembourg** (Map p252; 01 40 13 62 00; http://museeduluxembourg. fr; 19 rue de Vaugirard, 6e; most exhibitions €13; 10.30am-7pm Sat-Thu, to 10pm Fri; St-Sulpice, RER Luxembourg). Around the back of the museum, lemon and orange trees, palms, grenadiers and oleanders shelter from the cold in the palace's **orangery**.

✗ Take a Break

Park picnics aside, nearby options include family-style French cuisine at historic **Polidor** (Map p252; 01 43 26 95 34; www.polidor.com; 41 rue Monsieur le Prince, 6e; menus €22 & €35, mains €13-20; noon-2.30pm & 7pm-12.30am Mon-Sat, to 11pm Sun; Odéon).

The Pont Neuf

Cruising the Seine

The lifeline of Paris, the Seine sluices through the city, spanned by 37 bridges. Cruises along the river are an idyllic way to observe its Unesco World Heritage–listed riverbanks.

Great For...

☑ **Don't Miss**

Floating past Parisian landmarks such as the Louvre and Notre Dame.

Boat Trips & Cruise Companies

A plethora of companies run day- and night-time boat tours (usually lasting around an hour) with commentary in multiple languages.

An alternative to traditional boat tours is the Batobus (p238), a handy hop-on, hop-off service that stops at quintessentially Parisian attractions: the Eiffel Tower, Champs-Élysées, Musée d'Orsay, Musée du Louvre, St-Germain des Prés, Hôtel de Ville, Notre Dame and Jardin des Plantes. Single- and multiday tickets allow you to spend as long as you like sightseeing between stops.

Vedettes de Paris (Map p246; ☎01 44 18 19 50; www.vedettesdeparis.fr; Port de Suffren, 7e; adult/child €15/7; ☉11.30am-7.30pm May-Sep, 11.30am-5.30pm Oct-Apr; Ⓜ Bir Hakeim, RER Pont de l'Alma) **These one-hour sightseeing cruises**

ⓘ Need to Know

There are no barriers at the water's edge; keep a close eye on young children.

✕ Take a Break

Many cruise companies offer brunch, lunch and dinner cruises with high-quality food.

★ Top Tip

Floodlights illuminate the iconic riverside buildings at night.

---

on smaller boats are a more intimate experience than the major companies. It runs themed cruises too, including imaginative 'Mysteries of Paris' tours for kids (adult/child €15/9).

Vedettes du Pont Neuf (Map p250; ☎01 46 33 98 38; www.vedettesdupontneuf.com; square du Vert Galant, 1er; adult/child €14/7; ⊙10.30am–9pm; Ⓜ Pont Neuf) One-hour cruises depart year-round from Vedettes' centrally located dock at the western tip of Île de la Cité; commentary is in French and English. Tickets are cheaper if you buy in advance online (adult/child €10/5). Check the website for details of its one-hour lunch cruises (adult/child €41/35), two-hour dinner (€71/35) and Champagne cruises (adult/child €104/35).

Bateaux Parisiens (Map p246; ☎08 25 01 01 01; www.bateauxparisiens.com; Port de la Bourdonnais, 7e; adult/child €15/7; Ⓜ Bir Hakeim,

RER Pont de l'Alma) This vast operation runs hour-long river circuits with audioguides in 14 languages (every 30 minutes 10am to 11pm April to September, hourly 10.30am to 10pm October to March), and a host of themed lunch and dinner cruises. It has two locations: one by the Eiffel Tower, the other south of Notre Dame.

Bateaux-Mouches (Map p246; ☎01 42 25 96 10; www.bateaux-mouches.fr; Port de la Conférence, 8e; adult/child €13.50/6; Ⓜ Alma Marceau) Bateaux-Mouches, the largest river cruise company in Paris, is a favourite with tour groups. Departing just east of the Pont de l'Alma on the Right Bank, cruises (70 minutes) run regularly from 10am to 10.30pm April to September and every 40 minutes from 11am to 9.20pm the rest of the year. Commentary is in French and English.

Paris Canal Croisières (Map p246; ☎01 42 40 96 97; www.pariscanal.com; quai Anatole France, 7e; adult/child €22/14; ⊙Mar–mid-Nov; Ⓜ Solférino, RER Musée d'Orsay) Seasonal 2½-hour Seine-and-canal cruises depart from quai Anatole France near the Musée d'Orsay (morning cruises) and from Parc de la Villette (afternoon cruises).

Entrance hall, Centre Pompidou

Centre Pompidou

The primary-coloured, inside-out Centre Pompidou building houses France's national modern and contemporary art museum, the Musée National d'Art Moderne (MNAM), showcasing creations from 1905 to the present day.

Great For...

☑ Don't Miss

The sweeping panorama of Paris from the rooftop.

Galleries and exhibitions, hands-on workshops, dance performances, a bookshop, a design boutique, cinemas and other entertainment venues here are an irresistible cocktail.

Architecture & Views

Former French President Georges Pompidou wanted an ultracontemporary artistic hub and he got it: competition-winning architects Renzo Piano and Richard Rogers designed the building inside out, with utilitarian features like plumbing, pipes, air vents and electrical cables forming part of the external façade.

Viewed from a distance (such as from Sacré-Cœur), the Centre Pompidou's primary-coloured, boxlike form amid a sea of muted grey Parisian rooftops makes it look like a child's Meccano set abandoned

on someone's elegant living-room rug.
Although the Centre Pompidou is just six
storeys high, the city's low-rise cityscape
means stupendous views extend from
its roof (reached by external escalators
enclosed in tubes). Rooftop admission is
included in museum and exhibition admission – or buy a panorama ticket (€5) just
for the roof.

Musée National d'Art Moderne

Europe's largest collection of modern art
fills the bright and airy, well-lit galleries of
the National Museum of Modern Art, covering two complete floors of the Pompidou.
For art lovers, this is one of the jewels of
Paris. On a par with the permanent collection are the two temporary exhibition halls
(on the ground floor/basement and the top
floor), which showcase some memorable

blockbuster exhibits. Also of note is the
fabulous children's gallery on the 1st floor.

The permanent collection changes every
two years, but the basic layout generally
stays the same. The 5th floor showcases
artists active between 1905 and 1970 (give
or take a decade); the 4th floor focuses
on more contemporary creations, roughly
from the 1990s onward.

The dynamic presentation of the 5th
floor mixes up works by Picasso, Matisse,
Chagall and Kandinsky with lesser-known
contemporaries from as far afield as Argentina and Japan, as well as more famous
cross-Atlantic names such as Arbus,
Warhol, Pollock and Rothko.

One floor down on the 4th, you'll find
monumental paintings, installation pieces,
sculpture and video take centre stage. The
focus here is on contemporary art, architecture and design.

Tours & Guides

Guided tours in English take place at 2pm on Saturday and sometimes Sunday (€4.50; reserve online). The museum no longer provides audioguides; instead, visitors are encouraged to download the Centre Pompidou app (which unfortunately receives only so-so reviews) and bring headphones.

Atelier Brancusi

West of the Centre Pompidou main building, this reconstruction of the **studio** (Map p250; www.centrepompidou.fr; 55 rue de Rambuteau, 4e; incl in admission to Centre Pompidou adult/child €14/free; ☺2-6pm Wed-Mon; Ⓜ Rambuteau) of Romanian-born sculptor Constantin Brancusi (1876–1957) – known for works such as *The Kiss* and *Bird in*

Space – contains over 100 sculptures in stone and wood. You'll also find drawings, pedestals and photographic plates from his original Paris studio.

Street Fun

The full-monty Pompidou experience is as much about hanging out in the busy streets and squares around it, packed with souvenir shops and people, as absorbing the centre's contents. West of the Centre Pompidou, fun-packed place Georges Pompidou and its nearby pedestrian streets attract bags of buskers, musicians, jugglers and mime artists. Don't miss place Igor Stravinsky with its fanciful mechanical fountains of skeletons, hearts, treble clefs, and a big pair of ruby-red lips by Jean Tinguely and Niki de Saint Phalle.

Forum des Halles

What's Nearby?

Église St-Eustache — Church

(Map p250; www.st-eustache.org; 2 impasse St-Eustache, 1er; 🕑9.30am-7pm Mon-Fri, 9am-7.15pm Sat & Sun; MLes Halles, RER Châtelet–Les Halles) Just north of the gardens adjoining the city's old marketplace, now the Forum des Halles, is one of the most beautiful churches in Paris. Majestic, architecturally magnificent and musically outstanding, St-Eustache was constructed between 1532 and 1632 and is primarily Gothic. Artistic highlights include a work by Rubens, Raymond Mason's colourful bas-relief of market vendors (1969) and Keith Haring's bronze triptych (1990) in the side chapels.

Outside the church is a gigantic sculpture of a head and hand entitled *L'Écoute* (Listen; 1986) by Henri de Miller.

One of France's largest organs, above the church's western entrance, has 101 stops and 8000 pipes dating from 1854. Free organ recitals at 5.30pm on Sunday are a must for music lovers; there are also various concerts during the week – schedules and prices are listed online.

Forum des Halles — Notable Building

(Map p250; www.forumdeshalles.com; 1 rue Pierre Lescot, 1er; 🕑shops 10am-8pm Mon-Sat, 11am-7pm Sun; MLes Halles, RER Châtelet–Les Halles) Paris' main wholesale food market stood here for nearly 800 years before being replaced by this underground shopping mall in 1971. Long considered an eyesore by many Parisians, the mall's exterior was finally demolished in 2011 to make way for its golden-hued translucent canopy, unveiled in 2016. Below, four floors of stores (over 100), some 20 eateries and entertainment venues including cinemas and a swimming pool extend down to the city's busiest metro hub.

Bourse de Commerce — Museum

(Map p250; www.collectionpinaultparis.com; 2 rue de Viarmes, 1er; MLes Halles, RER Châtelet–Les Halles) Paris' newest art museum is housed in an eye-catching 18th-century rotunda that once held the city's grain market and stock exchange. Japanese architect Tadao Ando designed the ambitious new interior, where three floors of galleries will display contemporary art from the $1.4 billion collection of François Pinault. It's slated to open in early 2019.

> ★ **Travel with Children**
>
> The Centre Pompidou runs art workshops (for kids aged three to 12) and teen events in Studio 13/16.

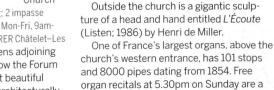

KLEV VICTOR/SHUTTERSTOCK ©

> ★ **Top Tip**
>
> Spilling out from the canopied centre of the Forum des Halles, new gardens will have *pétanque* (a variant on the game of bowls) courts, chess tables, a central patio and pedestrian walkways – it's expected to be completed by mid- to late 2018.

MAKAI TAMORI/SHUTTERSTOCK ©

Cimetière du Père Lachaise

Paris is a collection of villages and this sprawling cemetery of cobbled lanes and elaborate tombs, with a 'population' of over one million, qualifies as one in its own right.

Great For...

☑ Don't Miss

Oscar Wilde, Jim Morrison, Édith Piaf and countless other famous names.

The world's most visited cemetery was founded in 1804, and initially attracted few funerals because of its distance from the city centre. The authorities responded by exhuming famous remains and resettling them here. Their marketing ploy worked and Cimetière du Père Lachaise has been Paris' most fashionable final address ever since.

Famous Occupants

Paris residency was the only criterion needed to be buried in Père Lachaise, hence the cemetery's cosmopolitan population, which includes Irish playright Oscar Wilde and 1960s rock god Jim Morrison. Other famous occupants buried here are the composer Chopin; the playwright Molière; the poet Apollinaire; writers Balzac, Proust, Gertrude Stein and Colette; the actors Si-

ⓘ Need to Know

Map p254; ☎01 55 25 82 10; www.pere-lachaise.com; 16 rue du Repos & 8 bd de Ménilmontant, 20e; ⊙8am–6pm Mon–Fri, 8.30am–6pm Sat, 9am–6pm Sun mid-Mar–Oct, shorter hours Nov–mid-Mar; Ⓜ️Père Lachaise, Gambetta

✕ Take a Break

Book ahead for neobistro fare at nearby Le Servan (p130).

★ Top Tip

Arriving at Gambetta metro station allows you to walk downhill through the cemetery.

What's Nearby?

L'Atelier des Lumières Museum

(Map p254; www.atelier-lumieres.com; 38-40 rue St-Maur, 11e; adult/child €14.50/9.50; ⊙10am–6pm Sun-Thu, to 10pm Fri & Sat; Ⓜ️Voltaire) A former foundry dating from 1835 that supplied iron for the French navy and railroads now, since opening in 2018, houses Paris' first digital art museum. The 1500-sq-metre La Halle mounts dazzling light projections that take over the bare walls. Long programs lasting around 30 minutes are based on historic artists' works; there's also a shorter contemporary program. Screenings are continuous. In the separate Le Studio space, you can discover emerging and established digital artists.

mone Signoret, Sarah Bernhardt and Yves Montand; the painters Pissarro, Seurat, Modigliani and Delacroix; the *chanteuse* Édith Piaf alongside her two-year-old daughter; and the dancer Isadora Duncan.

Visiting

The cemetery has five entrances, two of which are on bd de Ménilmontant.

To save time searching for famous graves, pick up cemetery maps at the **conservation office** (Bureaux de la Conservation; ☎01 55 25 82 10; 16 rue du Repos, 20e; ⊙8.30am-12.30pm & 2-5pm Mon-Fri; Ⓜ️Philippe Auguste, Père Lachaise) near the main bd de Ménilmontant entrance.

Alternatively, pre-book a themed guided tour led by entertaining cemetery historian Thierry Le Roi (www.necro-romantiques.com).

Cimetière du Père Lachaise

A HALF-DAY TOUR

There is a certain romance to getting lost in Cimetière du Père Lachaise, a jungle of graves spun from centuries of tales. But to search for one grave among one million in this 44-hectare land of the dead is no joke – narrow the search with this itinerary.

From the main bd de Ménilmontant entrance (metro Père Lachaise or Philippe Auguste), head up av Principale, turn right onto av du Puits and collect a map from ❶ the Bureaux de la Conservation.

Backtrack along av du Puits, turn right onto av Latérale du Sud, scale the stairs and bear right along chemin Denon to New Realist artist ❷ Arman, film director ❸ Claude Chabrol and ❹ Chopin.

Follow chemin Méhul downhill, cross av Casimir Périer and bear right onto chemin Serré. Take the second left (chemin Lebrun – unsigned), head uphill and near the top leave the footpath to weave through graves on your right to rock star ❺ Jim Morrison. Back on chemin Lauriston, continue uphill to roundabout ❻ Rond-Point Casimir Périer.

Admire the funerary art of contemporary photographer ❼ André Chabot, av de la Chapelle. Continue uphill for energising city views from the ❽ chapel steps, then zig-zag to ❾ Molière & La Fontaine, on chemin Molière.

Cut between graves onto av Tranversale No 1 – spot potatoes atop ❿ Parmentier's headstone. Continue straight onto av Greffülhe and left onto av Tranversale No 2 to rub ⓫ Monsieur Noir's shiny crotch.

Navigation to ⓬ Édith Piaf and the ⓭ Mur des Fédérés is straightforward. End with angel-topped ⓮ Oscar Wilde near the Porte Gambetta entrance.

TOP TIPS

➡ Père Lachaise is a photographer's paradise any time of the day or year, but best are sunny autumn mornings after the rain.

➡ Cemetery-lovers will appreciate themed guided tours (two hours) led by entertaining cemetery historian Thierry Le Roi (www.necro-romantiques.com).

Chopin, Division 11
Add a devotional note to the handwritten letters and flowers brightening the marble tomb of Polish composer/pianist Frédéric Chopin (1810–49), who spent his short adult life in Paris. His heart is buried in Warsaw.

Monuments aux Morts

Main Entrance

av du Puits

av Latérale du Sud

chemin Denon

4

10

3

9

chemin Méhul

av Principale

1

2

❶

Bureaux de la Conservation

8

7

av Casimir Périer

chemin Maiso

Porte du Repos

73

chemin S

Jim Morrison, Division 6
The original bust adorning the disgracefully dishevelled grave of Jim Morrison (1943–71), lead singer of The Doors, was stolen. Pay your respects to rock's greatest legend – no chewing gum or padlocks please.

André Chabot, Division 20

Contemporary photographer André Chabot (b 1941) shoots funerary art, hence the bijou 19th-century chapel he's equipped with monumental granite camera – and a QR code – in preparation for the day he departs.

BRUNO DE HOGUES / GETTY IMAGES ©

Molière & La Fontaine, Division 25

Parisians refused to leave their local *quartier* for Père Lachaise so in 1817 the authorities moved in popular playwright Molière (1622–73) and poet Jean de la Fontaine (1621–95). The marketing strategy worked.

BRUNO DE HOGUES / GETTY IMAGES ©

Oscar Wilde, Division 89

Irish writer Oscar Wilde (1854–1900) was forever scandalous: check the enormous packet of the sphinx on his tomb, sculpted by British-American sculptor Jacob Epstein 11 years after Wilde died.

ALIZADA STUDIOS / SHUTTERSTOCK ©

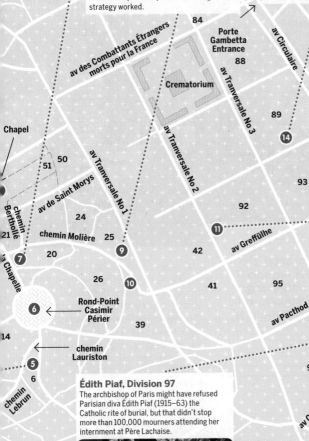

av des Combattants Étrangers morts pour la France

84

Porte Gambetta Entrance

88

Crematorium

av Circulaire

av Tranversale No 3

89

14

Chapel

51 50

av Tranversale No 1

av de Saint Morys

93

Monsieur Noir, Division 92

Cemetery sex stud Mr Black, alias 21-year-old journalist Victor Noir (1848–70), was shot by Napoléon III's nephew in a botched duel. Urban myth means women rub his crotch to boost fertility.

chemin Berthollet

21

24

92

11

chemin Molière 25

7

20

9

la Chapelle

26

10

41

95

av Pacthod

42

94

av Greffülhe

Rond-Point Casimir Périer

6

39

Commemorative war memorials

12 97 13

14

chemin Lauriston

96

76

5

6

chemin Lebrun

Édith Piaf, Division 97

The archbishop of Paris might have refused Parisian diva Édith Piaf (1915–63) the Catholic rite of burial, but that didn't stop more than 100,000 mourners attending her internment at Père Lachaise.

Porte de la Réunion

Mur des Fédérés, Division 76

This plain brick wall was where 147 Communard insurgents were lined up and shot in 1871. Equally emotive is the sculpted walkway of commemorative war memorials surrounding the mass grave.

av Circulaire

IRINA KVYACHINKOVA / SHUTTERSTOCK ©

Marché Bastille

Street Markets

Not simply places to shop, the city's street markets are social gatherings for the entire neighbourhood, and visiting one will give you a true appreciation for Parisian life.

Great For...

☑ **Don't Miss**

The city is also home to some wonderful covered food markets.

Stall after stall of cheeses, stacked baguettes, sun-ripened tomatoes, freshly lopped pigs' trotters, horsemeat sausages, spit-roasted chickens, glass bottles of olives and olive oils, quail eggs, duck eggs, boxes of chanterelle mushrooms and knobbly truffles, long-clawed langoustines and prickly sea urchins on beds of crushed ice – along with belts, boots, wallets, cheap socks, chic hats, colourful scarves, striped t-shirts, wicker baskets, wind-up toys, buckets of flowers... Paris' street markets are a feast for the senses.

Top Choices

Marché Bastille (Map p254; bd Richard Lenoir, 11e; ⊙7am-2.30pm Thu, to 3pm Sun; Ⓜ Bastille, Bréguet–Sabin) If you only get to one open-air street market in Paris, this one – stretching

Cheese stall, Marché d'Aligre

PREMIER PHOTO/SHUTTERSTOCK ©

place d'Aligre, 12e; ⊗8am-1pm Tue-Sun; Ⓜ Ledru-Rollin) takes place on the square.

Marché Raspail (Map p246; bd Raspail, btwn rue de Rennes & rue du Cherche Midi, 6e; ⊗7am-2.30pm Tue & Fri, organic market 9am-1.30pm Sun; Ⓜ Rennes) 🍃 A traditional open-air market on Tuesday and Friday, Marché Raspail is especially popular on Sunday, when it's filled with *biologique* (organic) produce.

Marché Biologique des Batignolles (34 bd des Batignolles, 17e; ⊗9am-3pm Sat; Ⓜ Place de Clichy, Rome) 🍃 Abuzz with market stalls, this busy boulevard in northern Paris is renowned for its organic produce. Many of the stalls offer tastings and everything is super fresh.

Marché de Belleville (Map p254; bd de Belleville, 11e & 20e; ⊗7am-2.30pm Tue & Fri; Ⓜ Belleville) Belleville Market has filled busy thoroughfare bd de Belleville with open-air fruit, veg and other fresh-produce stalls since 1860. Food shopping aside, it provides a fascinating insight into the large, vibrant community of this eastern neighbourhood, home to artists, students and immigrants from Africa, Asia and the Middle East.

between the Bastille and Richard Lenoir metro stations – is among the very best. Its 150-plus stalls are piled high with fruit and vegetables, meats, fish, shellfish, cheeses and seasonal specialities such as truffles. You'll also find clothing, leather handbags and wallets, and a smattering of antiques.

Marché d'Aligre (Map p254; rue d'Aligre, 12e; ⊗8am-1pm Tue-Sun; Ⓜ Ledru-Rollin) A favourite with chefs and locals, this chaotic street market's stalls are piled with fruit, vegetables and seasonal delicacies such as truffles. Behind them, specialist shops stock cheeses, coffee, chocolates, meat, seafood and wine. More are located in the adjoining covered market hall, **Marché Beauvau** (Map p254; place d'Aligre, 12e; ⊗9am-2pm & 4-7.30pm Tue-Sat, 9am-2pm Sun; Ⓜ Ledru-Rollin). The small but bargain-filled flea market **Marché aux Puces d'Aligre** (Map p254;

S-F/SHUTTERSTOCK ©

Day Trip: Château de Versailles

This monumental, 700-room palace and sprawling estate – with its gardens, fountains, ponds and canals – is a Unesco World Heritage–listed wonder situated an easy 40-minute train ride from central Paris.

Great For...

☑ Don't Miss

Summertime 'dancing water' displays set to music by baroque- and classical-era composers.

Amid magnificently landscaped formal gardens, this splendid and enormous palace was built in the mid-17th century during the reign of Louis XIV – the Roi Soleil (Sun King) – to project the absolute power of the French monarchy, which was then at the height of its glory. The château has undergone relatively few alterations since its construction, though almost all the interior furnishings disappeared during the Revolution and many of the rooms were rebuilt by Louis-Philippe (r 1830–48).

Some 30,000 workers and soldiers toiled on the structure, the bills for which all but emptied the kingdom's coffers.

Work began in 1661 under the guidance of architect Louis Le Vau (Jules Hardouin-Mansart took over from Le Vau in the mid-1670s); painter and interior designer Charles Le Brun; and landscape artist

View of the Château de Versailles from the Fountain of Apollo

❶ Need to Know

☎01 30 83 78 00; www.chateauversailles.fr; place d'Armes; adult/child passport ticket incl estate-wide access €20/free, with musical events €27/free, palace €18/free except during musical events; ◷9am-6.30pm Tue-Sun Apr-Oct, to 5.30pm Tue-Sun Nov-Mar; Ⓜ RER Versailles-Château–Rive Gauche

✗ Take a Break

Rue de Satory and rue de la Paroisse are lined with restaurants.

★ Top Tip

Arrive early morning and avoid Tuesday, Saturday and Sunday, which are Versailles' busiest days.

André Le Nôtre, whose workers flattened hills, drained marshes and relocated forests as they laid out the seemingly endless **gardens** (free except during musical events; ◷gardens 8am-8.30pm Apr-Oct, to 6pm Nov-Mar, park 7am-8.30pm Apr-Oct, 8am-6pm Nov-Mar), ponds and fountains.

Le Brun and his hundreds of artisans decorated every moulding, cornice, ceiling and door of the interior with the most luxurious and ostentatious of appointments: frescos, marble, gilt and woodcarvings, many with themes and symbols drawn from Greek and Roman mythology. The King's Suite of the Grands Appartements du Roi et de la Reine (King's and Queen's State Apartments), for example, includes rooms dedicated to Hercules, Venus, Diana, Mars and Mercury. The opulence reaches its peak in the Galerie des Glaces (Hall of

Mirrors), a 75m-long ballroom with 17 huge mirrors on one side and, on the other, an equal number of windows looking out over the gardens and the setting sun.

To access areas that are otherwise off limits and to learn more about Versailles' history, prebook a 90-minute **guided tour** (☎01 30 83 77 88; www.chateauversailles.fr; Château de Versailles; tours €10, plus palace entry; ◷English-language tours 9.30am Tue-Sun) of the Private Apartments of Louis XV and Louis XVI and the Opera House or Royal Chapel. Tours also cover the most famous parts of the palace.

The château is situated in the leafy, bourgeois suburb of Versailles, 22km southwest of central Paris. Take the frequent RER C5 (return €7.10) from Paris' Left Bank RER stations to Versailles-Château–Rive Gauche station.

Versailles

A DAY IN COURT

Visiting Versailles – even just the State Apartments – may seem overwhelming at first, but think of it as a house where people ate, drank, worked, slept and conspired and you'll be on the right path.

Some two decades into his long reign, Louis XIV began turning his father's hunting lodge into a palace large enough to house his entire court (to keep closer tabs on the 6000-strong army of courtiers). Sparing no expense, the Sun King employed the greatest artists and craftspeople of the day and by 1682 he'd created the most extravagant dormitory in history.

The royal schedule was as accurate and predictable as a Swiss watch. By following this itinerary of rooms you can recreate the king's day, starting with the ❶ **King's Bedchamber** and the ❷ **Queen's Bedchamber**, where the royal couple was roused at about the same time. The royal procession then leads through the ❸ **Hall of Mirrors** to the ❹ **Royal Chapel** for morning Mass and returns to the ❺ **Council Chamber** for late-morning meetings with ministers. After lunch the king might ride or hunt or visit the ❻ **King's Library**. Later he could join courtesans for an 'apartment evening' starting from the ❼ **Hercules Drawing Room** or play billiards in the ❽ **Diana Drawing Room** before supping at 10pm.

VERSAILLES BY NUMBERS

Rooms 700 (11 hectares of roof)

Windows 2153

Staircases 67

Gardens and parks 800 hectares

Trees 200,000

Fountains 50 (with 620 nozzles)

Paintings 6300 (measuring 11km laid end to end)

Statues and sculptures 2100

Objets d'art and furnishings 5000

Visitors 5.3 million per year

Queen's Bedchamber
Chambre de la Reine
The queen's life was on constant public display and even the births of her children were watched by crowds of spectators in her own bedchamber. DETOUR » The Guardroom, with a dozen armed men at the ready.

Guardroom

South Wing

LUNCH BREAK

Contemporary French cuisine at Alain Ducasse's restaurant Ore, or a picnic in the park.

Hercules Drawing Room
Salon d'Hercule
This salon, with its stunning ceiling fresco of the strong man, gave way to the State Apartments, which were open to courtiers three nights a week. DETOUR» Apollo Drawing Room, used for formal audiences and as a throne room.

Hall of Mirrors
Galerie des Glaces
The solid-silver candelabra and furnishings in this extravagant hall, devoted to Louis XIV's successes in war, were melted down in 1689 to pay for yet another conflict. DETOUR» The antithetical Peace Drawing Room, adjacent.

WALTER.G / SHUTTERSTOCK ©

King's Bedchamber
Chambre du Roi
The king's daily life was anything but private and even his *lever* (rising) at 8am and *coucher* (retiring) at 11.30pm would be witnessed by up to 150 sycophantic courtiers.

Council Chamber
Cabinet du Conseil
This chamber, with carved medallions evoking the king's work, is where the monarch met his various ministers (state, finance, religion etc) depending on the days of the week.

Peace Drawing Room

Hall of Mirrors

Marble Courtyard

Apollo Drawing Room

King's Library
Bibliothèque du Roi
The last resident, bibliophile Louis XVI, loved geography and his copy of *The Travels of James Cook* (in English, which he read fluently) is still on the shelf here.

ntrance

Entrance

North Wing

To Royal Opera

Diana Drawing Room
Salon de Diane
With walls and ceiling covered in frescoes devoted to the mythical huntress, this room contained a large billiard table reserved for Louis XIV, a keen player.

Royal Chapel
Chapelle Royale
This two-storey chapel (with gallery for the royals and important courtiers, and the ground floor for the B-list) was dedicated to St Louis, patron of French monarchs. DETOUR» The sumptuous Royal Opera.

COJATO / BUDGET TRAVEL ©

SAVVY SIGHTSEEING

Avoid Versailles on Monday (closed), Tuesday (Paris' museums close, so visitors flock here) and Sunday, the busiest day. Also, book tickets online so you don't have to queue.

Minting equipment, Musée du 11 Conti

Monnaie de Paris

The 18th-century royal mint, Monnaie de Paris, houses the Musée du 11 Conti, an interactive museum exploring the history of French coinage from antiquity onwards, plus edgy contemporary-art exhibitions.

Great For...

☑ Don't Miss
The magnificent building and courtyards.

The Building

The impeccably restored, neoclassical building, with one of the longest façades on the Seine stretching 116m long, squirrels away five sumptuous courtyards, the Hôtel de Conti designed by Jules Hardouin-Mansart in 1690, engraving workshops, the original foundry (now the museum boutique) and Guy Savoy's flagship restaurant (p140).

The Mint

Coins were minted at the Monnaie de Paris until 1973 when manufacturing was moved to the town of Pessac on the Atlantic Coast. The Ministry of Finance still uses the Paris mint however to produce commemorative medals and coins, many of which are sold in the museum's stylish boutique alongside glass jars of honey from hives on the

Stained glass depicting mint workers, Monnaie de Paris

ℹ Need to Know

Map p250; ☏01 40 46 56 66; www.monnaie deparis.fr; 11 quai de Conti, 6e; adult/child €10/free; ⏱11am-7pm Tue & Thu-Sun, to 9pm Wed; Ⓜ Pont Neuf

✕ Take a Break

On-site Frappé by Bloom (p184) has farm-sourced cafe fare and fabulous cocktails.

★ Top Tip

Skip ticket queues by buying tickets online or at the automatic ticket machines.

building's rooftop, medallions featuring the Louvre or Eiffel Tower, and other classy souvenirs.

What's Nearby

Musée National Eugène Delacroix
Museum

(Map p250; ☏01 44 41 86 50; www.musee-dela croix.fr; 6 rue de Furstenberg, 6e; adult/child €7/ free; ⏱9.30am-5pm Wed-Mon, to 9pm 1st Thu of month; Ⓜ Mabillon) In a courtyard off a pretty tree-shaded square, this museum is housed in the romantic artist's home and studio at the time of his death in 1863. It contains a collection of his oil paintings, watercolours, pastels and drawings, including many of his more intimate works, such as *An Unmade Bed* (1828) and his paintings of Morocco.

A ticket from the Musée du Louvre (p52) allows same-day entry here (you can also

buy tickets here and skip the Louvre's ticket queues).

Église St-Germain des Prés
Church

(Map p246; ☏01 55 42 81 18; www.eglise-saint germaindespres.fr; 3 place St-Germain des Prés, 6e; ⏱9am-7.45pm; Ⓜ St-Germain des Prés) Paris' oldest standing church was built in the 11th century on the site of a 6th-century abbey and was the main place of worship in Paris until the arrival of Notre Dame. It's since been altered many times. The oldest part, **Chapelle de St-Symphorien** is to the right as you enter; St Germanus (496–576), the first bishop of Paris, is believed to be buried there.

An English brochure (€10) is available; proceeds go towards the current restoration works ongoing until 2020 (the church will stay open throughout). Free early-afternoon organ concerts are held on the last Sunday of the month; check the website's calendar for times. Other concerts take place on Thursdays and Fridays at 8.30pm; details including prices are listed online.

ANMBPH/SHUTTERSTOCK ©

Jardin des Tuileries

Filled with fountains, classical sculptures and magnificent panoramas at every turn, this quintessentially Parisian 28-hectare formal park constitutes part of the Banks of the Seine Unesco World Heritage Site.

Great For...

☑ Don't Miss

Monet's enormous mural-like Water Lilies in the Musée de l'Orangerie.

The park was laid out in its present form in 1664 by André Le Nôtre, who also created the gardens at Versailles.

Musée de l'Orangerie   Museum

(Map p246; ☎01 44 77 80 07; www.musee-orangerie.fr; place de la Concorde, 1er; adult/child €9/free; ☺9am-6pm Wed-Mon; MConcorde) Monet's extraordinary cycle of eight enormous *Decorations des Nymphéas* (Water Lilies) occupies two huge oval rooms purpose-built in 1927 on the artist's instructions. The lower level houses more of Monet's impressionist works and many by Sisley, Renoir, Cézanne, Gauguin, Picasso, Matisse and Modigliani, as well as Derain's *Arlequin et Pierrot*. The orangery, along with photography gallery Jeu de Paume, is all that remains of the former Palais des Tuileries, which was razed during the Paris Commune in 1871. Audioguides cost €5.

Statue on the Arc de Triomphe du Carrousel

ℹ️ Need to Know

Map p246; rue de Rivoli, 1er; ⏱7am-9pm Apr–late Sep, 7.30am-7.30pm late Sep–Mar; Ⓜ Tuileries, Concorde

✕ Take a Break

Famed hot chocolate at Angelina (p173) comes with a pot of whipped cream.

★ Top Tip

Place de la Concorde (Map p246; 8e; Ⓜ Concorde) offers a 360-degree panorama at the park's northwestern end.

du Carrousel, the gardens next to the Louvre (p52). The eastern counterpoint to the more famous Arc de Triomphe (p42), it is one of several monuments in the historical axis, which terminates with the statue of Louis XIV next to the Pyramide du Louvre.

Jeu de Paume   Gallery

(Map p246; ☎01 47 03 12 50; www.jeudepaume. org; 1 place de la Concorde, 1er; adult/child €10/ free; ⏱11am-9pm Tue, to 7pm Wed-Sun; Ⓜ Concorde) The Galerie du Jeu de Paume, which stages innovative photography exhibitions, is housed in an erstwhile *jeu de paume* (royal tennis court) of the former Palais des Tuileries in the northwestern corner of the Jardin des Tuileries. Cinema screenings and concert performances also take place – check the agenda online.

What's Nearby?

Arc de Triomphe du Carrousel   Monument

(Map p246; place du Carrousel, 1er; Ⓜ Palais Royal–Musée du Louvre) This triumphal arch, erected by Napoléon to celebrate his 1805 battlefield successes, rises from the **Jardin**

Le Grand Musée du Parfum   Museum

(Map p246; ☎01 42 65 25 44; www.grand museeduparfum.fr; 73 rue du Faubourg St-Honoré, 8e; adult/child €14.50/5; ⏱10.30am-7pm Tue-Sun; Ⓜ Miromesnil) There are several perfume museums in Paris, but this is the only one that's not run by a major brand. It reveals the chemical processes and showcases the art of fragrance creation.

Musée Maxim's   Museum

(Map p246; ☎01 42 65 30 47; http://maxims-de-paris.com; 3 rue Royale, 8e; adult/child €25/ free; ⏱English tours 2pm Tue & Wed; Ⓜ Concorde) During the belle époque, Maxim's bistro was the most glamorous place to be in Paris, but for art nouveau buffs the real treasure is the upstairs museum. Its 12 rooms are filled with some 550 pieces of art nouveau artworks, objets d'art and furniture.

VICHIE81/GETTY IMAGES ©

Sainte-Chapelle

This gemlike Holy Chapel is Paris'
most exquisite Gothic monument.
Try to save it for a sunny day,
when Paris' oldest, finest stained
glass is at its dazzling best.

Sainte-Chapelle was built in just six years
(compared with nearly 200 years for Notre
Dame) and consecrated in 1248. The chapel
was conceived by Louis IX to house his
personal collection of holy relics, including
the famous Ste-Couronne (Holy Crown),
acquired by the French king in 1239 from
the emperors of Constantinople for a sum of
money easily exceeding the amount it cost
to build the chapel. The wreath of thorns is
safeguarded today in the treasury at Notre
Dame.

Statues, foliage-decorated capitals,
angels and so on decorate this sumptuous,
bijou chapel. But it is the 1113 scenes depict-
ed in its 15 floor-to-ceiling stained-glass windows – 15.5m high in the nave, 13.5m in the
apse – that stun visitors. From the bookshop
in the former ground-floor chapel reserved
for palace staff, spiral up the staircase to the

Great For...

☑ **Don't Miss**

The ethereal experience of classical-
and sacred-music concerts amid the
stained glass.

❶ Need to Know

Map p250; 📱01 53 40 60 80, concerts 01 42 77 65 65; www.sainte-chapelle.fr; 8 bd du Palais, 1er; adult/child €10/free; joint ticket with Conciergerie €15/free; ⏱9am-7pm Apr-Sep, to 5pm Oct-Mar; Ⓜ Cité

✕ Take a Break

Enjoy artistically presented dishes at Seine-side Sequana (p136).

★ Top Tip

Combination tickets pre-purchased at the Conciergerie allow you to skip the ticket queues.

What's Nearby?

Conciergerie   Monument

(Map p250; 📱01 53 40 60 80; www.paris-conci ergerie.fr; 2 bd du Palais, 1er; adult/child €9/free, joint ticket with Sainte-Chapelle €15; ⏱9.30am-6pm; Ⓜ Cité) A royal palace in the 14th century, the Conciergerie later became a prison. During the Reign of Terror (1793–94) alleged enemies of the Revolution were incarcerated here before being brought before the Revolutionary Tribunal next door in the **Palais de Justice**. Top-billing exhibitions take place in the beautiful, Rayonnant Gothic **Salle des Gens d'Armes**, Europe's largest surviving medieval hall.

Of the almost 2800 prisoners held in the dungeons during the Reign of Terror (in various 'classes' of cells, no less) before being sent in tumbrels to the guillotine, star prisoner was Queen Marie-Antoinette – see a reproduction of her cell.

To get the most out of your visit, rent a HistoPad (a tablet-device guide €6.50) to take part in an interactive, 3D treasure hunt.

upper chapel, where only the king and his close friends were allowed.

Before arriving, download the 'Sainte Chapelle Windows' app to 'read' the window biblical story – from Genesis through to the resurrection of Christ. Once here, rent an audioguide (€3) or join a free 45-minute guided tour in English (daily between 11am and 3pm).

Sainte-Chapelle's location within the Palais de Justice (Law Courts) means security is tight; be sure to leave pocket knives, scissors and the like at your accommodation. Even combination ticket-holders still need to go through the security queue.

You can peek at Sainte-Chapelle's exterior from across the street (albeit not a patch on its interior), by the law courts' magnificently gilded 18th-century gate facing rue de Lutèce.

Ossuaries in the Catacombs

MIKHAIL GNATKOVSKIY/SHUTTERSTOCK ©

Les Catacombes

Paris' most macabre sight is its series of subterranean passages lined with skulls and bones. It's a 1.5km walk through the creepy ossuary and definitely not for the faint-hearted.

In 1785 it was decided to rectify the hygiene problems of Paris' overflowing cemeteries by exhuming the bones and storing them in disused quarry tunnels; the Catacombes were created in 1810.

The route through Les Catacombes begins at a small, dark-green belle époque building in the centre of a grassy area of av Colonel Henri Roi-Tanguy, adjacent to place Denfert Rochereau. After descending 20m below street level (via 130 narrow, dizzying spiral steps), you follow the dark, subterranean passages to reach the ossuary itself, with a mind-boggling number of bones and skulls of millions of Parisians neatly packed along the walls.

The exit is via a minimalist all-white 'transition space' with a gift shop onto 21bis av René Coty, 14e. Bag searches are carried out to prevent visitors 'souveniring' bones.

Great For...

☑ Don't Miss

Combining a visit to Les Catacombes with a wander through Cimetière du Montparnasse.

STEFANO EMBER/SHUTTERSTOCK ©

Denfert Rochereau Ⓜ Les Catacombes

Av du Général Leclerc

Bd St-Jacques

St-Jacques Ⓜ

Denfert Rochereau

ⓘ Need to Know

Map p246; ☎01 43 22 47 63; www.cata combes.paris.fr; 1 av Colonel Henri Roi-Tanguy, 14e; adult/child €13/free, online booking incl audioguide €29/5; ☉10am-8.30pm Tue-Sun; ⓂDenfert Rochereau

✕ Take a Break

Pick up picnic fare on foodie street rue Daguerre and head to a nearby park.

★ Top Tip

Wear sturdy shoes for the uneven, often muddy surface and loose stones.

Visiting

A maximum of 200 people are allowed in the tunnels at a time and queues can be huge – when the queue extends beyond a 20-minute wait, you'll be handed a coupon with a return entry time later that day. Last entry is at 7.30pm. Online bookings are pricier but include an audioguide and guarantee a timeslot, whereas standing in the queue does not, as online ticket holders have priority.

Renting an audioguide greatly enhances the experience.

Bear in mind that the catacombes are not suitable for young children. Also be aware the only toilets are by the exit, flash photography isn't permitted and the temperature is a cool 14°C below ground.

What's Nearby?

Cimetière du Montparnasse   Cemetery

(Map p246; www.paris.fr; 3 bd Edgar Quinet, 14e; ☉8am-6pm Mon-Fri, 8.30am-6pm Sat, 9am-6pm Sun; ⓂEdgar Quinet) FREE This 19-hectare cemetery opened in 1824 and is Paris' second largest after Père Lachaise (p78). Famous residents include writer Guy de Maupassant, playwright Samuel Beckett, sculptor Constantin Brancusi, photographer Man Ray, industrialist André Citroën, Captain Alfred Dreyfus of the infamous Dreyfus Affair, legendary singer Serge Gainsbourg and philosopher-writer couple Jean-Paul Sartre and Simone de Beauvoir.

Cooking class, Le Cordon Bleu

Cooking & Wine-Tasting Courses

If dining in the city's restaurants whets your appetite, Paris has some outstanding cookery schools. And where there's food in Paris, wine is never more than an arm's length away.

Great For...

☑ Don't Miss

Even during a lightning-quick trip there are myriad short-course options, but book ahead.

Le Cordon Bleu (Map p246; ☎01 85 65 15 00; www.cordonbleu.edu/paris; 13-15 quai André Citroën, 15e; Ⓜ Javel–André Citroën, RER Javel) One of the world's foremost culinary arts schools, the Le Cordon Bleu campus overlooks the Seine and Statue of Liberty, with views of the nearby Eiffel Tower from its terrace. Prices start at €140 for themed three-hour classes (food and wine pairing, vegetarian cuisine, eclairs, choux pastry etc) and €470 for two-day courses. There are also evening wine tastings (€90), chef demonstrations (€50) and classes for kids (eight to 12 years, €90).

La Cuisine Paris (Map p254; ☎01 40 51 78 18; https://lacuisineparis.com; 80 quai de l'Hôtel de Ville, 4e; 2hr cooking class/walking tours from €69/80; Ⓜ Pont Marie, Hôtel de Ville) Classes in English range from how to make bread and

Making croissants

ALEKSEIGL/SHUTTERSTOCK ©

Cook'n With Class (☑01 42 57 22 84; https://cooknwithclass.com; 6 rue Baudelique, 18e; ⊙2hr classes from €95; ⓂSimplon, Jules Joffrin) A bevy of international chefs, small classes and an enchanting Montmartre location are ingredients for success at this informal cooking school, which organises market visits, gourmet food tours and six-course dinners with the chef and sommelier as well as cookery classes. Classes are taught in English.

Ô Chateau (Map p250; ☑01 44 73 97 80; http://o-chateau.com; 68 rue Jean-Jacques Rousseau, 1er; ⊙4pm-midnight Mon-Sat; 🛜; ⓂLes Halles, RER Châtelet–Les Halles) Wine aficionados can thank this young, fun, cosmopolitan wine bar for bringing affordable tasting to Paris. Choose from 50 *grands vins* served by the glass (or 1000-plus by the bottle!). Or sign up in advance for a 'tour de France' of French wines (€59) or a guided cellar tasting in English over lunch (€75) or dinner (€99).

Meeting the French (☑01 42 51 19 80; www.meetingthefrench.com; tours & courses from €15) French table decoration, market tours, baking with a Parisian baker – the repertoire of cultural and gourmet tours offered by Meeting the French is truly outstanding. All courses and tours are in English.

croissants to macarons as well as market classes and gourmet 'foodie walks'.

Le Foodist (☑06 71 70 95 22; www.lefoodist.com; 59 rue du Cardinal Lemoine, 5e; ⓂCardinal Lemoine) Ceate your own eclairs and choux pastry, macarons or croissants at this culinary school. Market tours and wine and cheese tastings and pairings are also available. Instruction is in English. Three-hour classes start at €99.

Wine Tasting in Paris (☑06 76 93 32 88; www.wine-tasting-in-paris.com; 14 rue des Boulangers, 5e; tastings from €46; ⊙tastings 5-7.30pm Tue, Thu & Sat; ⓂJussieu) The comprehensive French Wine Tour (€62, 2½ hours, six wines) covers tasting methodology, wine vocabulary and French wine-growing regions. Foodies will adore the tasty, lunchtime cheese-wine pairing (€46, 1½ hours, four wines). All classes are in English.

Monet's studio

Day Trip: Maison et Jardins de Claude Monet

Monet lived in Giverny from 1883 until his death in 1926, in a rambling house – surrounded by flower-filled gardens – that's now the immensely popular Maison et Jardins de Claude Monet.

Great For...

☑ Don't Miss

Monet's trademark lily pond, immortalised in his *Nymphéas* (Water Lilies) series.

Monet's home for the last 43 years of his life is now a delightful house-museum. His pastel-pink house and Water Lily studio stand on the periphery of the Clos Normand – its symmetrically laid-out gardens burst with flowers. Monet bought the Jardin d'Eau (Water Garden) in 1895 and set about creating his trademark lily pond, as well as the famous Japanese bridge (since rebuilt).

The charmingly preserved house and beautiful bloom-filled gardens (rather than Monet's works) are the draws here.

Draped with purple wisteria, the Japanese bridge blends into the asymmetrical foreground and background, creating the intimate atmosphere for which the 'painter of light' was renowned.

Seasons have an enormous effect on Giverny. From early to late spring, daffodils,

Spring flowers, Jardins de Claude Monet

SEAN HEATLEY/SHUTTERSTOCK ©

tulips, rhododendrons, wisteria and irises appear, followed by poppies and lilies. By June, nasturtiums, roses and sweet peas are in flower. Around September, there are dahlias, sunflowers and hollyhocks.

Combined tickets with Paris' **Musée Marmottan Monet** (☏01 44 96 50 33; www. marmottan.fr; 2 rue Louis Boilly, 16e; adult/child €11/7.50; ☼10am-6pm Tue, Wed & Fri-Sun, to 9pm Thu; Ⓜ La Muette) cost €20.50/12 per adult/child, and combined adult tickets with Paris' Musée de l'Orangerie (p90) cost €18.50.

Visiting

The tiny village of Giverny is 74km north-west of Paris. From Paris' Gare St-Lazare there are up to 15 daily trains to Vernon (from €9, 45 minutes to one hour), 7km

to the west of Giverny, from where buses, taxis and cycle/walking tracks run to Giverny.

Shuttle buses (single/return €5/10, 20 minutes, four daily Monday to Friday Easter to October, five daily Saturday and Sunday Easter to October) meet most trains from Paris at Vernon. There are limited seats, so arrive early for the return trip from Giverny. Tickets are sold on board; check the live shuttle schedule on www.sngo-giverny.fr.

Rent bikes (cash only) at the **Café L'Ar-rivée de Giverny** (☏02 32 21 16 01; 1-3 place de la Gare, Vernon; per day €14; ☼8am-11pm), opposite the train station in Vernon, from where Giverny is a signposted 5km along a direct (and flat) cycle/walking track.

Taxis (☏02 32 51 10 24) usually wait outside the train station in Vernon and charge around €15 for the one-way trip to Giverny. There's no taxi rank in Giverny, however, so you'll need to phone one for the return trip.

The village has an ATM located along rue Claude Monet. There is a public toilet by the car park (only open Easter to October).

SONGQUAN DENG/SHUTTERSTOCK ©

Palais Garnier

The fabled 'phantom of the opera' lurked in this opulent opera house designed in 1860 by Charles Garnier (then an unknown 35-year-old architect), which offers behind-the-scenes tours.

Few other Paris monuments have provided artistic inspiration in the way that the Palais Garnier has. From Degas' ballerinas to Gaston Leroux' Phantom and Chagall's ceiling, the layers of myth painted on gradually over the decades have bestowed a particular air of mystery and drama to its ornate interior. Designed in 1860 by Charles Garnier, the opera house was part of Baron Haussmann's massive urban renovation project.

A prop man at the opera set up beehives on the roof in 1983 – the honey is now sold at the gift shop when available.

The opera house is open to visitors during the day, and the building is a fascinating place to explore even if you're not taking in a show. Highlights include the opulent Grand Staircase, the library-museum (1st floor) and the horseshoe-shaped auditori-

Great For...

☑ Don't Miss

Chagall's ceiling mural (1964), above the massive chandelier, which depicts scenes from 14 operas.

ⓘ Need to Know

Map p246; ☏08 92 89 90 90; www.
operadeparis.fr; cnr rues Scribe & Auber, 9e;
self-guided tours adult/child €12/8, guided
tours adult/child €15.50/8.50; ⊙self-guided
tours 10am-5pm, guided tours 11am &
2.30pm; MOpéra)

✗ Take a Break

Close at hand, Place de la Madeleine
(p152) is a gourmet fantasyland.

★ Top Tip

Catching a performance (p190) here is
a treat.

The church is a popular venue for
classical-music concerts (some free);
check the posters outside or the website
for dates.

um (2nd floor), with its extravagant gilded
interior and red velvet seats.

Visits are either unguided (audioguides
available; €5), or you can reserve a spot
online for an English-language guided tour.
Check the website for updated schedules.

What's Nearby

Église de la Madeleine　Church

(Map p246; Church of St Mary Magdalene; www.
eglise-lamadeleine.com; place de la Madeleine,
8e; ⊙9.30am-7pm; MMadeleine) Place de la
Madeleine is named after the 19th-century
neoclassical church at its centre, the Église
de la Madeleine. Constructed in the style
of a massive Greek temple, 'La Madeleine'
was consecrated in 1842 after almost a
century of design changes and construction delays.

Jardin du Palais Royal　Gardens

(Map p250; www.domaine-palais-royal.fr; 2 place
Colette, 1er; ⊙8am-10.30pm Apr-Sep, to 8.30pm
Oct-Mar; MPalais Royal–Musée du Louvre) The
Jardin du Palais Royal is a perfect spot to
sit, contemplate and picnic between boxed
hedges, or shop in the trio of beautiful
arcades that frame the garden: the **Galerie
de Valois** (east), **Galerie de Montpensier**
(west) and **Galerie Beaujolais** (north).
However, it's the southern end of the
complex, polka-dotted with sculptor Daniel
Buren's 260 black-and-white striped
columns, that has become the garden's
signature feature.

Walking Tour: Seine-Side Meander

The Seine and its surrounds are Paris at its most seductive. Descend the steps along the quays wherever possible to stroll along the water's edge.

Start Place de la Concorde
Distance 7km
Duration Three hours

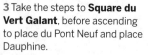

3 Take the steps to **Square du Vert Galant**, before ascending to place du Pont Neuf and place Dauphine.

2 Walk through the Jardin de l'Oratoire to the **Cour Carrée** (p53) and exit at the Jardin de l'Infante.

PAVEL L PHOTO AND VIDEO/SHUTTERSTOCK ©

Classic Photo: Enjoy fountain views in this elegant 28-hectare garden.

1 After taking in the panorama at place de la Concorde, stroll through the **Jardin des Tuileries** (p90).

MING TANG-EVANS/LONELY PLANET ©

7 End your romantic meander at the tranquil **Jardin des Plantes** (p106). Cruise back along the Seine by Batobus.

RRRAINBOW/GETTY IMAGES ©

N
0   500 m
0   0.25 miles

4 Curl up with a volume of poetry in the magical **Shakespeare & Company** (p159) bookshop.

ALESSIO CATELLI/SHUTTERSTOCK ©

Take a Break...

Morning or night, try hip **Café Saint Régis** (p136).

5 Cross to Île St-Louis and share an ice cream from *glacier* (ice-cream maker) **Berthillon** (p136).

6 Wander among late-20th-century unfenced sculptures at the **Musée de la Sculpture en Plein Air** (p109).

Jardin du Palais Royal

Palais-Royal – Musée du Louvre

R du Louvre

Louvre Rivoli

Pont Neuf

Q du Louvre

Pont Neuf

Q des Grands Augustins

Île de la Cité

Bd du Palais

Châtelet

Hôtel de Ville

Cité

4E

Q de l'Hôtel de Ville

St-Michel

Bd St-Germain

St-Michel– Notre Dame

Sq Jean XXIII

Pont St-Louis

Pont Marie

Île St-Louis

Pont de Sully

Bd St-Germain

Q Henri IV

Jardin du Luxembourg

R Cuvier

Q St-Bernard

Seine

Jardin des Plantes

Place Monge

FINISH

R Buffon

Place Monge

Gare d'Austerlitz

Tombeau de Napoléon 1er

MANJIK /SHUTTERSTOCK ©

Hôtel des Invalides

Flanked by the 500m-long Esplanade des Invalides lawns, this massive military complex built in the 1670s by Louis XIV to house 4000 invalides (disabled war veterans) contains Napoléon's tomb.

Great For...

☑ Don't Miss
France's largest military museum, the Musée de l'Armée.

On 14 July 1789, a mob broke into the building and seized 32,000 rifles before heading on to the prison at Bastille and the start of the French Revolution.

In the **Cour d'Honneur**, the nation's largest collection on the history of the French military is displayed at the **Musée de l'Armée** (Map p246; Army Museum; www.musee-armee.fr; 129 rue de Grenelle, 7e; included in Hôtel des Invalides entry; ☺10am-6pm Apr-Oct, to 5pm Nov-Mar; MVarenne, La Tour Maubourg). South is **Église St-Louis des Invalides**, once used by soldiers, and **Église du Dôme** (Map p246; www.musee-armee.fr; 129 rue de Grenelle, 7e; included in Hôtel des Invalides entry; ☺10am-7pm Jul & Aug, to 6pm Apr-Jun, Sep & Oct, to 5pm Nov-Mar; MVarenne) which, with its sparkling golden dome (1677–1735), is one of the finest religious edifices erected under Louis XIV and was the inspiration

Statue of Napoleon I

KRULIKOVSHUTTERSTOCK ©

ⓘ Need to Know

Map p246; www.musee-armee.fr; 129 rue de Grenelle, 7e; adult/child €12/free; ⏰10am–6pm; ⓂVarenne, La Tour Maubourg

✗ Take a Break

Coutume Café (p183) brews up some of Paris' best coffee from its own-roasted beans.

★ Top Tip

Atmospheric classical concerts (ranging from €5 to €30) take place regularly here year-round.

for the United States Capitol building. It received the remains of Napoléon in 1840. The extravagant **Tombeau de Napoléon 1er**, in the centre of the church, comprises six coffins fitting into one another like a Russian doll. Scale models of towns, fortresses and châteaux across France fill the esoteric **Musée des Plans-Reliefs**.

Admission includes entry to all Hôtel des Invalides sights. Their individual hours often vary – check the website for updates.

What's Nearby?

Musée Yves Saint Laurent Paris · Museum

(Map p246; ☏01 44 31 64 00; www.museeysl paris.com; 5 av Marceau, 16e; adult/child €10/7; ⏰11am–6pm Tue-Thu, Sat & Sun, to 9pm Fri; ⓂAlma-Marceau) Housed in the legendary designer's studios (1974 to 2002), this museum holds retrospectives of YSL's avant-garde designs, from early sketches to finished pieces. Temporary exhibitions give an insight into the creative process of designing a haute couture collection and the history of fashion throughout the 20th century. The building can only accommodate a small number of visitors at a time, so buy tickets online or expect to queue outside.

Petit Palais · Gallery

(Map p246; Musée des Beaux-Arts de la Ville de Paris; ☏01 53 43 40 00; www.petitpalais.paris. fr; av Winston Churchill, 8e; suggested donation €2; ⏰10am-6pm Tue-Sun, to 9pm Fri; ⓂChamps-Élysées–Clemenceau) **FREE** This architectural stunner was built for the 1900 Exposition Universelle, and is home to the **Musée des Beaux-Arts de la Ville de Paris** (City of Paris Museum of Fine Arts). It specialises in medieval and Renaissance objets d'art, such as porcelain and clocks, tapestries, drawings, and 19th-century French paintings and sculpture; there are also paintings by such artists as Rembrandt, Colbert, Cézanne, Monet, Gauguin and Delacroix.

Statue, Jardin des Plantes

CHRISTIAN MUELLER/SHUTTERSTOCK ©

Jardin des Plantes

Founded in 1626 as a medicinal herb garden for Louis XIII, Paris' 24-hectare botanic gardens are an idyllic spot to stroll or visit its museums or zoo.

Great For...

☑ Don't Miss

The gardens' beautiful glass-and-metal Grandes Serres (greenhouses).

Visually defined by the double alley of plane trees that run the length of the park, these sprawling gardens allow you to escape the city concrete for a spell.

Highlights here include peony and rose gardens, an alpine garden, and the gardens of the École de Botanique, used by students of the school and green-fingered Parisians. The gorgeous glass-and-metal **Grandes Serres** (Map p252; www.jardindesplantes.net; Jardin des Plantes; adult/child €7/5; ☉10am-6pm Apr-Sep, to 5pm Oct-Mar; ⓂJussieu) – a series of four greenhouses – have been in use since 1714, and several of Henri Rousseau's jungle paintings, sometimes on display in the Musée d'Orsay, were inspired by his frequent visits here.

Dinosaur skeletons, Galeries d'Anatomie Comparée et de Paléontologie

CHRISTIAN MUELLER/SHUTTERSTOCK ©

❶ Need to Know

Map p252; www.jardindesplantes.net; place Valhubert & 36 rue Geoffroy-St-Hilaire, 5e; ⏱7.30am-8pm early Apr–mid-Sep, shorter hours rest of year; ⓂGare d'Austerlitz, Censier Daubenton, Jussieu

✕ Take a Break

Bring a picnic with you (but watch out for the automatic sprinklers!).

★ Top Tip

A tranquil way to travel to/from here is by Batobus (p238) along the Seine.

Museums & Zoo

Muséum National d'Histoire Naturelle   Museum

(Map p252; www.mnhn.fr; place Valhubert & 36 rue Geoffroy-St-Hilaire, 5e; ⓂGare d'Austerlitz, Censier Daubenton, Jussieu) Despite the name, the National Museum of Natural History is not a single building, but a collection of sites throughout France. Its historic home is in the Jardin des Plantes, and it's here you'll find the greatest number of branches: taxidermied animals in the excellent **Grande Galerie de l'Évolution** (Map p252; ☎01 40 79 54 79; www.grandegaleriedelevolution.fr; 36 rue Geoffroy-St-Hilaire, 5e; adult/child €9/free, with Galeries des Enfants €11/9; ⏱10am-6pm Wed-Mon; ⓂCensier Daubenton); fossils and dinosaur skeletons in the **Galeries d'Anatomie Comparée et de Paléontologie** (Map p252; ☎01 40 79 56 01;

www.mnhn.fr; 2 rue Buffon, 5e; adult/child €7/ free; ⏱10am-6pm Wed-Mon Apr-Sep, to 5pm Wed-Mon Oct-Mar; ⓂGare d'Austerlitz); and meteorites and crystals in the **Galerie de Minéralogie et de Géologie** (Map p252; ☎01 40 79 56 01; www.galeriedemineralogieet geologie.fr; 36 rue Geoffroy-St-Hilaire, 5e; adult/ child €7/5; ⏱10am-6pm Wed-Mon Apr-Sep, to 5pm Wed-Mon Oct-Mar; ⓂCensier Daubenton).

Created in 1793, the National Museum of Natural History became a site of significant scientific research in the 19th century. Of the three museums here, the four-floor Grande Galerie de l'Évolution is a particular winner if you're travelling with kids: life-sized elephants, tigers and rhinos play safari, and imaginative exhibits on evolution, extinction and global warming fill 6000 sq metres. The temporary exhibits are generally excellent. Within this building is a separate attraction, the **Galerie des Enfants** (Map p252; www.galeriedesenfants.fr; 36 rue Geoffroy-St-Hilaire, 5e; adult/child €11/9; ⏱10am-6pm Wed-Mon; ⓂCensier Daubenton) – a hands-on science museum tailored to children from ages six to 12.

La Ménagerie   Zoo

(Map p252; Le Zoo du Jardin des Plantes; www.zoodujardindesplantes.fr; 57 rue Cuvier, 5e; adult/child €13/10; ⏱9am-6pm Mon-Sat, to 6.30pm Sun Mar-Oct, to 5pm or 5.30pm Nov-Feb; MGare d'Austerlitz) Like the Jardin des Plantes in which it's located, this 170-species zoo is more than a tourist attraction, also doubling as a research centre for the reproduction of rare and endangered species. During the Prussian siege of 1870, the animals of the day were themselves endangered, when almost all were eaten by starving Parisians.

What's Nearby?

Mosquée de Paris   Mosque

(Map p252; ☏01 45 35 97 33; www.mosqueedeparis.net; 2bis place du Puits de l'Ermite, 5e; adult/child €3/2; ⏱9am-noon & 2-7pm Sat-Thu Apr-Sep, 9am-noon & 2-6pm Sat-Thu Oct-Mar; MPlace Monge) Paris' central mosque, with a striking 26m-high minaret, was completed in 1926 in an ornate art deco Moorish style. You can visit the interior to admire the intricate tile work and calligraphy. A separate entrance leads to the wonderful North African-style **hammam** (Map p252; ☏01 43 31 14 32; www.la-mosquee.com; 39 rue Geoffroy-St-Hilaire, 5e; admission €18, spa package from €43; ⏱10am-9pm Wed-Mon), **restaurant** (Map p252; ☏01 43 31 14 32; www.restaurantauxportesdelorient.com; 39 rue Geoffroy-St-Hilaire, 5e; mains €10-28; ⏱kitchen noon-midnight) and **tearoom** (Map p252; ☏01 43 31 38 20; www.restaurantauxportes-delorient.com; 39 rue Geoffroy-St-Hilaire, 5e; ⏱noon-midnight), and a small *souk* (actually more of a gift shop). Visitors must be modestly dressed.

Mosquée de Paris

Musée de la Sculpture en Plein Air
Museum

(Map p252; quai St-Bernard, 5e; Ⓜ Gare d'Austerlitz) FREE Along quai St-Bernard, this open-air sculpture museum (also known as the Jardin Tino Rossi) has more than 50 late-20th-century unfenced sculptures, and makes a great picnic spot. A salad beneath a César or a baguette beside a Brancusi is a pretty classy way to see the Seine up close.

> ★ **Top Tip**
>
> The natural history museum's Grande Galerie de l'Évolution includes imaginative exhibits on evolution and humankind's effect on the global ecosystem – rare specimens of endangered and extinct species dominate the Hall of Threatened and Extinct Species on level 2.

EQROY/SHUTTERSTOCK ©

Institut du Monde Arabe
Museum

(Map p252; Arab World Institute; ☎ 01 40 51 38 38; www.imarabe.org; 1 place Mohammed V, 5e; adult/child €8/4; ⊙ 10am-6pm Tue-Fri, to 7pm Sat & Sun; Ⓜ Jussieu) The Arab World Institute was jointly founded by France and 18 Middle Eastern and North African nations in 1980, with the aim of promoting cross-cultural dialogue. It hosts temporary exhibitions and a fascinating museum of Arabic culture and history (4th to 7th floors). The stunning building, designed by French architect Jean Nouvel, was inspired by latticed-wood windows (*mashrabiya*) traditional to Arabic architecture: thousands of modern-day photo-electrically sensitive apertures cover its sparkling glass façade.

Station F
Research Centre

(https://stationf.co/fr/campus/; 55 bd Vincent Auriol, 13e; ⊙ tours noon Mon, Wed & Fri; Ⓜ Chevaleret, Bibliothèque) FREE The world's largest start-up campus was unveiled with much pomp and ceremony by French president, Emmanuel Macron, in mid-2017. At any one time, some 3000 resident entrepreneurs from all over the world beaver away on ground-breaking new ideas and businesses, supported by 30 hi-tech incubators and accelerators in this unique start-up ecosystem. Guided tours take visitors on a 45-minute waltz through the gargantuan steel, glass and concrete hangar – a railway depot constructed in 1927–29 to house new trains servicing nearby Gare de Austerlitz.

☑ **Don't Miss**

The Institut de Monde Arabe has incredible views from the top (9th)-floor roof terrace (open 10am to 6pm Tuesday to Sunday).

Walking Tour: Paris' Covered Passages

Stepping into Paris' *passages couverts* (covered shopping arcades) is a superb way to get a feel for what life was like in early-19th-century Paris. This walking tour is tailor-made for a rainy day, but it's best avoided on a Sunday, when some arcades shut.

Start Galerie Véro Dodat

Distance 3km

Duration Two hours

Take a Break...
Dine and drink within the arcades.

Classic Photo: Stroll through this elegant passage, designed by Jacques Billaud.

3 The 1826-built **Galerie Colbert** features a huge glass dome and rotunda.
KIEV.VICTOR/SHUTTERSTOCK ©

7 There's lots to explore in **Passage Verdeau**: vintage comic books, antiques, old postcards and more.

4 The 1824-built **Passage Choiseul** has discount and vintage clothing, beads and costume jewellery, and cheap eateries
KIEV.VICTOR/SHUTTERSTOCK ©

R St-Augustin

R des Petits Champs

R de Richelieu

R Vivienne

4

3 **2**

Ⓜ Pyramides

Av de l'Opéra

Jardin du Palais Royal

R de Valois

1ER

Pl Colette

R du Colonel Driant

R de Rohan

Jardin des Tuileries

Jardin du Carrousel

Palais Royal – Musée du Louvre Ⓜ

R de Rivoli

R Croix des Petits Champs

R Richer

N 0 | 200 m
0 | 0.1 miles

FINISH

7

6

6 Inside **Passage Jouffroy** (1847) there's a wax museum, the Musée Grévin, and wonderful boutiques.

Passage des Panoramas

Grands Boulevards M

Bd Poissonnière

5

R Vivienne

Pl de la Bourse

M Bourse

R Montmartre

R Notre Dame des Victoires

R de Réaumur

5 Paris' oldest covered arcade (1800), **Passage des Panoramas**, was expanded in 1834 and is full of eateries and unusual shops.

KIEV.VICTOR/SHUTTERSTOCK ©

2 Built in 1826, **Galerie Vivienne** is decorated with floor mosaics and bas-reliefs on the walls.

Pl des Victoires

R d

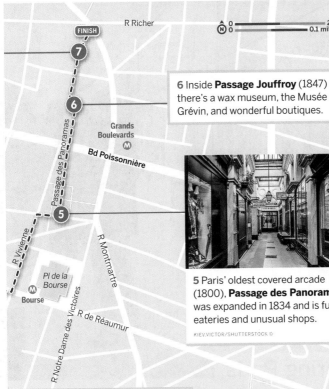

R du Boulot

R du Louvre

R Coquillière

1

START

1 Galerie Véro Dodat retains its 19th-century skylights, murals, Corinthian columns, and shop-fronts including furniture restorers.

ANDERSPHOTO/SHUTTERSTOCK ©

Graffiti, Rue Dénoyez

CHINATOWN/ALAMY STOCK PHOTO ©

Discovering Paris' Street Art

The City of Light inspires artists of all genres, including urban art, and vibrant street art continues to splash colour across neighbourhoods city-wide.

Great For...

☑ Don't Miss

Check out works by French and international artists, including Banksy, at Art 42.

Locations

Rue Dénoyez (Map p254; 20e; M Belleville)
One block east of bd de Belleville, narrow rue Dénoyez has some of Paris' most dazzling street art. Everything on the small cobbled street, from litter bins and flower pots to lamp posts and window shutters, is covered in colourful graffiti. Artists' workshops pepper the paved street where local kids kick footballs around and street art 'happenings' break out on summer nights.

Le MUR (Map p254; www.lemur.fr; rue Oberkampf, 11e; M Parmentier) Meaning 'the wall' but also standing for Modulable Urbain Réactif (Modular Urban Reactive), street-art canvas Le MUR is overseen by an arts collective, with hundreds of murals painted on it to date.

ℹ Need to Know

City funds are set aside to create *murs d'expression* (street-art murals) in all 20 *arrondissements*.

✕ Take a Break

Next to Le MUR, Café Charbon (p178) is great for a drink or bistro fare.

★ Top Tip

See graffiti street artists in action at the workrooms in hip-hop centre La Place (p190).

over Paris), among others. Compulsory guided tours, generally lasting 1½ to two hours, lead you through 4000 sq metres of subterranean rooms. Entry's free but you need to reserve tours online (ideally several weeks in advance, although last-minute cancellations can arise). Tours in French depart from 6.30pm to 8.30pm on Tuesdays and from 2.30pm to 5.30pm on the first Sunday of the month.

L'Aerosol (www.laerosol.fr; 54 rue de l'Évangile, 18e; adult/child €5/3; ⊘11am-9pm Wed-Sun; Ⓜ RER Rosa-Parks, Marx Dormoy) Street art is showcased at this cavernous museum inside a former SNCF freight railway station. French and international artists here include Mr Chat, Speedy Graphito, Invader and Banksy. You can test out your own tagging skills on the walls outside (BYO aerosols) or ask about taking a street-art course.

Galerie Itinerrance (http://itinerrance.fr; 24 bd du Général d'Armée Jean Simon, 13e; ⊘noon-7pm Tue-Sat; Ⓜ Bibliothèque) FREE Testament to the 13e's ongoing creative renaissance, this gallery showcases graffiti and street art, and can advise on self-guided and guided street-art tours of the neighbourhood that take in many landmark works by artists represented by the gallery. Across the train tracks in nearby Chinatown, don't miss the striking twinset of monumental wall murals by Portuguese artist Pantónio showcased on high-rise apartment blocks at 20-22 ave d'Ivry.

Tours

Street Art Paris (☎09 50 75 19 92; http://streetartparis.fr; 2½hr tour €20) Learn about the history of graffiti on fascinating tours taking in Paris' vibrant street art. Tours take place in Belleville and Montmartre and on the Left Bank. If you're inspired to try it yourself, book into a 2½-hour mural workshop (€35).

Street Art Museums & Galleries

Art 42 (http://art42.fr; 96 bd Bessières, 17e; ⊘tours in English 7pm Tue, 4pm 1st Sun of month; Ⓜ Porte de Clichy) FREE Street art and post-graffiti now have their own dedicated space at this 'anti-museum', with works by Banksy, Bom.K, Miss Van, Swoon, and Invader (who's behind the Space Invader motifs on buildings all

TAKASHI IMAGES/SHUTTERSTOCK ©

Musée National Picasso

An exquisite 17th-century mansion in Le Marais is the wonderfully intimate setting for an exceptional collection of works by long-time Paris resident, Pablo Picasso.

One of Paris' most beloved art collections is showcased inside the mid-17th-century Hôtel Salé, an exquisite private mansion owned by the city since 1964. The Musée National Picasso is a staggering art museum devoted to Spanish artist Pablo Picasso (1881–1973), who spent much of his life living and working in Paris. The collection includes more than 5000 drawings, engravings, paintings, ceramic works and sculptures by the *grand maître* (great master), although they're not all displayed at the same time.

The extraordinary collection was donated to the French government by the artist's heirs in lieu of paying inheritance taxes. In addition to the permanent collection, the museum mounts two major temporary exhibitions per year (included in the admission price).

Great For...

☑ **Don't Miss**

The museum's bi-annual temporary exhibitions.

ⓘ Need to Know

Map p254; ☏ 01 85 56 00 36; www.musee picassoparis.fr; 5 rue de Thorigny, 3e; adult/ child €12.50/free; ⊙10.30am-6pm Tue-Fri, 9.30am-6pm Sat & Sun; Ⓜ Chemin Vert, St-Paul

✖ Take a Break

Stop by the museum's 'rooftop cafe', overlooked by an ancient stone sphinx.

★ Top Tip

To best appreciate the artworks and building's history, rent an audioguide (€5).

What's Nearby

Musée d'Art et d'Histoire du Judaïsme   Museum

(Map p254; ☏01 53 01 86 62; www.mahj.org; 71 rue du Temple, 3e; adult/child €9/free; ⊙11am-6pm Tue-Fri, 10am-6pm Sat & Sun; Ⓜ Rambuteau) Inside the Hôtel de St-Aignan, dating from 1650, this museum traces the evolution of Jewish communities from the Middle Ages to the present, including French Jewish history. Highlights include documents relating to the Dreyfus Affair, and artworks by Chagall, Modigliani and Soutine. Creative workshops (adult/child from €9/7) for children, adults and families complement excellent temporary exhibitions (from €8.50/5.50). To learn more about Le Marais' Jewish history, take a guided walking tour of the neighbourhood (including museum entrance €12/9; English available).

Pavillon de l'Arsenal   Museum

(Map p254; www.pavillon-arsenal.com; 21 bd Morland, 4e; ⊙11am-7pm Tue-Sun; Ⓜ Sully–Morland) FREE Built in 1879 as a museum, this magnificent glass-roofed building with arched wrought-iron girders wasn't actually used as one until over a century later, when it opened as a centre for Parisian urbanism and architecture. Interpretative information is in French but it's fascinating for anyone with an interest in the evolution of Paris. There's a small but excellent architectural bookshop on the ground floor.

Marché des Enfants Rouges   Market €

(Map p254; 39 rue de Bretagne & 33bis rue Charlot, 3e; ⊙8.30am-1pm & 4-7.30pm Tue-Sat, 8.30am-2pm Sun, individual stall hours vary; Ⓜ Filles du Calvaire) Paris' oldest covered market (built 1615) is secreted behind an inconspicuous green-metal gate. A glorious maze of stalls selling ready-to-eat dishes from around the globe, as well as produce, cheese and flower stalls, it's a great place to meander and to dine at communal tables.

DINING OUT

Produce-laden markets, intimate bistros, gastronomic temples and more

Dining Out

The inhabitants of some cities rally around local sports teams, but in Paris, they rally around la table. Pistachio macarons, shots of tomato consommé, decadent bœuf bourguignon, a gooey wedge of Camembert running onto the cheese plate… food is not fuel here, it's the reason you get up in the morning.

Paris doesn't have its own 'local' cuisine, but is the crossroads for the regional flavours of France. Dishes from the hot south favour olive oil, garlic and tomatoes; the cooler, pastoral northern regions turn to cream and butter; and coastal areas concentrate on seafood. The freshness of ingredients and reliance on natural flavours combined with refined, often very complex cooking methods – and, of course, wine – means you're in a gourmet's paradise.

In This Section

Price Ranges/Tipping

The following price ranges refer to the cost of a two-course meal.

€ Less than €20

€€ €20 to €40

€€€ More than €40

Tipping A *pourboire* (tip) is unnecessary, as service is always included in the bill. It's not uncommon to round up the bill for good service.

Montmartre & Northern Paris
Neobistros, wine bars and world cuisine (p125)

Champs-Élysées & Grands Boulevards
Big-name chefs, backstreet bistros (p122)

Louvre & Les Halles
Trendy restaurants on the rise (p123)

Le Marais, Ménilmontant & Belleville
Premier foodie destination (p129)

Eiffel Tower & Western Paris
Gastronomic palaces and museum restaurants (p122)

Seine

Eiffel Tower

St-Germain & Les Invalides
Chic cafes, *haute cuisine* (p138)

The Islands
Romantic setting but limited options (p136)

Latin Quarter
Cheap eats and Left Bank treasures (p136)

Bastille & Eastern Paris
Balances tradition and innovation (p133)

Seine

Montparnasse & Southern Paris
Historic brasseries, neighbourhood favourites (p142)

Useful Phrases

I'd like to reserve a table for... *Je voudrais réserver une table pour...*

...(eight) o'clock (*vingt*) *heures*

...two/three people *deux/trois personnes*

I don't eat... *Je ne mange pas...*

Please bring the bill. *Apportez-moi l'addition, s'il vous plaît.*

Must try/Classic dishes

Bœuf bourguignon Beef marinated and cooked in young red wine with mushrooms, onions, carrots and bacon.

Confit de canard Duck cooked slowly in its own fat.

Entrecôte Thin, boneless rib-eye steak.

Tarte Tatin Upside-down apple tart.

The Best...

Experience Paris' top restaurants and cafes

Classic Bistros

Le Chardenoux (p134) Listed historical monument.

Le Bistrot Paul Bert (p134) Legendary address with vintage decor.

Chez Paul (p134) Paris as your grandmother knew it.

Chez Dumonet (p140) The quintessential Parisian bistro experience.

Wine-Bar Dining

Le Verre Volé (p126) Excellent wines, expert advice and hearty *plats du jour* (daily specials).

Café de la Nouvelle Mairie (p136) Latin Quarter favourite for by-the-glass wines and seasonal bistro dishes.

Neobistros

Marrow (p128) Inventive ingredients and knock-out paired cocktails.

Richer (p122) Brilliant-value bistro fare.

Le Beurre Noisette (p143) Creative, locally loved cooking.

Clover (p139) Watch the chefs at work in the combined dining space/kitchen.

Le Servan (p130) Daily changing creations near Père Lachaise.

Crêpes

Breizh Café (p129) Among the most authentic Breton crêpes in town.

Crêperie Pen-Ty (p126) Northern Paris' best crêperie, with traditional Breton aperitifs.

Little Breizh (p138) Innovative twists such as Breton sardines.

Seafood

Le Dôme (p143) Magnificent shellfish platters in a timeless art deco brasserie.
Huîtrerie Regis (p139) Oyster heaven.

Traditional French

Bouillon Racine (p138) Traditional fare inspired by age-old recipes.
Chez La Vieille (p124) Homage to the former wholesale markets Les Halles.
Brasserie Bofinger (p131) The city's oldest brasserie, pictured above.

Lonely Planet's Top Choices

Tomy & Co (p138) Tomy Gousset uses organic produce from his own garden.
Restaurant AT (p137) Abstract-art-like masterpieces made from rare ingredients.
Restaurant Guy Savoy (p140) Resplendent triple-Michelin-starred flagship.
Bouillon Racine (p138) Classical French cooking in an art nouveau showpiece.

Vegetarian & Vegan

Abattoir Végétal (p125) Plant-filled vegan cafe in Montmartre.
Soul Kitchen (p127) Market-driven vegetarian dishes.
Raw Cakes (p143) Not only cakes but yes, it's all raw.

⊗ Eiffel Tower & Western Paris

Arnaud Nicolas   French €€

(Map p246; ☑01 45 55 59 59; http://arnaud nicolas.paris/en; 46 ave de la Bourdonnais, 7e; 2-/3-course lunch menu €28/32, tasting menu €62; ☺2-9.45pm Mon, noon-1.45pm & 2-9.45pm Tue-Sat; MÉcole Militaire) The upmarket hybrid – restaurant and boutique – of chef Arnaud Nicolas combines two natural French loves: gastronomy and charcuterie. Be it a posh pork pie (flavoured with herbs, or foie gras and quail pie with pear and pistachio perhaps), fancy terrine or a simple plate of cold cuts, this sleek address serves it to astonishing effect. End with a sublime dark chocolate soufflé.

L'Astrance   Gastronomy €€€

(Map p246; ☑01 40 50 84 40; www.astrances taurant.com; 4 rue Beethoven, 16e; 3-/5-course lunch menus €75/170, 7-course dinner menu €250; ☺12.15 & 8.15pm Tue-Fri, closed Aug; MPassy) It's almost two decades since Pascal Barbot's dazzling cuisine at the triple-Michelin-starred L'Astrance made its debut, but it's shown no signs of losing its cutting edge. Look beyond the complicated descriptions on the menu and expect exquisite elements making up intricate plates that are as spectacular as the artworks adorning Paris' grand galleries. Reserve one to two months in advance.

Le Jules Verne   Gastronomy €€€

(Map p246; ☑01 45 55 61 44; www.lejules verne-paris.com; 2nd fl, Eiffel Tower, Champ de Mars, 7e; 5-/6-course menus €190/230, 3-course lunch menu €105; ☺noon-1.30pm & 7-9.30pm; MBir Hakeim, RER Champ de Mars–Tour Eiffel) Book way ahead (online only) to feast on Michelin-starred cuisine and the most beautiful view of Paris at this magical spot on the Eiffel Tower's 2nd floor, accessed by a private lift (elevator) in the south pillar. Cuisine is contemporary, with a five- or six-course 'experience' menu allowing you to taste the best of chef Pascal Féraud's stunning gastronomic repertoire.

⊗ Champs-Élysées & Grands Boulevards

Richer   Bistro €

(Map p250; www.lericher.com; 2 rue Richer, 9e; mains €17-21; ☺noon-2.30pm & 7.30-10.30pm; MPoissonière, Bonne Nouvelle) Run by the same team as across-the-street neighbour **L'Office** (Map p250; ☑01 47 70 67 31; www. office-resto.com; 3 rue Richer, 9e; 2-/3-course lunch menus €22/27, mains €23-29; ☺noon-2pm & 7.30-10.30pm Mon-Fri), Richer's pared-back, exposed-brick decor is a smart setting for genius creations like smoked duck breast ravioli in miso broth, and quince and lime cheesecake for dessert. It doesn't take reservations, but it serves snacks and Chinese tea, and has a full bar (open until midnight). Fantastic value.

Ladurée   Pastries €€

(Map p246; ☑01 40 75 08 75; www.laduree.com; 75 av des Champs-Élysées, 8e; pastries from €2.60, mains €18-47, 2-/3-course menu €35/42; ☺7.30am-11pm Sun-Thu, 7.30am-midnight Fri & Sat; ☝; MGeorge V) One of Paris' oldest patisseries, Ladurée has been around since 1862 and first created the lighter-than-air, ganache-filled macaron in the 1930s. Its tearoom is the classiest spot to indulge on the Champs. Alternatively, pick up some pastries to go – from croissants to its trademark macarons, it's all quite heavenly. A three-course children's menu costs €19.

Détour   French €€

(Map p246; ☑01 45 26 21 48; www.facebook. com/DetourRestaurant; 15 rue de la Tour des Dames, 9e; lunch menu €28, dinner menu €35-50; ☺noon-1.30pm Wed-Sat, 7.30-10.30pm Tue-Sat; MTrinité) As the name suggests, Adrien Cachot's 16-seat neobistro is off the beaten path, both literally and figuratively. Diners choose between just two options (meat or fish), leaving the rest in the hands of the highly original chef. Expect dishes like sweet carrots puréed with miso and topped with shaved Mimolette, or veal tartare with coffee vinaigrette and truffled egg cream.

Le Jules Verne

86 Champs — Pastries €€

(Map p246; ☎01 70 38 77 38; www.86champs.
com; 86 av Champs-Élysées, 8e; ⏱8.30am-
11.30pm Sun-Thu, to 12.30am Fri & Sat; Ⓜ George
V) A swirling fantasy of floral aromas –
verveine, rose, lavender – lures visitors
into this opulent shrine to French pastries.
It's half Pierre Hermé (of macaron fame),
half Occitane (Provençe-themed beauty
products); after you're done browsing the
boutique, head to the horseshoe-shaped
dessert bar in the back, where you can dine
on whimsical creations prepared in front
of you.

Le Hide — French €€

(Map p246; ☎01 45 74 15 81; www.lehide.fr; 10
rue du Général Lanrezac, 17e; 2-/3-course menus
€36/48; ⏱6-10.30pm Mon-Sat; Ⓜ Charles de
Gaulle–Étoile) A perpetual favourite, Le Hide is
a tiny neighbourhood bistro serving scrump-
tious traditional French fare: snails, baked
shoulder of lamb, and monkfish with *beurre
blanc* (white sauce). Unsurprisingly, this
place fills up faster than you can scamper
down the steps of the nearby Arc de Triomphe (p42) – reserve well in advance.

Lasserre — Gastronomy €€€

(Map p246; ☎01 43 59 02 13; www.restaurant-
lasserre.com; 17 av Franklin D Roosevelt, 8e;
3-course lunch menu €60, tasting menu €190,
mains €85-130; ⏱noon-2pm Thu & Fri, 7-10pm
Tue-Sat; Ⓜ Franklin D Roosevelt) Since 1942,
this exceedingly elegant restaurant in
the Triangle d'Or has hosted style icons,
including Audrey Hepburn, and is still a su-
perlative choice for a Michelin-starred meal
to remember. A bellhop-attended lift, white-
and-gold chandeliered decor, extraordinary
retractable roof and flawless service set the
stage for inspired creations like roast blue
lobster *à la Parisienne* with tarragon sauce.
Dress code required.

⊗ Louvre & Les Halles

Fou de Pâtisserie — Patisserie €

(Map p250; 45 rue Montorgueil, 2e; ⏱11am-
8pm Mon-Fri, 10am-8pm Sat, 10am-6pm Sun;
Ⓜ Les Halles, Sentier, RER Châtelet–Les Halles)
Single-name patisseries scatter across the
city, but for a greatest-hits range from its finest pastry chefs – Cyril Lignac, Christophe

📖 Menu Advice

Carte Menu, as in the written list of what's cooking, listed in the order you'd eat it: starter, main course, cheese, then dessert. Note that an entrée is a starter, not the main course (as in the US).

Menu Not at all what it means in English, *le menu* in French is a *prix-fixe* menu: a multicourse meal at a fixed price. It's by far the best-value dining there is and most restaurants chalk one on the board.

À la carte Order whatever you fancy from the menu (as opposed to opting for a *prix-fixe* menu).

Formule Similar to a *menu, une formule* is a cheaper lunchtime option comprising a main plus starter or dessert. Wine or coffee is sometimes included.

Plat du jour Dish of the day, invariably good value.

Menu enfant Two- or three-course meal for kids (generally up to the age of 12) at a fixed price; usually includes a drink.

Menu dégustation Fixed-price tasting menu served in many top-end restaurants, consisting of at least five modestly sized courses.

Adam (L'Éclair de Génie), Jacques Genin, Pierre Hermé and Philippe Conticini included – head to this one-stop concept shop.

Stohrer   Patisserie €
(Map p250; www.stohrer.fr; 51 rue Montorgueil, 2e; ⏰7.30am-8.30pm; MÉtienne Marcel, Sentier) Opened in 1730 by Nicolas Stohrer, the Polish pastry chef of queen consort Marie Leszczyńska (wife of Louis XV), Stohrer's house-made specialities include its own inventions, the *baba au rhum* (rum-soaked sponge cake) and *puits d'amour* (caramel-topped, vanilla cream–filled puff pastry). The beautiful pastel murals were added in 1864 by Paul-Jacques-Aimé Baudry, who also decorated the Palais Garnier's Grand Foyer.

Maison Maison   Mediterranean €€
(Map p250; 📞09 67 82 07 32; www.facebook.com/maisonmaisonparis; opposite 16 quai du Louvre, 1er; 2-/3-course lunch menu €20/25, small plates €7-16; ⏰10am-2am Wed-Sun, 6pm-2am Tue; MPont Neuf) Halfway down the stairs by Pont Neuf is this wonderfully secret space beneath the *bouquinistes*, where you can watch the bateaux-mouches float by as you dine on artful creations like beetroot and pink grapefruit-cured bonito or gnocchi with white asparagus and broccoli pesto. In nice weather, cocktails at the glorious riverside terrace are not to be missed.

Balagan   Israeli €€
(Map p246; 📞01 40 20 72 14; www.balagan-paris.com; 9 rue d'Alger, 1er; lunch menus from €24, mains €23-28; ⏰noon-2pm Mon-Sat, 7-10pm daily; MTuileries) Cool navy blues and creamy diamond tiling contrast with the chic vibe at this Israeli hotspot. Come here to sample delectable small plates: deconstructed kebabs, crispy halloumi cheese with dates, onion confit Ashkenazi chicken liver, or, our favourite, a spicy, succulent tuna tartare with fennel, cilantro, capers and pistachios. Mains, like the seabream black pasta, are just as praiseworthy.

Chez La Vieille   French €€
(Map p250; 📞01 42 60 15 78; www.chezlavieille.fr; 1 rue Bailleul, 1er; mains €24-26; ⏰noon-2.30pm Fri & Sat, 6-10.30pm Tue-Sat; MLouvre–Rivoli) In salvaging this history-steeped eatery within a 16th-century building, star chef Daniel Rose pays homage to the former wholesale markets, the erstwhile legendary owner Adrienne Biasin (many of her timeless dishes have been updated, from terrines and rillettes to veal blanquette), and the soul of Parisian bistro cooking itself. Dine at the street-level bar or upstairs in the peacock-blue dining room.

Bambou   Southeast Asian €€
(Map p250; 📞01 40 28 98 30; www.bambouparis.com; 23 rue des Jeûneurs, 2e; mains €18-29; ⏰noon-2.30pm & 7-11pm, bar to 1am; 📞; MSentier) This spectacular Southeast Asian restaurant occupies a 500-sq-m former

fabric warehouse, with vintage birdcages and a giant metal dragon adorning the main dining room, a downstairs billiards room/bar, a vast terrace and a Zen-like garden. Chef Antonin Bonnet's specialities include squid with black pepper and basil, and aromatic shrimp pad thai.

Frenchie — Bistro €€€

(Map p250; ☎01 40 39 96 19; www.frenchie-restaurant.com; 5 rue du Nil, 2e; 4-course lunch menu €45, 5-course dinner menu €74, with wine €175; ☺6.30-11pm Mon-Fri, noon-2.30pm Thu & Fri in summer; Ⓜ Sentier) Tucked down an inconspicuous alley, this tiny bistro with wooden tables and old stone walls is always packed and for good reason: excellent-value dishes are modern, market-driven and prepared with unpretentious flair by French chef Gregory Marchand. Reserve well in advance or arrive early and pray for a cancellation (it does happen). Alternatively, head to neighbouring **Frenchie Bar à Vins** (6 rue du Nil, 2e; dishes €9-23; ☺6.30-11pm). No reservations at the latter – write your name on the sheet of paper strung outside and wait for your name to be called.

During the day, swing by its adjacent deli-style takeaway outlet **Frenchie to Go** (Map p250; ☎01 40 26 23 43; www.frenchietogo.com; 9 rue du Nil, 2e; dishes €8-18; ☺8.30am-4.30pm Mon-Fri, 9.30am-5.30pm Sat & Sun; 🛜).

Verjus — Modern American €€€

(Map p250; ☎01 42 97 54 40; http://verjusparis.com; 52 rue de Richelieu, 1er; menu €78, with wine €133; ☺7-11pm Mon-Fri; Ⓜ Bourse, Pyramides) Opened by American duo Braden Perkins and Laura Adrian, Verjus was born out of their former clandestine supper club, the Hidden Kitchen. The restaurant builds on that tradition, offering a chance to sample some excellent, creative cuisine in a casual space. The tasting menu is a series of small plates, using ingredients sourced straight from producers. Reserve well in advance.

If you're just after an aperitif or a prelude to dinner, the downstairs **Verjus Bar à Vins** (Map p250; 47 rue de Montpensier, 1er; ☺6-11pm Mon-Fri) serves a handful of charcuterie and cheese plates. For lunch or a more casual

dinner, don't miss nearby **Ellsworth** (Map p250; ☎01 42 60 59 66; www.ellsworthparis.com; 34 rue de Richelieu, 1er; 2-/3-course lunch menu €22/28, mains €12-30; ☺12.15-2.15pm & 7-10.30pm Mon-Sat, 11.30am-3pm Sun; Ⓜ Pyramides), Verjus' sister restaurant.

Le Grand Véfour — Gastronomy €€€

(Map p250; ☎01 42 96 56 27; www.grand-vefour.com; 17 rue de Beaujolais, 1er; lunch/dinner menu €115/315, mains €99-126; ☺noon-2.30pm & 7.30-10.30pm Mon-Fri; Ⓜ Pyramides) Holding two Michelin stars, this 18th-century jewel on the northern edge of the Jardin du Palais Royal has been a dining favourite since 1784; the names ascribed to each table span Napoléon and Victor Hugo to Colette (who lived next door). Expect a voyage of discovery from chef Guy Martin in one of the most beautiful restaurants in the world.

⊗ Montmartre & Northern Paris

Du Pain et des Idées — Bakery €

(Map p249; http://dupainetdesidees.com; 34 rue Yves Toudic, 10e; breads €1.20-7, pastries €2.50-6.50; ☺6.45am-8pm Mon-Fri; Ⓜ Jacques Bonsergent) This traditional bakery with an exquisite interior from 1889 is famed for its naturally leavened bread, orange-blossom brioche and *escargots* (scroll-like 'snails') in four sweet flavours. Its mini savoury *pavés* (breads) flavoured with reblochon cheese and fig, or goat's cheese, sesame and honey are perfect for lunch on the run. A wooden picnic table sits on the pavement outside.

Abattoir Végétal — Vegan €

(Map p249; 61 rue Ramey, 18e; 3-course lunch menu €18, mains €13-16, Sunday brunch adult/child €25/5; ☺9am-6pm Tue & Wed, 9am-11.45pm Thu & Fri, 10am-11.45pm Sat, 10.30am-4.30pm Sun; 🛜✍; Ⓜ Jules Joffrin) Mint-green wrought-iron chairs and tables line the pavement outside the 'plant slaughterhouse' (it occupies a former butcher shop), while the light, bright interior has bare-bulb downlights, distempered walls and greenery-filled hanging baskets. Each day there's a choice of three raw and cooked organic dishes per course, cold-pressed juices and craft beers. Gluten-free options are plentiful.

Le Verre Volé   Bistro €
(Map p254; ☑01 48 03 17 34; http://leverrevole. fr; 67 rue de Lancry, 10e; mains €11-22, sandwiches €7.90; ⏱bistro 12.30-2.30pm & 7.30-11.30pm, wine bar 10am-2am; ☎; Ⓜ Jacques Bonsergent) The tiny 'Stolen Glass' – a wine shop with a few tables – is one of Paris' most popular wine bar–restaurants, with outstanding natural and unfiltered wines and expert advice. Unpretentious, hearty *plats du jour* are excellent. Reserve in advance for meals, or stop by to pick up a gourmet sandwich (such as mustard-smoked burrata with garlic-pork sausage) and a bottle.

Holybelly 5   Cafe €
(Map p245; https://holybellycafe.com; 5 rue Lucien Sampaix, 10e; dishes €6.50-16.50; ⏱9am-5pm; ☎☑; Ⓜ Jacques Bonsergent) Light-filled Holybelly's regulars never tire of its outstanding coffee, cuisine and service. Sarah Mouchot's breakfast pancakes (with eggs, bacon, bourbon butter and maple syrup) and chia-seed porridge are legendary, while her lunch menu features everything from beetroot gnocchi to slow-cooked pork belly with sweet potato purée. Wash them down with a Bloody Mary or Deck & Donahue beer. No reservations.

Le Petit Château d'Eau   French €
(Map p245; ☑01 42 08 72 81; 34 rue du Château d'Eau, 10e; mains €13.50-17.50; ⏱kitchen noon-3pm Mon, noon-3pm & 7-11.30pm Tue-Sat, bar 8am-3.30pm Mon, 8am-2am Tue-Fri, 9am-2am Sat; Ⓜ Jacques Bonsergent) Scarcely changed in a century, with lemon- and lime-tiled walls, zinc bar and burgundy banquettes, this neighbourhood treasure endures in defiance of the post-industrial co-working cafes that have sprung up around it. Classical cooking spans duck with honey sauce to beef entrecôte with roast garlic potatoes, or just stop by for a morning coffee or afternoon kir.

Crêperie Pen-Ty   Crêpes €
(Map p249; ☑01 48 74 18 49; 65 rue de Douai, 9e; galettes €4-15, crêpes €4.90-10.40; ⏱noon-2.30pm & 7.30-11.15pm Mon-Fri, 12.30-4pm & 6.30-11.30pm Sat, 12.30-4pm & 6.30-10.30pm Sun; Ⓜ Place de Clichy) Hailed as the best crêperie in northern Paris, Pen-Ty is well worth the detour. Book ahead, and don't miss the selection of authentic Breton aperitifs like *chouchen* (a type of mead) and *pastis marin* (an aniseed and seaweed liquor), along with superb savoury *galettes* (made with buckwheat flour) and sweet crêpes. There is a takeaway window too.

Fric-Frac   Sandwiches €
(Map p254; ☑01 42 85 87 34; http://fricfrac. fr; 79 quai de Valmy, 10e; sandwiches €11.50-15; ⏱noon-3pm & 7.30-11pm Tue-Fri, noon-11pm Sat & Sun; Ⓜ Jacques Bonsergent) Traditional snack croque monsieur (a toasted cheese and ham sandwich) gets a contemporary makeover at this quayside space. Gourmet Winnie (Crottin de Chavignol cheese, dried fruit, chestnut honey, chives and rosemary) and exotic Shaolin (king prawns, lemongrass paste, shitake mushrooms and Thai basil) are among the creative combos served with salad and fries. Eat in or head to the canal.

L'affineur Affiné   Cheese €
(Map p249; ☑09 66 94 22 15; www.laffineuraffine. com; 51 rue Notre Dame de Lorette, 9e; cheese platters €6.50-39, weekend brunch €20; ⏱kitchen noon-2.30pm Mon, noon-2.30pm & 5.30-9pm Wed-Sat, 11.30am-2pm & 5.30-7pm Sun, shop 10.30am-2.30pm Mon, to 9pm Wed-Sat, to 7pm Sun; Ⓜ St-Georges) With 120 French cheeses, this *fromagerie* (cheese shop) is a fabulous place to stock up and taste them at its on-site *bar à fromages* (cheese bar). Let the staff know your preferences and they'll prepare platters of two to 15 varieties, with charcuterie available as well as paired wines. Weekend brunch is a multicourse feast.

Le Grenier à Pain   Bakery €
(Map p249; http://legrenierapain.com; 38 rue des Abbesses, 18e; ⏱7.30am-8pm Thu-Mon; Ⓜ Abbesses) A past winner of Paris' annual 'best baguette' prize, this enchanting bakery with a semi-open kitchen is an ideal place to pick up picnic fare. Join the queue for a crusty baguette sandwich, Provence-style

Madeleine cake, Mesdemoiselles Madeleines

fougasse bread and alluring mini breads topped with fig and goat's cheese or bacon and olives. End on a sweet high with a fruit-bejewelled loaf cake.

Mesdemoiselles
Madeleines   Pastries €

(Map p249; www.mllesmadeleines.com; 37 rue des Martyrs, 9e; madeleines small €0.70, large €2.50-4.50; ⊘10.30am-7pm Tue-Sat, 10.30am-2pm & 3.30-6.30pm Sun; ⓂSt-Georges) Shell-shaped French madeleine cakes, immortalised by Marcel Proust, are the sole product of this ingenious spot, in a dazzling array of flavours: 'simple' (Tahitian vanilla; Ethiopian coffee), 'savoury' (red onion, chives and crème fraîche; basil, feta and pine nuts), and 'gourmet' (Rhône valley raspberries with raspberry coulis; caramelised hazelnuts, salted caramel mousse and a caramel shell), along with bite-sized mini-madeleines.

Pain Pain   Bakery €

(Map p249; www.pain-pain.fr; 88 rue des Martyrs, 18e; sandwiches & pastries €2.20-5.25; ⊘7am-8pm Tue-Sat, 7.30am-7.30pm Sun; ⓂAbbesses)

Sébastien Mauvieux is famed for his baguettes (his accolades include Paris' 'best baguette' prize) and bakes delicious corn bread, rye and chestnut loaves and other varieties of *pain*. Pick up a sandwich to take away, along with exquisite pastries, such as a layered Opéra cake with yuzu and raspberries or signature Zéphyr tart with white chocolate and sweetened Chantilly cream.

Soul Kitchen   Vegetarian €

(Map p249; ☎01 71 37 99 95; 33 rue Lamarck, 18e; 3-course lunch menus €14, snacks €3-4.50; ⊘8.30am-6pm Tue-Fri, 10am-6.30pm Sat & Sun; ☞☏♿; ⓂLamarck–Caulaincourt) This vegetarian eatery with a shabby-chic vintage interior and tiny open kitchen serves market-driven dishes including creative salads, homemade soups, savoury tarts, burritos and wraps – all gargantuan in size and packed with seasonal veggies. Round off lunch or snack between meals with muffins, cakes and mint-laced *citronnade maison* (homemade lemonade). Families should check out the sage-green 'games' cupboard.

Marrow   Bistro €€

(Map p254; ☑09 81 34 57 00; 128 rue du Faubourg
St-Martin, 10e; mains €11-19; ☺6-10pm Tue-Sat, bar
to 2am, closed Aug; Ⓜ Gare de l'Est) Hay-smoked
quail with peat vinaigrette, grilled octopus
and fennel confit, and breaded roast bone
marrow are among the adventurous flavour
combinations from Hugo Blanchet, who
partnered with mixologist Arthur Combe to
open this neobistro that's taking Paris' foodie
scene by storm. Rough stone walls, blond
wood tables and a small pavement terrace
create a relaxed backdrop.

Le Bistrot de la Galette   Bistro €€

(Map p249; ☑01 46 06 19 65; http://bistrotdela
galette.fr; 102ter rue Lepic, 18e; mains €14-17;
☺11am-10pm Tue-Sun; Ⓜ Abbesses, Lamarck–
Caulaincourt) ✐ In the shadow of Montmartre windmill Moulin de la Galette, this
vintage-fitted bistro is the creation of pastry
chef Gilles Marchal, who uses locally hand-
milled flour in *feuilletés* (delicately laminated
pastry puffs) that accompany most dishes,
such as *Galette Parisienne* (roast ham, sau-
téed mushrooms and Comté) and *Galette
Provençale* (shredded roast lamb, aubergine,

garlic and sun-dried tomatoes). Traditional
bistro staples are also available daily, alongside all-natural wines and craft beers.

Matière à.   Modern French €€

(Map p254; ☑09 70 38 61 48; www.matiere-a.
com; 15 rue Marie et Louise, 10e; 2-/3-course
lunch menus €21/25, 4-course dinner menus €46;
☺noon-2pm & 7.30pm-11pm Mon-Fri, 7.30pm-
11pm Sat; Ⓜ Goncourt, Jacques Bonsergent) The
short but stunning seasonal menu changes
daily at this unique space. *Table d'hôte*–style
dining for up to 14 is around a shared oak
table lit by dozens of naked light bulbs. In
the kitchen is young chef Anthony Courteille,
who prides himself on doing everything *fait
maison* (homemade), including bread and
butter to die for. Reservations essential.

Le Bel Ordinaire   Mediterranean €€

(Map p250; ☑01 46 27 46 67; www.lebelordi
naire.com; 54 rue de Paradis, 10e; 2-/3-course
midweek lunch menus €18/22, dishes €5-15;
☺kitchen noon-2.30pm & 7-10.30pm, bar 11am-
11.30pm; 🛜; Ⓜ Poissonnière) Floor-to-ceiling,
wall-to-wall open shelves lined with bottles
and gourmet products (hams, cheeses,

Le Verre Volé (p126)

shellfish, preserves, straw baskets of farm eggs and fresh fruit and vegetables) fire up your appetite for tapas-style small plates such as tuna gravlax with grated apple, smoked burrata with sesame pesto, cuttlefish-ink risotto with blue cheese at this contemporary wine bar. Over 300 winemakers are represented. Seating is at a long communal oak table, high counters and, in fine weather, out on the terrace.

Aspic   Bistro €€€

(Map p249; ☑09 82 49 30 98; 24 rue de la Tour d'Auvergne, 9e; 7-course tasting menu €65, with wine €100; ⊘7.30-9.30pm Tue-Sat; MﾠAnvers) Chef Quentin Giroud ditched the high-flying world of finance for the stoves, and this small vintage-style space with a semi-open kitchen is testament to his conviction. Weekly changing, no-choice tasting menus feature inspired creations like peppercorn pancetta with kaffir lime butter, warm octopus with cashew purée, skin-on plaice with popcorn capers, and celeriac with mustard shoots and grated raw cauliflower.

⊗ Le Marais, Ménilmontant & Belleville

La Maison Plisson   Cafe, Deli €

(Map p254; http://lamaisonplisson.com; 93 bd Beaumarchais, 3e; mains €8-15; ⊘9.30am-9pm Mon, 8.30am-9pm Tue-Sat, 9.30am-8pm Sun; MﾠSt-Sébastien–Froissart) This gourmand's dream incorporates a covered-market-style, terrazzo-floored food hall filled with exquisite, mostly French produce: meat, vegetables, cheese, wine, chocolate, jams, freshly baked breads and much more. If your appetite's whet, its cafe, opening to twin terraces, serves charcuterie, foie gras and cheese planks, bountiful salads and delicacies such as olive oil-marinated, Noilly Prat–flambéed sardines.

Jacques Genin   Pastries €

(Map p254; ☑01 45 77 29 01; www.jacquesgenin. fr; 133 rue de Turenne, 3e; pastries €9; ⊘11am-7pm Tue-Fri & Sun, to 7.30pm Sat; MﾠOberkampf, Filles du Calvaire) Wildly creative *chocolatier*

🗨 Dining Tips

Bread Order a meal and within seconds a basket of fresh bread will be brought to the table. Butter is rarely an accompaniment. Except in the most upmarket of places, don't expect a side plate – simply put it on the table.

Water Asking for *une carafe d'eau* (jug of tap water) is perfectly acceptable, although some waiters will presume you don't know this and only offer mineral water, which you have to pay for.

Service To state the obvious, France is not a service-oriented country. No one is working for tips here, so to get around this, think like a Parisian – acknowledge the expertise of your *serveur* by asking for advice (even if you don't really want it). Being witty and speaking French with an accent will often help your cause.

Dress Smart casual is best. How you look is very important, and Parisians favour personal style above all else.

Jacques Genin is famed for his flavoured caramels, *pâtes de fruits* (fruit jellies) and exquisitely embossed *bonbons de chocolat* (chocolate sweets). But what completely steals the show at his elegant chocolate showroom is the *salon de dégustation* (aka tearoom), where you can order a pot of outrageously thick hot chocolate and legendary Genin *mille-feuille*, assembled to order.

Breizh Café   Crêpes €

(Map p254; ☑01 42 72 13 77; https://breizhcafe. com; 109 rue Vieille du Temple, 3e; crêpes & galettes €6.80-18.80; ⊘11.30am-11pm Mon-Sat, to 10pm Sun; MﾠSt-Sébastien–Froissart) Everything at the Breizh ('Breton' in Breton) is 100% authentic, including its organic-flour crêpes and *galettes* that top many Parisians' lists for the best in the city. Other specialities include Cancale oysters and 20 types of cider. Tables are limited and there's often a wait; book ahead or try its neighbouring deli,

L'Épicerie (Map p254; 01 42 71 39 44; https://
breizhcafe.com; 111 rue Vieille du Temple, 3e;
crêpes & galettes €6.80-18.80; 11.30am-10pm).

Café Méricourt   Cafe €

(Map p254; www.cafemericourt.com; 22 rue
de la Folie Méricourt, 11e; 2-course midweek
lunch menus €15, mains €8.50-14; 9am-6pm;
; St-Ambroise) With a pretty pepper-
mint-green façade and airy, plant-filled
interior, Méricourt is a delightful backstreet
find. Breakfast (honey-ricotta pancakes with
roasted pineapple, spinach-wrapped eggs
with feta, congee rice porridge) is served
until 3pm, with lunch options from 11am.
Parisian-roasted coffee, homemade ginger
beer and lemonade, natural wines and cocktails make it easy to while away a few hours.

Chambelland   Bakery €

(Map p254; 01 43 55 07 30; http://chambel
land.com; 14 rue Ternaux, 11e; lunch menus €10-
12, pastries €2.50-5.50; 9am-8pm Tue-Sat, to
6pm Sun; Parmentier) Using rice and buckwheat flour from its own mill in southern
France, this pioneering 100% gluten-free
bakery creates exquisite cakes and pastries
as well as sourdough loaves and brioches
peppered with nuts, seeds, chocolate and
fruit. Stop for lunch at one of the handful of
formica tables in this relaxed space, strewn
with sacks of flour and books.

L'As du Fallafel   Felafel €

(Map p254; 34 rue des Rosiers, 4e; takeaway
€5.50-8.50, mains €12-18; noon-midnight Sun-
Thu, to 4pm Fri; ; St-Paul) The lunchtime
queue stretching halfway down the street
from this place says it all. This Parisian
favourite, 100% worth the inevitable wait, is
the address for kosher, perfectly deep-fried
falafel (chickpea balls) and turkey or lamb
shawarma sandwiches. Do as every Parisian does and get them to take away.

Testament to its popularity, a second
takeaway window has opened at 44 rue des
Rosiers to cope with demand.

Miznon   Israeli €

(Map p254; 01 42 74 83 58; 22 rue des Écouffes,
4e; pita sandwiches €6-12.50; noon-11pm Sun-
Thu, to 4pm Fri; ; St-Paul, Hôtel de Ville) Pa-

risians can't get enough of this hip outpost
of celebrity chef Eyal Shani's famed Tel Aviv
restaurant. Head past the grocery crates to
the bar to order a warm, fluffy pita (such as
lamb, fish or roasted cauliflower) and phenomenal house-made hummus. Don't miss
the sweet *banane au chocolat* pita to finish.
Takeaway's available if you can't get a seat.

Pastelli   Gelato €

(Map p254; Mary; 60 rue du Temple, 3e; gelato
1/2/3/4 scoops €3.50/5/6.50/7.50; 11am-
10pm; Rambuteau) The youngest winner
of Milan's prestigious Cone d'Oro (Golden
Cone), artisan gelato maker Mary Quarta
has over 100 different flavours in her
all-natural repertoire, and serves around a
dozen different freshly made small batches
each day at her light, white-painted Haut
Marais shop. Standouts include avocado,
black sesame, peach Champagne bellini
and coffee-laced tiramisu.

Au Passage   Bistro €€

(Map p254; 01 43 55 07 52; www.restaurant-
aupassage.fr; 1bis passage St-Sébastien, 11e;
small plates €9-18, meats to share €25-70; 7-
10.30pm Tue-Sat; St-Sébastien-Froissart)
Rising-star chefs continue to make their
name at this *petit bar de quartier* (little
neighbourhood bar). Choose from a
good-value, uncomplicated selection *of petites assiettes* (small tapas-style plates) of
cold meats, raw or cooked fish, vegetables
and so on, and larger meat dishes to share
such as slow-roasted lamb shoulder or *côte
de bœuf* (rib steak). Advance reservations
are essential. Some 200 natural wines are
available by the bottle.

Le Servan   Bistro €€

(Map p254; 01 55 28 51 82; http://leservan.
com; 32 rue St-Maur, 11e; 3-course lunch
menu €27, mains €25-38; 7.30-10.30pm
Mon, noon-2.30pm & 7.30-10.30pm Tue-Fri;
Voltaire, Rue St-Maur, Père Lachaise) Ornate
cream-coloured ceilings with moulded
cornices and pastel murals, huge windows
and wooden floors give this neighbourhood neobistro near Père Lachaise a light,
airy feel on even the greyest Parisian day.

Sweetbread wontons, cockles with chilli and sweet basil, and roast pigeon with tamarind *jus* are among the inventive creations on the daily changing menu. Reserve to avoid missing out.

Robert et Louise   French €€

(Map p254; ☎01 42 78 55 89; http://robertet louise.com; 64 rue Vieille du Temple, 4e; 2-course lunch menus €14, mains €13-26; ⊗7-11pm Tue & Wed, noon-3pm & 7-11pm Thu & Fri, noon-11pm Sat & Sun; MRambuteau) Going strong since 1958, this wonderfully convivial 'country inn' with red gingham curtains and rustic timber beams offers simple and inexpensive French food, including *côte de bœuf* (side of beef for two or three people) cooked on an open fire. Arrive early to snag the farmhouse table next to the fireplace – the makings of a jolly Rabelaisian evening.

Brasserie Bofinger   Brasserie €€

(Map p254; ☎01 42 72 87 82; www.bofingerparis. com; 5-7 rue de la Bastille, 4e; 2-/3-course menus €26/32, mains €19.50-29.50; ⊗noon-3pm & 6.30pm-midnight Mon-Fri, noon-3.30pm & 6.30pm-midnight Sat, noon-11pm Sun; 🛜💺;

MBastille) Founded in 1864, Bofinger is reputedly Paris' oldest brasserie, though its polished art nouveau brass, glass and mirrors indicate redecoration a few decades later. Alsatian-inspired specialities include six kinds of sauerkraut, along with oysters (€11 to €35 per half-dozen) and magnificent seafood platters (€30 to €140). Ask for a seat downstairs beneath the *coupole* (stained-glass dome). Kids are catered for with a two-course children's menu (€14.50).

CAM   Asian €€

(Map p254; ☎06 26 41 10 66; www.cam-paris.fr; 55 rue au Maire, 3e; mains €12.50-24; ⊗7pm-11pm Wed-Sat; MArts et Métiers) Don't be fooled by the façade reading 'CAM Import Export' – this former miniature Eiffel Tower wholesaler has been stripped back to create a hip space for small pan-Asian plates that fire up the spice (bonito head with spring onion relish; smoked cuttlefish with ginger dressing; fermented soy-marinated steak with lettuce, mint and cilantro) accompanied by well-priced natural wines. No reservations.

Jacques Genin (p129)

🍴 The Five Basic Cheese Types

The choices on offer at a *fromagerie* (cheese shop) can be overwhelming, but vendors are usually very generous with their guidance and pairing advice.

Fromage à pâte demi-dure 'Semi-hard cheese' means uncooked, pressed cheese. Among the finest are Tomme de Savoie, Cantal, St-Nectaire and Ossau-Iraty.

Fromage à pâte dure 'Hard cheese' is always cooked and then pressed. Popular varieties are Beaufort, Comté, Emmental and Mimolette.

Fromage à pâte molle 'Soft cheese' is moulded or rind-washed. Camembert and Brie de Meaux are both made from raw cow's milk. Munster, Chaource, Langres and Époisses de Bourgogne are rind-washed, fine-textured cheeses.

Fromage à pâte persillée 'Marbled' or 'blue cheese' is so called because the veins often resemble *persille* (parsley). Roquefort is a ewe's-milk veined cheese that is to many the king of French cheeses. Fourme d'Ambert is a mild cow's-milk cheese from Rhône-Alpes. Bleu du Haut Jura is a mild, blue-veined mountain cheese.

Fromage de chèvre 'Goat's-milk cheese' is usually creamy and both sweet and slightly salty when fresh, but hardens and gets much saltier as it matures. Among the best varieties are Ste-Maure de Touraine, Crottin de Chavignol, Cabécou de Rocamadour and soft, slightly aged Chabichou.

Istr Seafood, Breton €€

(Map p254; 📞01 43 56 81 25; 41 rue Notre Dame de Nazareth, 3e; half-dozen oysters €12-20, mains €13-25, 2-/3-course lunch menus €19/24; ⏱kitchen noon-2.30pm & 6-10pm Tue-Fri, 6-11pm Sat, bar to 2am Tue-Sat; Ⓜ Temple) Fabulously patterned wallpaper and a gleaming zinc bar set the stage for innovative Breton-inspired cuisine. The region's famed *istr* ('oyster' in Breton) is the star of the show here, served plain, as a Bloody Mary–style shot, or with sauces such as soy and ginger. Other creations include buckwheat chips with smoked haddock fishcakes. It doubles as a rocking bar.

La Cave de l'Insolite Bistro €€

(Map p254; 📞01 53 36 08 33; www.lacavedelinsolite.fr; 30 rue de la Folie Méricourt, 11e; 2-/3-course midweek lunch menus €18/20, mains €18-21; ⏱noon-2.30pm & 7.30-10.30pm Tue-Sat, to 10pm Sun; 📶; Ⓜ St-Ambroise, Parmentier) Brothers Axel and Arnaud, who have worked at some of Paris' top addresses, run this rustic-chic wine bar with barrels, timber tables and a wood-burning stove. Duck pâté with cider jelly, haddock rillettes with lime and endive confit, and beef with mushroom and sweetbread sauce are among the seasonal dishes; its 100-plus hand-harvested wines come from small-scale French vineyards.

Le Clown Bar French €€

(Map p254; 📞01 43 55 87 35; www.clown-bar-paris.com; 114 rue Amelot, 11e; mains €28-34; ⏱kitchen noon-2.30pm & 7-10.30pm Wed-Sun, bar 8am-2am; Ⓜ Filles du Calvaire) The former staff dining room of the city's winter circus, the 1852-built Cirque d'Hiver, is a historic monument with colourful clown-themed ceramics and mosaics, painted glass ceilings and its original zinc bar. Modern French cuisine spans line-caught whiting with whelks to Mesquer pigeon stuffed with anchovies.

Anahi South American €€

(Map p254; 📞01 83 81 38 00; www.anahi-paris.com; 49 rue Volta, 3e; mains €16-39, 2-/3-course midweek lunch menus €29/35; ⏱7-11pm Sun-Thu, to 11.30pm Fri & Sat; Ⓜ Temple) History infuses Anahi, a 1920s butcher that became an '80s fashion-magnet steakhouse and is now overseen by rare meat importer and restaurateur Riccardo Giraudi. Features include its glorious art deco painted-glass ceiling. Premium charcoal-grilled steaks are the house speciality; other South American dishes include Black Angus empanadas, Wagyu quesadillas and sea bass ceviche.

⊗ Bastille & Eastern Paris

Mokonuts   Cafe €
(Map p254; ☑09 80 81 82 85; 5 rue St-Bernard, 11e; mains €2-3.50, mains €7-18; ☺8.45am-6pm Mon-Fri, closed Aug; 🛜🖊; ⓂFaidherbe-Chaligny) Much-loved hole-in-the-wall Mokonuts, with a beautiful mosaic-tiled floor, makes a cosy refuge for snacks like flourless chocolate layer cake, clementine almond cake and pecan pie. Sea bream with chickpeas and capers, and lamb shoulder with hummus are among the all-organic lunchtime mains. Natural wines and craft beers feature on the drinks list.

Farine & O   Bakery €
(Map p254; 153 rue du Faubourg St-Antoine, 11e; pastries €2.50-5.50; ☺7.30am-8.30pm Wed-Mon; ⓂLedru-Rollin) *Pâtissier* Olivier Magne, a winner of the prestigious Meilleur Ouvrier de France master craftsman competition, hails from the Cantal region of France and has now brought his talents to the capital. Magne's stunning creations include a mini choux pastry Paris-Brest with chestnut cream, blackcurrant and lemon brioche, and an apricot-filled *cuillère* ('spoon'), along with his signature sourdough loaves.

CheZaline   Sandwiches €
(Map p254; 85 rue de la Roquette, 11e; sandwiches €5.50-8.50; ☺11am-5.30pm Mon-Fri; ⓂVoltaire) A former horse-meat butcher's shop (*chevaline,* hence the spin on the name; look for the gold horse head above the door) is now a fabulous deli for baguettes filled with ingredients such as Prince de Paris ham and house-made garlic pesto, salads and homemade terrines. There's a handful of seats (and plenty of parks nearby). Prepare to queue at lunchtime.

Buffet   Bistro €€
(Map p254; ☑01 83 89 63 82; www.restaurant buffet.fr; 8 rue de la Main d'Or, 11e; 2-/3-course lunch menu €16.50/19, small plates €5-15; ☺7.30-11pm Tue, noon-2.30pm & 7.30-11pm Wed-Sat; ⓂLedru-Rollin) Tucked away on a charming Bastille backstreet behind a mulberry-coloured façade, Buffet has burgundy leather seating, wooden tables, mirrors and terrazzo floors. Despite its name, there's no smorgasbord but a short daily changing blackboard menu of bistro dishes like lemon sole with hand-cut chips, lamb shoulder with prunes, and chestnut and chocolate mousse that belies the complexity of the cooking.

Les Déserteurs   French €€
(Map p254; ☑01 48 06 95 85; 46 rue Trousseau, 11e; menus €30-49; ☺7.30-9.45pm Tue, 12.30-2pm & 7.30-9.45pm Wed-Sat; ⓂLedru-Rollin) Deserting their previous workplace, Les Déserteurs' chef Daniel Baratier and sommelier Alexandre Céret have combined their talents here at their own premises. In a contemporary space with high blonde oak tables, grey-painted walls and open kitchen, they serve exquisitely presented multi-course *menus* (no à la carte) with an emphasis on market-sourced vegetables, complemented by small-scale, pan-European wines. Dishes change daily but might include smoked asparagus with a soft egg yolk in wild garlic sauce, followed by maple syrup–filled choux pastry with caramelised almonds.

Passerini   Italian €€
(Map p254; ☑01 43 42 27 56; www.passerini. paris; 65 rue Traversière, 12e; lunch menus €24-48, dinner mains €18-42; ☺6-10pm Tue, noon-2.30pm & 6-10pm Wed-Sat, closed early May & Aug; ⓂLedru-Rollin) Rome native Giovanni Passerini is one of the finest Italian chefs cooking in Europe today. Delectable specialities include roast pigeon with smoked ricotta, and tagliolini with red Sicilian shrimp, and are complemented by natural wines sourced from small vineyards. Pastas are made fresh and are also sold at its adjoining deli, Pastificio Passerini.

Le Bistrot Paul Bert   Bistro €€

(Map p254; ☑01 43 72 24 01; 18 rue Paul Bert,
11e; 2-/3-course lunch/dinner menu €19/41;
☺noon-2pm & 7.30-11pm Tue-Sat, closed Aug;
Ⓜ Faidherbe-Chaligny) When food writers
list Paris' best bistros, Paul Bert's name
consistently pops up. The timeless vintage
decor and classic dishes like *steak-frites* and
hazelnut-cream Paris-Brest pastry reward
booking ahead. Look for its siblings in the
same street: **L'Écailler du Bistrot** (Map p254;
☑01 43 72 76 77; 22 rue Paul Bert, 11e; oysters
per half-dozen €9-20, mains €32-46, seafood
platters per person from €40; ☺noon-2.30pm &
7.30-11pm Tue-Sat) for seafood; **La Cave Paul
Bert** (Map p254; ☑01 58 53 50 92; 16 rue Paul
Bert, 11e; ☺noon-midnight, kitchen noon-2pm &
7.30-11.30pm), a wine bar with small plates;
and **Le 6 Paul Bert** (Map p254; ☑01 43 79 14
32; www.le6paulbert.com; 6 rue Paul Bert, 12e;
6-course menu €60, mains €24-35; ☺noon-2pm &
7.30-11pm Tue-Sat) for modern cuisine.

Chez Paul   Bistro €€

(Map p254; ☑01 47 00 34 57; www.chezpaul.com;
13 rue de Charonne, 11e; 2-/3-course weekday
lunch menu €18/21, mains €17-27; ☺noon-
12.30am; Ⓜ Ledru-Rollin) This is Paris as your
grandmother knew it: chequered red-and-
white napkins, faded photographs on the
walls, old red banquettes and traditional
French dishes such as pig trotters, *an-
douillette* (a feisty tripe sausage) and *tête
de veau et cervelle* (calf head and brains).
If offal isn't for you, alternatives include a
steaming bowl of *pot au feu* (beef stew).

Septime   Gastronomy €€€

(Map p254; ☑01 43 67 38 29; www.septime-
charonne.fr; 80 rue de Charonne, 11e; 4-course
lunch menu €42, with wine €70, 7-course dinner
menu €80, with wine €135; ☺7.30-10pm Mon,
12.15-2pm & 7.30-10pm Tue-Fri; Ⓜ Charonne)
The alchemists in Bertrand Grébaut's
Michelin-starred kitchen produce truly
beautiful creations, served by blue-aproned
waitstaff. The menu reads like an obscure
shopping list: each dish is a mere listing of
three ingredients, while the mystery *carte
blanche* dinner *menu* puts you in the hands
of the innovative chef. Reservations require

planning and perseverance – book at least
three weeks in advance.

Its nearby wine bar Septime La Cave
(p181) is ideal for a pre- or post-meal drink.
For stunning seafood tapas, its sister restaurant **Clamato** (Map p254; http://clamato-
charonne.fr; 80 rue de Charonne, 11e; tapas €8-16,
dozen oysters €18-48; ☺7-11pm Wed-Fri, from noon
Sat & Sun) is right next door.

Le Chardenoux   Bistro €€€

(Map p254; ☑01 43 71 49 52; www.restaurant
lechardenoux.com; 1 rue Jules Vallès, 11e;
2-/3-course lunch menus €25/30, 3-course dinner
menu €41; ☺noon-2.30pm & 7-11pm; Ⓜ Charonne)
Dating from 1908, this picture-perfect Parisian bistro with a polished-timber façade,
patterned tiled floors, marble-topped tables,
mirrored walls, bevelled frosted-glass
screens and a centrepiece zinc bar is a listed
historic monument. Star chef Cyril Lignac
recreates classical French dishes: Aubrac
beef tartare and *frites*, chicken in white wine,
and brioche toast with poached pears and
hazelnut caramel.

It's across the road (to the east) from
Lignac's chocolate boutique/tearoom **La
Chocolaterie Cyril Lignac** (Map p254; www.
cyrillignac.com; 25 rue Chanzy, 11e; pastries €1.40-
4; ☺8am-7pm; Ⓜ Charonne) and (to the south)
from his bakery/pastry shop **La Pâtisserie**
(Map p254; www.gourmand-croquant.com; 24 rue
Paul Bert, 11e; pastries €3-6.50; ☺7am-7pm Mon,
to 8pm Tue-Sun; Ⓜ Charonne, Faidherbe-Chaligny).

Table   French €€€

(Map p254; ☑01 43 43 12 26; www.tablerest
aurant.fr; 3 rue de Prague, 12e; 2-/3-course lunch
menu €25/29, mains €39-69; ☺noon-3pm &
7.45-10.30pm Mon-Fri, 7.30-10pm Sat; Ⓜ Ledru-Rollin) Unusual and rare artisan products
sourced from all over France decide the
day's menu at Michelin-starred Table,
styled like a contemporary *table d'hôte*,
with diners seated at the curvaceous
zinc bar while talented food writer/chef
Bruno Verjus performs in his open kitchen.
Delicious meats are spit-roasted on the
rotisserie and Verjus delights in talking food
with diners. To enter, press the button and
wait for the glass door to slide open.

Paris on a Plate

A classic *baguette ordinaire* legally has three ingredients (flour, yeast and salt) and weighs 250g.

Avoid baguettes with a mesh-like patterned base or overly uniform colouring (signs they're industrially produced).

Know Your Baguette

A *baguette tradition* ('une tradi') is a shorter, pointier version with a coarse, hand-crafted surface.

JIRI HERA/SHUTTERSTOCK ©

Best Bakeries

Du Pain et des Idées (p125) This traditional *boulangerie* is famed for its delicious baked treats.

Le Grenier à Pain (p126) Past winner of Paris' 'best baguette' prize; pick up picnic supplies here.

Pain Pain (p127) Another past winner of the 'best baguette' prize; a good spot for a takeaway pastry or sandwich.

Daily Bread

Some 80% of Parisians eat bread with every meal, hence the near-constant aroma of freshly baking baguettes and other varieties wafting from Paris' *boulangeries* (bakeries), with around 1200 *boulangeries* city-wide, or 11.5 per sq km.

The shape of a baguette (meaning 'stick' or 'wand') evolved when Napoléon ordered army bakers to create loaves for soldiers to stuff down their trouser legs on the march.

⊗ The Islands

Berthillon   Ice Cream €

(Map p252; www.berthillon.fr; 29-31 rue
St-Louis en l'Île, 4e; 1/2/3/4 scoops take away
€3/4.50/6/7.50; ☺10am-8pm Wed-Sun,
closed mid-Feb–early Mar & Aug; ⓂPont Marie)
Founded here in 1954, this esteemed
glacier (ice-cream maker) is still run by the
same family today. Its 70-plus all-natural,
chemical-free flavours include fruit sorbets
(pink grapefruit, raspberry and rose) and
richer ice creams made from fresh milk
and eggs (salted caramel, candied Ardèche
chestnuts, Armagnac and prunes, ginger-
bread, liquorice, praline and pine kernels).
Watch for tempting new seasonal flavours.

Café Saint Régis   Cafe €

(Map p252; ☎01 43 54 59 41; www.cafesaint
regisparis.com; 6 rue Jean du Bellay, 4e;
breakfast & snacks €3.50-15.50, mains €18-32;
☺6.30am-2am, kitchen 8am-midnight; ⓢ;
ⓂPont Marie) Waiters in long white aprons,
a ceramic-tiled interior and retro vintage
decor make hip Le Saint Régis a deliciously
Parisian hang-out any time of day – for
eating or drinking. From breakfast pastries,
organic eggs and bowls of fruit-peppered
granola to mid-morning pancakes or waffles, lunchtime salads, burgers, dusk-time
oysters and late-night cocktails, it is *the*
hobnobbing hotspot on the islands.

Le Caveau
du Palais   Modern French €€

(Map p250; ☎01 43 26 04 28; www.caveaudu
palais.fr; 19 place Dauphine, 1er; mains €20-27;
☺noon-2.30pm & 7-10pm; ⓂPont Neuf) Even
when the western Île de la Cité shows few
other signs of life, the Caveau's half-timbered
dining areas and (weather permitting) alfres-
co terrace are packed with diners tucking
into bountiful fresh fare: pan-seared scallops
with artichokes, grilled codfish with smoked
haddock cream and coriander-spiced cauliflower, or vegetable risotto. More informal
dishes are served at its adjacent wine bar, **Le
Bar du Caveau** (Map p250; www.barducaveau.fr;
17 place Dauphine, 1er; ☺bar 8am-6.30pm Mon-Fri,
kitchen noon-4pm Mon-Fri).

Sequana   Modern French €€€

(Map p250; ☎01 43 29 78 81; http://sequana.
paris; 72 quai des Orfèvres, 1er; 2-/3-/4-course
lunch menu €24/32/50, 4-/6-course dinner menu
€50/70; ☺noon-2.30pm & 7.30-11pm Tue-Fri,
7.30-11pm Sat; ⓂPont Neuf) At home in a chic
steel-grey dining room with 1950s style
banquet seating on Île de la Cité's southwestern tip, sleek Sequana evokes the
Gallo-Roman goddess of the River Seine. In
the kitchen are well-travelled Philippe and
Eugénie whose childhood in Senegal finds
its way into colourful combos such as wild
turbot with spinach, mallard and butternut
pumpkin, parsnip and China black tea.

⊗ Latin Quarter

Café de la Nouvelle Mairie   Cafe €

(Map p252; ☎01 44 07 04 41; 19 rue des Fossés
St-Jacques, 5e; mains €10-20; ☺8am-midnight
Mon-Fri, kitchen noon-2.30pm & 8-10.30pm Mon-
Thu, 8-10pm Fri; ⓂCardinal Lemoine) Shhhh...
Hidden away on a small, fountained square,
this hybrid cafe-restaurant and wine bar
is a tip-top neighbourhood secret, serving
blackboard-chalked natural wines by the
glass and delicious seasonal bistro fare
from oysters and ribs (*à la française*) to
grilled lamb sausage over lentils. It takes
reservations for dinner but not lunch –
arrive early.

La Bête Noire   Mediterranean €

(Map p252; ☎06 15 22 73 61; www.facebook.
com/labetenoireparis; 58 rue Henri Barbusse,
5e; mains lunch €12-15, dinner €20, brunch
€25; ☺8am-5pm Tue, 8am-11pm Wed-Fri,
9.30am-5.30pm Sat & Sun; ⓢⓍ; ⓂRER Port
Royal) Funky music and a small, fashion-
ably minimalist interior with open kitchen
ensure bags of soul at this off-the-radar
'cantine gastronomique', showcase for
the sensational home cooking of passionate chef-owner Maria. Inspired by her
Russian-Maltese heritage, she cooks just
one meat and one vegetarian dish daily
using seasonal products sourced from local
farmers and small producers, washed down
with Italian wine.

Le Coupe-Chou
French €€

(Map p252; 01 46 33 68 69; www.lecoupechou. com; 9 & 11 rue de Lanneau, 5e; menu lunch €15, 2-/3-course dinner €27/33, mains €17.50-29.50; noon-1.30pm & 7-10.30pm Mon-Sat, 7-10.30pm Sun Sep-Jun, 7-10.30pm Jul & Aug; MMaubert-Mutualité) This maze of candlelit rooms inside a vine-clad 17th-century townhouse is overwhelmingly romantic. Ceilings are beamed, furnishings are antique, open fireplaces crackle and background classical music mingles with the intimate chatter of diners. As in the days when Marlene Dietrich dined here, advance reservations are essential. Timeless French dishes include Burgundy snails, steak tartare and bœuf bourguignon.

Les Papilles
Bistro €€

(Map p252; 01 43 25 20 79; www.lespapilles paris.fr; 30 rue Gay Lussac, 5e; 2-/4-course menus €28/35; noon-2pm & 7-10.30pm Tue-Sat; MRaspail, RER Luxembourg) This hybrid bistro, wine cellar and épicerie (specialist grocer) with a sunflower-yellow façade is one of those fabulous Parisian dining experiences. Meals are served at simply dressed tables wedged beneath bottle-lined walls, and fare is market driven: each weekday cooks up a different *marmite du marché* (market casserole). But what really sets it apart is its exceptional wine list.

It only seats around 15 people; reserve a few days in advance to guarantee a table. After your meal, stock your own *cave* (wine cellar) at Les Papilles' *cave à vins*.

Restaurant AT
Gastronomy €€€

(Map p252; 01 56 81 94 08; www.atsushi tanaka.com; 4 rue du Cardinal Lemoine, 5e; 6-course lunch menu €55, 12-course dinner tasting menu €105; 12.15-2pm & 8-9.30pm Mon-Sat; MCardinal Lemoine) Trained by some of the biggest names in gastronomy (Pierre Gagnaire included), chef Atsushi Tanaka showcases abstract artlike masterpieces incorporating rare ingredients (charred bamboo, kohlrabi turnip cabbage, juniper berry powder, wild purple fennel, Nepalese Timut pepper) in a blank-canvas-style dining space on stunning outsized plates. Ingeniously, dinner menus can be paired with wine (€70) or juice (€45). Reservations essential.

Septime (p134)

⊗ St-Germain & Les Invalides

Au Pied de Fouet   Bistro €
(Map p246; 📞01 42 96 59 10; 3 rue St-Benoît, 6e; mains €9-12.50; ⊙noon-2.30pm & 7-11pm Mon-Sat; Ⓜ St-Germain des Prés) At this tiny, lively, cherry-red bistro, wholly classic dishes such as *entrecôte* (steak), *confit de canard* (duck cooked slowly in its own fat) with creamy potatoes and *foie de volailles sauté* (pan-fried chicken livers) are astonishingly good value. Round off your meal with a *tarte tatin* (upside-down apple tart), wine-soaked prunes, or deliciously rich *fondant au chocolat*.

Little Breizh   Crêpes €
(Map p250; 📞01 43 54 60 74; www.facebook. com/LittleBreizhCreperie; 11 rue Grégoire de Tours, 6e; crêpes €5-15; ⊙noon-2.30pm & 7-10.30pm Tue-Sat; 📝; Ⓜ Odéon) As authentic as you'd find in Brittany, but with some innovative twists (such as Breton sardines, olive oil and sundried tomatoes; goat's cheese, stewed apple, hazelnuts, rosemary and honey; smoked salmon, dill cream, pink peppercorns and lemon), the crêpes at this sweet spot are infinitely more enticing than those sold on nearby street corners. Hours can fluctuate; book ahead.

L'Avant Comptoir de la Terre   French €
(Map p252; www.hotel-paris-relais-saint-germain. com; 3 Carrefour de l'Odéon, 6e; tapas €5-10; ⊙noon-11pm; Ⓜ Odéon) Squeeze in around the zinc bar (there are no seats and it's tiny) and feast on amazing tapas (crab custard tarts with Pernod foam, Iberian ham or salmon tartare croquettes, duck confit hot dogs, blood-sausage macarons, and prosciutto and artichoke waffles), with wines by the glass, in a chaotically sociable atmosphere.

For seafood tapas, head to neighbouring **L'Avant Comptoir de la Mer** (Map p252; 📞01 42 38 47 55; 3 Carrefour de l'Odéon, 6e; tapas €5-25, oysters per six €17; ⊙noon-11pm); for porcine tapas, nearby **L'Avant Comp-**toir du Marché (Map p252; 15 rue Lobineau, 6e; tapas €3.50-20; ⊙noon-11pm; Ⓜ Mabillon). Or for gourmet bistro dining, try for a lunchtime table or evening reservation at **Le Comptoir** (Map p252; 📞01 44 27 07 97; 9 Carrefour de l'Odéon, 6e; lunch mains €14-30, dinner menu €60; ⊙noon-6pm & 8.30-11.30pm Mon-Fri, noon-11pm Sat & Sun).

La Crèmerie   French €
(Map p252; 📞01 43 54 99 30; 9 rue des Quatre-Vents, 6e; small plates €7-20; ⊙11am-2pm & 6-10pm Tue-Sat, 6-10pm Sun & Mon; Ⓜ Odéon) Beneath an original glass-covered ceiling, this marble-walled *caviste* (wine cellar) is a delicious flashback to 1880s Paris. With a stock of 400-odd wines and an exquisite array of France's finest gourmet goods, it is a delightful spot for an early-evening *apéro* (predinner drink) accompanied by tapas-style dishes (smoked-trout terrine, goat's cheese and olives, black-pudding-topped toast) or a fully-fledged meal.

Reservations essential. If you fail to snag a table, try its big sister nearby, **La Grande Crèmerie** (Map p250; 📞01 43 26 09 09; www. lagrandecremerie.fr; 8 rue Grégoire de Tours, 6e; small plates €6-14; ⊙6pm-midnight; Ⓜ Odéon).

Tomy & Co   Gastronomy €€
(Map p246; 📞01 45 51 46 93; 22 rue Surcouf, 7e; 2-course lunch menu €27, 3-course/tasting dinner menu €47/68, mains wine pairings €45; ⊙noon-2pm & 7.30-9.30pm Mon-Fri; Ⓜ Invalides) Tomy Gousset's restaurant near Mademoiselle Eiffel has been a sensation since day one. The French-Cambodian chef works his magic on inspired seasonal dishes using produce from his organic garden. Winter ushers in aromatic black truffles (themed tasting menu €95), and spectacular desserts – chocolate tart with fresh figs, Cambodian palm sugar and fig ice cream anyone? – are equally seasonal. Reservations essential.

Bouillon Racine   Brasserie €€
(Map p252; 📞01 44 32 15 60; www.bouillonracine. com; 3 rue Racine, 6e; 2-course weekday lunch menu €16.90, 3-course menu €35, mains €16-27.50; ⊙noon-11pm; 🍴; Ⓜ Cluny-La Sorbonne)

Inconspicuously situated in a quiet street, this heritage-listed art nouveau 'soup kitchen', with mirrored walls, floral motifs and ceramic tiling, was built in 1906 to feed market workers. The food, inspired by age-old recipes, is superbly executed (stuffed, spit-roasted suckling pig, pork shank in Rodenbach red beer, scallops and shrimps with lobster coulis). Finish off your foray into gastronomic history with an old-fashioned sherbet. Two-course children's menus (€14.50) mean kids don't miss out.

Anicia · French €€

(Map p246; 01 43 35 41 50; http://anicia-bistrot.com; 97 rue du Cherche Midi, 6e; 2-/3-course weekday lunch menu €24/29, 3-/5-course dinner menu €49/58, mains €27-34; noon-10.30pm Tue-Sat; Duroc, Vaneau) An advance online booking is essential at this glorious 'bistro nature', showcase for the earthy but refined cuisine of chef François Gagnaire who ran a Michelin-starred restaurant in the foodie town of Puy-en-Velay in the Auvergne before uprooting to the French capital. He still sources dozens of regional products – Puy lentils, Velay snails, St-Nectaire cheese – from small-time producers in central France, to stunning effect.

Clover · Bistro €€

(Map p246; 01 75 50 00 05; www.clover-paris.com; 5 rue Perronet, 7e; 2-/3-course lunch menu €37/47, 3-/5-course dinner menu €60/73; 12.30-2pm & 7-10pm Tue-Fri, 12.30-2.30pm & 7-10pm Sat; St-Germain des Prés) Dining at hot-shot chef Jean-François Piège's casual bistro is like attending a private party: the galley-style open kitchen adjoining the 20 seats (online reservations open just 15 days in advance) is part of the dining-room decor, putting customers at the front and centre of the culinary action. Light, luscious dishes span tomato gazpacho with pea sorbet to cabbage leaves with smoked herring *crème* and chestnuts. Scallops are cooked on the shell on a flagstone-size rock at diners' tables; innovative desserts include caramelised banana with parsley ice cream or rum-marinated butternut squash.

🍽 Traditional Bakery: Poilâne

Pierre Poilâne opened his *boulangerie* (bakery) **Poilâne** (Map p246; 01 45 48 42 59; www.poilane.com; 8 rue du Cherche Midi, 6e; 7am-8.30pm Mon-Sat; Sèvres-Babylone) upon arriving from Normandy in 1932. Today his granddaughter Apollonia runs the company, which still turns out wood-fired, rounded sourdough loaves made with stone-milled flour and Guérande sea salt. A clutch of other outlets include one in the **15e** (Map p246; www.poilane.com; 49 bd de Grenelle, 15e; 7am-8.30pm Tue-Sun; Dupleix).

Traditional French loaves of bread
EQROY/SHUTTERSTOCK ©

Huîtrerie Regis · Seafood €€

(Map p250; http://huitrerieregis.com; 3 rue de Montfaucon, 6e; dozen oysters from €26; noon-2.30pm & 6.30-10.30pm Mon-Fri, noon-10.45pm Sat, noon-10pm Sun; Mabillon) Hip, trendy, tiny and white, this is *the* spot for slurping oysters on crisp winter days – inside or on the tiny pavement terrace sporting sage-green Fermob chairs. Oysters arrive live from the Bassin de Marennes-Oléron and come only by the dozen. Wash them down with a glass of chilled Muscadet. No reservations, so arrive early. A twinset of tables are set on the pavement; otherwise it's all inside.

L'Étable Hugo Desnoyer · French €€

(Map p252; 01 42 39 89 27; www.hugodesnoyer.com; 15 rue Clément, 6e; lunch menu €24.50, mains €30-40; noon-2.30pm & 7.30-10.30pm Tue-Sat; Mabillon) Duck beneath the elegant stone arches of **Marché St-Germain** (http://marchesaintgermain.com; 4-6 rue Lobineau, 6e; ⊙8am-8pm Tue-Sat, to 1.30pm Sun; MMabillon) to uncover the stylish steakhouse of Paris' superstar butcher Hugo Desnoyer. Vegetarians be warned, there are some delicious veggie dishes too, but some of the walls in the sharp design interior are clad in ginger-and-cream cow-hide and the menu is essentially for meat lovers.

Semilla   Neobistro €€

(Map p250; ☑01 43 54 34 50; www.semillaparis. com; 54 rue de Seine, 6e; 2-/3-course weekday lunch menu €34/40, mains €24-40; ⊙12.30-2.30pm & 7-11pm Mon-Sat, to 10pm Sun, closed early–mid-Aug; MMabillon) Stark concrete floor, beams and an open kitchen (in front of which you can book front-row 'chef seats') set the factory-style scene for edgy, modern, daily changing dishes such as scallops cooked in Vin Jaune wine with crunchy endives or trout with passionfruit and ginger. Desserts are equally creative and irresistible. Be sure to book.

If you don't have a reservation, head to its adjoining wine bar, **Freddy's** (Map p250; 54 rue de Seine, 6e; small plates €6-10; ⊙noon-midnight), serving small tapas-style plates.

Chez Dumonet   Bistro €€

(Map p246; Joséphine; ☑01 45 48 52 40; 117 rue du Cherche Midi, 6e; mains €24-40; ⊙noon-2.30pm & 7.30-9.30pm Mon-Fri; MDuroc) Fondly known by its former name, Joséphine, this lace-curtained, mosaic-tiled place with white-clothed tables inside and out is the Parisian bistro of many people's dreams, serving timeless standards such as confit of duck and grilled châteaubriand steak with Béarnaise sauce. Order its enormous signature Grand Marnier soufflé at the start of your meal. Mains, unusually, come in full or half-portion size.

Le Timbre   Bistro €€

(Map p246; ☑01 45 49 10 40; www.facebook. com/restaurantletimbre; 3 rue Ste-Beuve, 6e; 2-/3-course lunch menu €23/28, 3-/4-course dinner menu €36/45; ⊙7.30-11pm Tue, noon-3pm & 7.30-11pm Wed-Sat; MVavin) As tiny as the postage stamp for which it's named, Le

Timbre is run by husband-and-wife team Charles Danet (in the kitchen) and Agnès Peyre (front of house) and has a local following for its daily changing menu of original dishes with a sharp contemporary twist (caramelised endives with Parmesan *crème* and brioche; turbot and clams with marinated cabbage and potato terrine).

Les Fables
de la Fontaine   Gastronomy €€

(Map p246; ☑01 44 18 37 55; www.lesfablesdela fontaine.net; 131 rue St-Dominique, 7e; 2-course weekday lunch menu €28, mains €21-29; ⊙noon-2.30pm & 7-10.30pm; MÉcole Militaire, RER Pont de l'Alma) Prices at this Michelin-starred restaurant are a serious bargain and the lunchtime *menu* is a steal. Chefs Julia Sedef-djian and David Bottreau create true works of art: on-the-shell oysters in vivid green cucumber jelly with green apple and lemon caviar; almond-crusted veal with mashed artichokes and king trumpet mushrooms; and banana soufflé with rum ice cream.

Restaurant
Guy Savoy   Gastronomy €€€

(Map p250; ☑01 43 80 40 61; www.guysavoy. com; 11 quai de Conti, 6e, Monnaie de Paris; lunch menu via online booking €130, tasting menu €415; ⊙noon-2pm & 7-10.30pm Tue-Fri, 7-10.30pm Sat; MPont Neuf) If you're considering visiting a three-Michelin-star temple of gastronomy, this should certainly be on your list. The world-famous chef needs no introduction (he trained Gordon Ramsay, among others) but his flagship, entered via a red-carpeted staircase, is ensconced in the gorgeous-ly refurbished neoclassical Monnaie de Paris (p88). Monumental cuisine to match includes Savoy icons like artichoke and black-truffle soup with layered brioche.

Les Climats   French €€€

(Map p246; ☑01 58 62 10 08; http://lesclimats. fr; 41 rue de Lille, 7e; lunch/dinner menu €45/130, mains €52-72; ⊙12.15-2.30pm & 7-10pm Tue-Sat; MSolférino) Like the neighbouring Musée d'Orsay, this is a magnificent art nouveau treasure – a 1905-built former home for female telephone, telegram and postal

Clockwise from top: Macaroons; *Haute cuisine* dish; Le Dôme (p143)

When to Eat: Parisian Meal Times

Petit déjeuner (breakfast) The French kick-start the day with a slice of baguette smeared with unsalted butter and jam and *un café* (espresso) or – for kids – hot chocolate. Parisians might grab a coffee and croissant on the way to work, but otherwise croissants (eaten straight, never with butter or jam) are more of a weekend treat or *goûter* (afternoon snack) along with *pains au chocolat* (chocolate-filled croissants) and other *viennoiseries* (sweet pastries).

Déjeuner (lunch) The traditional main meal of the day, lunch incorporates a starter and main course with wine, followed by a short, sharp *café*. During the work week this is less likely to be the case – many busy Parisians now grab a sandwich to go – but the standard hour-long lunch break, special *prix-fixe* menus and *tickets restaurant* (company-funded meal vouchers) ensure that many restaurants fill up at lunch.

Apéritif Otherwise known as an *apéro,* the premeal drink is sacred. Cafes and bars get packed out from around 5pm onwards as Parisians wrap up work for the day and relax over a chit-chat-fuelled glass of wine or beer.

Diner (dinner) Traditionally lighter than lunch, but a meal that is being treated more and more as the day's main meal.

workers – featuring soaring vaulted ceilings and original stained glass, along with a lunchtime summer garden and glassed-in winter garden. Exquisite Michelin-starred dishes complement its 150-page list of wines, sparkling wines and whiskies purely from the Burgundy region.

Restaurant David Toutain
Gastronomy €€€

(Map p246; ☏01 45 50 11 10; http://davidtoutain. com; 29 rue Surcouf, 7e; 3-course lunch menu €55,

tasting menus €80-140, wine pairings €70-100; ⊗12.30-2pm & 8-10pm Mon, noon-2pm & 8-10pm Tue-Fri; MInvalides) Prepare to be wowed: David Toutain pushes the envelope at his eponymous Michelin-starred restaurant with some of the most creative high-end cooking in Paris. Mystery *dégustation* (tasting) courses include unlikely combinations such as smoked eel in green-apple-and-black-sesame mousse, cauliflower, white chocolate and coconut truffles, or candied celery and truffled rice pudding with artichoke praline. Stunning wine pairings are available.

⊗ Montparnasse & Southern Paris

La Butte aux Piafs
Bistro €

(☏09 70 38 55 11; www.labutteauxpiafs-paris. fr; 31 bd Auge Blanqui, 13e; mains €14.10-16.90; ⊗noon-midnight Mon-Fri, noon-3.30pm & 6pm-midnight Sat; MPlace d'Italie) A cinematic cluster of cherry-red chairs flag the pavement terrace of this neighbourhood bistro, *the* spot to lap up the quietly fashionable vibe of La Butte aux Cailles. Inside, flip-down cinema seats mix with an eclectic jumble of vintage seating, while menus featuring burgers, meal-sized salads and creative starters come bound in the sleeve of a vinyl single.

Le Petit Pan
Modern French €

(Map p246; ☏01 42 50 04 04; www.lepetitpan. fr; 18 rue Rosenwald, 15e; 2-/3-course lunch menu €16.50/20.50, small plates €2.50-13; ⊗noon-2.30pm & 7-11.30pm Tue-Sat; MPorte de Vanves) Parisians working in the 'hood fill this casual bistro to bursting at lunchtime thanks to a fantastic-value menu, but it is after dusk that the gourmet action kicks in with small plates of tapas *à la française* designed for sharing. Think cured ham, duck pâté with pork trotters or duck hearts fried in ginger, washed down with superb wines by the glass. Le Petit Pan also serves gourmet sandwiches, quiches and salads at lunchtime. To sink your teeth into a serious hunk of meat, nip over the street to big sister restaurant **Le Grand Pan** (Map p246;

☑01 42 50 02 50; www.legrandpan.fr; 20 rue Rosenwald, 15e; mains €14-30; ⊘noon-2pm & 7.30-11pm Mon-Fri).

Raw Cakes Vegan €

(Map p246; ☑09 86 12 73 48; 83 rue Daguerre, 14e; mains €10-15; ⊘10am-8pm Mon, 11am-10pm Tue-Thu, 10am-4pm Fri, noon-7pm Sun; MGaîté) A pretty lavender and fuchsia-pink façade fronts this much-welcomed cafe and cake shop where everything is 100% vegan, gluten-free and raw. Enticing nut and chickpea burgers, veggie-packed pizzas and meal-sized salads rub shoulders on the menu with fresh juices, smoothies and exquisite uncooked cakes. Sunday brunch (€25) is always a full house.

Le Cassenoix Modern French €€

(Map p246; ☑01 45 66 09 01; www.le-cassenoix. fr; 56 rue de la Fédération, 15e; 3-course menu €34; ⊘noon-2.30pm & 7-10.30pm Mon-Fri; MBir Hakeim) The Nutcracker is everything a self-respecting neighbourhood bistro should be. *'Tradition et terroir'* (tradition and regional produce) dictate the menu that inspires owner-chef Pierre Olivier Lenormand to deliver feisty dishes such as braised veal with mashed potato and caramelised onions or grilled hake with parsnips and hazelnut-parmesan crumble. Vintage ceiling fans add to the wonderful retro vibe. Book ahead.

Le Beurre Noisette Bistro €€

(Map p246; ☑01 48 56 82 49; www.restaurant beurrenoisette.com; 68 rue Vasco de Gama, 15e; 2-/3-course lunch menu €23/32, 3-/5-/7-course dinner menu €36/46/56, mains lunch/dinner €18/21; ⊘noon-2pm & 7-10.30pm Tue-Sat; MLourmel) *Beurre noisette* (brown butter sauce, named for its hazelnut colour) features in dishes such as tender veal loin with homemade fries and caramelised pork belly tender with braised red cabbage and apple at pedigreed chef Thierry Blanqui's neighbourhood neobistro. Filled with locals, the chocolate-toned dining room is wonderfully convivial – be sure to book. Fantastic value.

L'Accolade Bistro €€

(Map p246; ☑01 45 57 73 20; www.laccolade paris.fr; 208 rue de la Croix Nivert, 15e; 2-/3-course lunch menu €19.50/24.50, 4-course dinner menu €35; ⊘noon-2.30pm Mon, noon-2pm & 7-10.30pm Tue-Fri, 7-10.30pm Sat; MConvention) Seasonal market products reign supreme at this neighbourhood bistro where rising star, Nicolas Tardivel, woos a local crowd with his creative, modern French 'bistronomie' – bistro-style gastronomy. The lunchtime *plat du jour* (dish of the day), at €15 including coffee, is an excellent deal. Should you be open to temptation, the vanilla millefeuille, glazed with salted butter caramel, is sublime.

L'Assiette Bistro €€

(Map p246; ☑01 43 22 64 86; http://restaurant-lassiette.paris; 181 rue du Château, 14e; 2-course lunch menu €23, mains €25-45; ⊘noon-2.30pm & 7.30-10.30pm Tue-Fri, 12.30-2.30pm & 7.30-10.30pm Sat & Sun; MPernety, Gaîté) Consistently hailed as one of Paris' best bistros, The Plate is the culinary powerhouse of chef David Rathgebe, from Clermont-Ferrand in the foodie Auvergne. He mixes age-old traditional French dishes like *cassoulet maison* (Toulouse sausage and white bean stew) and *tête de veau* (rolled calf's head) with the occasional unexpected combo (sweetbreads with black truffle risotto) to delicious effect. Reservations essential.

Le Dôme Brasserie €€€

(Map p246; ☑01 43 35 25 81; www.restaurant-ledome.com; 108 bd du Montparnasse, 14e; mains €42-67, seafood platters €85-148; ⊘noon-3pm & 7-11pm; MVavin) A 1930s art deco extravaganza of the formal white-tablecloth and bow-tied waiter variety, monumental Le Dôme is one of the swishest places around for shellfish platters laden with fresh oysters, king prawns, crab claws and much more, followed by traditional creamy homemade millefeuille for dessert, wheeled in on a trolley and cut in front of you.

TREASURE HUNT

One of the world's premier
shopping destinations

Treasure Hunt

Paris has it all: broad boulevards lined with flagship fashion houses and international labels, famous grand magasins (department stores) and fabulous markets, along with tiny speciality shops and one-off boutiques. Fashion is Paris' forte. Browse haute couture creations, cutting-edge designs and original streetwear, along with statement-making accessories and adorable children's wear. Parisian fashion doesn't have to break the bank: you can find fantastic bargains at secondhand boutiques and outlet shops. But fashion is just the beginning. Paris is also a treasure chest of gourmet food, wine, tea, new and antiquarian books, stationery, classic and contemporary art, art supplies, antiques and collectables

In This Section

Useful Phrases

Look for signs indicating *cabines d'essayage* (fitting rooms).

Most shops offer free (and beautiful) gift wrapping – ask for *un paquet cadeau*.

A *ticket de caisse* (receipt) is essential for returning/exchanging an item (within one month of purchase).

If you're happy browsing, tell sales staff *Je regarde* (I'm just looking).

**Montmartre &
Northern Paris**
Gourmet food shops,
art, quintessential
souvenirs (p151)

**Champs-Élysées &
Grands Boulevards**
Haute couture houses,
famous department stores
(p150)

**Louvre &
Les Halles**
Cookware shops,
high-street chains,
covered arcades
(p150)

**Le Marais,
Ménilmontant &
Belleville**
Quirky homewares,
art galleries, up-and-
coming designers
(p153)

*Eiffel
Tower*

**St-Germain &
Les Invalides**
Art, antiques and
chic designer boutiques
(p160)

The Islands
Enchanting gift shops
and gourmet
boutiques (p159)

Seine

Latin Quarter
Late-opening
bookshops and
music shops (p159)

**Bastille &
Eastern Paris**
Great markets,
Viaduc des Arts
workshops (p158)

Opening Hours

Broadly 10am to 7pm Monday to
Saturday. Smaller shops may shut on
Monday and/or close from around noon
to 2pm for lunch. Larger stores hold
nocturnes (late-night shopping), usually
on Thursday, until around 10pm. Shops
in ZTIs (international tourist zones, eg
Le Marais) open late and on Sundays.

Sales

Paris' twice-yearly *soldes* (sales)
generally last five to six weeks, starting
around mid-January and again around
mid-June.

The Best...

Experience Paris' best shopping

Fashion

Galeries Lafayette (p150) Magnificent department store with free fashion shows.

Le Bon Marché (p160) Left Bank department store designed by Gustave Eiffel.

Andrea Crews (p154) Bold art and fashion collective.

Pigalle (p152) Leading Parisian menswear brand.

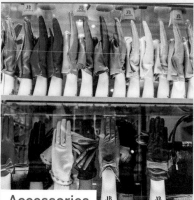

Accessories

JB Guanti (p162) Gorgeous gloves.

Alexandra Sojfer (p163) Handcrafted umbrellas.

Atelier 144 (p163) Beautiful hats.

Sabbia Rosa (p163) Exquisite lingerie made from French fabrics.

Jamin Puech (p157) One-of-a-kind handbags.

Art & Antiques

Marché aux Puces de St-Ouen (p155) One of Europe's largest flea markets, with over 2500 stalls.

Hôtel Drouot (p151) Famous auction house.

Deyrolle (p161) Historic taxidermist that starred in *Midnight in Paris*.

For Kids

Bonton Surplus (p161) Vintage-inspired fashion, furnishings and knick-knacks for babies, toddlers and children.

Finger in the Nose (p157) Streetwise Parisian label for kids.

Les Petits Bla-Blas (p157) *Atelier* (workshop) making children's clothes offering a personalisation service.

Gourmet Shops

La Grande Épicerie de Paris (p160) Now with a Right Bank outpost, too.

La Manufacture de Chocolat (p158) Alain Ducasse's bean-to-bar chocolate factory.

La Dernière Goutte (p162) Independent French wines.

Concept Stores

Merci (p153) Fabulously fashionable and unique: all profits go to a children's charity in Madagascar.

Empreintes (p153) Emporium showcasing some 6000 French artists and designers.

L'Exception (p150) Fashion, homewares, books and more from over 400 French designers.

Hermès (p162) Housed in an art deco ex-swimming pool.

Lonely Planet's Top Choices

Bouquinistes (p163) Vintage posters and other treasures.

Le Bonbon au Palais (p159) Artisan French sweets.

Shakespeare & Company (p159) A 'wonderland of books'.

Vintage & Discount Shops

Frivoli (p159) Brand-name cast-offs by the Canal St-Martin.

Chercheminippes (p160) Several specialist boutiques on one street.

Catherine B (p160) Stocking only Chanel and Hermès vintage pieces.

🅐 Champs-Élysées & Grands Boulevards

Galeries Lafayette   Department Store

(Map p246; ☑ 01 42 82 34 56; http://haussmann. galerieslafayette.com; 40 bd Haussmann, 9e; ⊘ 9.30am-8.30pm Mon-Sat, 11am-7pm Sun; 🛜; Ⓜ Chaussée d'Antin, RER Auber) Grande-dame department store Galeries Lafayette is spread across the main store (whose magnificent stained-glass dome is over a century old), men's store, and homewares store with a gourmet emporium.

Catch modern art in the 1st-floor **gallery** (☑ 01 42 82 81 98; www.galeriedesgaleries.com; ⊘ 11am-7pm Tue-Sun) **FREE**, take in a **fashion show** (☑ bookings 01 42 82 81 98; ⊘ 3pm Fri Mar-Jun & Sep-Dec by reservation), ascend to a free, windswept rooftop panorama, or take a break at one of its 24 restaurants and cafes.

The main store will stay open during renovations by architect Amanda Levete's studio AL_A. On the av des Champs-Élysées is a new Galeries Lafayette store (Map p246; 52 av Champs-Élysées; Ⓜ Franklin D Roosevelt).

Guerlain   Perfume

(Map p246; ☑ spa 01 45 62 11 21; www.guerlain. com; 68 av des Champs-Élysées, 8e; ⊘ 10.30am-8pm Mon-Sat, noon-8pm Sun; Ⓜ Franklin D Roosevelt) Guerlain is Paris' most famous parfumerie, and its shop (dating from 1912) is one of the most beautiful in the city. With its shimmering mirror and marble art deco interior, it's a reminder of the former glory of the Champs-Élysées. For total indulgence, make an appointment at its heavenly spa.

À la Mère de Famille   Food & Drinks

(Map p250; ☑ 01 47 70 83 69; www.lameredefamille.com; 35 rue du Faubourg Montmartre, 9e; ⊘ 9.30am-8pm Mon-Sat, 10am-7.30pm Sun; Ⓜ Le Peletier) Founded in 1761, this is the original location of Paris' oldest chocolatier. Its beautiful belle époque façade is as enchanting as the rainbow of sweets, caramels and chocolates inside.

Le Printemps   Department Store

(Map p246; ☑ 01 42 82 50 00; www.printemps. com; 64 bd Haussmann, 9e; ⊘ 9.35am-8pm Mon-Sat, to 8.45pm Thu, 11am-7pm Sun; 🛜; Ⓜ Havre Caumartin) Famous department store Le Printemps encompasses Le Printemps de la Mode (women's fashion) and Le Printemps de l'Homme (men's fashion), both with established and up-and-coming designer wear, and Le Printemps de la Beauté et Maison (beauty and homewares), offering a staggering display of perfume, cosmetics and accessories. There's a free panoramic rooftop terrace and luxury eateries.

🅐 Louvre & Les Halles

Didier Ludot   Fashion & Accessories

(Map p250; ☑ 01 42 96 06 56; www.didierludot. fr; 24 Galerie de Montpensier, 1er; ⊘ 10.30am-7pm Mon-Sat; Ⓜ Palais Royal–Musée du Louvre) In the rag trade since 1975, collector Didier Ludot sells the city's finest couture creations of yesteryear, hosts exhibitions and has published a book portraying the evolution of the little black dress.

L'Exception   Design

(Map p250; ☑ 01 40 39 92 34; www.lexception. com; 24 rue Berger, 1er; ⊘ 10am-8pm Mon-Sat, 11am-7pm Sun; Ⓜ Les Halles, RER Châtelet–Les Halles) Over 400 different French designers come together under one roof at this light-filled concept store, which showcases rotating collections of men's and women's fashion along with accessories, lingerie and swimwear. It also sells design books, cosmetics, vases and other gorgeous homewares, and has a small in-house coffee bar.

Legrand Filles & Fils   Food & Drinks

(Map p250; ☑ 01 42 60 07 12; www.caves-legrand. com; 1 rue de la Banque, 2e; ⊘ 11am-7pm Mon, 10am-7.30pm Tue-Sat; Ⓜ Bourse) Tucked inside Galerie Vivienne since 1880, Legrand sells fine wine and all the accoutrements: corkscrews, tasting glasses, decanters etc. It also has a fancy wine bar, *école du vin* (wine school; courses from €60 for two hours) and *éspace dégustation* with several tastings

Le Printemps

a month, including ones accompanied by live concerts; check its website for details.

E Dehillerin

Homewares

(Map p250; ☎01 42 36 53 13; www.edehillerin.fr; 18-20 rue Coquillière, 1er; ⊗9am-12.30pm & 2-6pm Mon, 9am-6pm Tue-Sat; ⓜLes Halles) Founded in 1820, this extraordinary two-level store – more like an old-fashioned warehouse than a shiny, chic boutique – carries an incredible selection of professional-quality *matériel de cuisine* (kitchenware). Poultry scissors, turbot poacher, professional copper cookware or an Eiffel Tower–shaped cake tin – it's all here.

La Samaritaine

Department Store

(Map p250; ☎01 56 81 28 40; www.lasamaritaine.com; 19 rue de la Monnaie, 1er; ⓜPont Neuf) One of Paris' four big department stores, the 10-storey La Samaritaine is finally emerging from a much contested and drawn-out 14-year overhaul. Pritzker Prize–winning Japanese firm Sanaa has preserved much of the art nouveau and art deco exterior, in addition to the glass ceiling topping the central Hall Jourdain.

Hôtel Drouot

Art, Antiques

(Map p250; ☎01 48 00 20 20; www.drouot.com; 7-9 rue Drouot, 9e; ⊗11am-6pm Mon-Fri, to 11pm Thu; ⓜRichelieu Drouot) Selling everything from antiques and jewellery to rare books and art, Paris' most established auction house has been in business for more than a century. Viewings are from 11am to 6pm the day before and from 11am to noon the morning of the auction. Pick up the catalogue *Gazette de l'Hôtel Drouot,* published Fridays, in-house or at newsstands.

⊙ Montmartre & Northern Paris

Fromagerie Alléosse

Cheese

(http://fromage-alleosse.com; 13 rue Poncelet, 17e; ⊗9am-1pm & 3.30-7pm Tue-Sat, 9am-1pm Sun; ⓜTernes) On stall-filled foodie street rue Poncelet, this heady *fromagerie* (cheese shop) has its own cheese-ripening *caves* (cellars). Its 250-plus cheeses are grouped into five main categories: *fromage de chèvre* (goat's milk), *fromage à pâte persillée* (veined or blue), *fromage à pâte*

🍴 Place de la Madeleine

Ultragourmet food shops garland **place de la Madeleine** (Map p246; place de la Madeleine, 8e; MMadeleine); many have in-house dining options. Notable names include the following:

La Maison de la Truffe (Map p246; 📞01 42 65 53 22; www.maison-de-la-truffe.com; 19 place de la Madeleine, 8e; ⏰10am-10pm Mon-Sat) Truffle dealers.

Hédiard (Map p246; 📞01 43 12 88 88; www.hediard.fr; 21 place de la Madeleine, 8e) Luxury food shop; reopened in 2019 after head-to-toe renovations.

Boutique Maille (Map p246; www.maille.com; 6 place de la Madeleine, 8e; ⏰10am-7pm Mon-Sat) Mustard specialist.

Fauchon (Map p246; 📞01 70 39 38 00; www.fauchon.fr; 26 & 30 place de la Madeleine, 8e; ⏰10am-8.30pm Mon-Sat) Paris' most famous caterer.

Patrick Roger (Map p246; 📞09 67 08 24 47; www.patrickroger.com; 3 place de la Madeleine, 8e; ⏰10.30am-7.30pm) Extravagant chocolate sculptures.

La Maison du Miel (Map p246; 📞01 47 42 26 70; www.maisondumiel.com; 24 rue Vignon, 9e; ⏰9.30am-7pm Mon-Sat) Honey specialist.

molle (soft), *fromage à pâte demi-dure* (semihard) and *fromage à pâte dure* (hard).

Belle du Jour   Fashion & Accessories
(Map p249; www.belle-de-jour.fr; 7 rue Tardieu, 18e; ⏰11am-1pm & 2-7pm Tue-Fri, 11am-1pm &

2-6pm Sat; MAnvers, Abbesses) Be whisked back in time to the elegance of belle époque Paris at this Montmartre shop specialising in perfume bottles. Gorgeous 19th-century atomisers, smelling salts and powder boxes in engraved or enamelled Bohemian, Baccarat and Saint-Louis crystal share shelf space with more contemporary designs.

Balades Sonores   Music
(Map p249; www.baladessonores.com; 1-3 av Trudaine, 9e; ⏰noon-8pm Mon-Sat; MAnvers) One of Paris' best vinyl shops sprawls over two adjacent buildings. The ground floor of 1 av Trudaine stocks contemporary pop, rock metal, garage and all genres of French music. Its basement holds secondhand blues, country, new wave and punk from the '60s to '90s. Next door, No 3 has soul, jazz, funk, hip-hop, electronica and world music. It's also a great place to pick up vintage memorabilia, turntables and streetwear, and info about upcoming gigs and DJ sets.

La Binouze   Drinks
(Map p249; 📞09 53 17 23 18; www.labinouze.fr; 72 rue de Rochechouart, 9e; ⏰noon-10pm Mon-Thu, noon-11pm Fri, 11am-11pm Sat, 11am-10pm Sun; MAnvers) Over 600 craft beers from across France and around the world are stocked at this beer emporium. Pick them up to take away or taste them on site, accompanied by *tartines* (open sandwiches) or cheese and charcuterie sharing boards. Two-hour guided tastings in English or French cost €30.

Pigalle   Fashion & Accessories
(Map p249; www.pigalle-paris.com; 7 rue Henry Monnier, 9e; ⏰noon-8pm Mon-Sat, 2-8pm Sun; MSt-Georges) Pick up a hoodie emblazoned with the black-and-white Pigalle logo from this leading Parisian menswear brand, created by designer and basketball player Stéphane Ashpool, who grew up in the 'hood.

O/HP/E   Design
(Map p254; 27 rue du Château d'Eau, 10e; ⏰2-7.30pm Tue, 8.30am-7.30pm Wed-Fri, 9.30am-7.30pm Sat, 9.30am-6.30pm Sun; MJacques Bonsergent) White-on-white concept store O/HP/E stocks chic homewares – ceramics, textiles, light fittings, candles and kitchen-

ware (rolling pins, mats, chopping boards, chopsticks et al) – along with cosmetics, stationery and gifts. Also here is an *épicerie* (specialist grocer) with gourmet delicacies (preserves, nougats, sugar-coated olives and chocolates) and a cafe with baked treats such as hazelnut praline tarts.

Spree Fashion & Accessories
(Map p249; ☏01 42 23 41 40; www.spree.fr; 16 rue de la Vieuville, 18e; ⊙11am-7.30pm Tue-Sat, 3-7pm Sun & Mon; Ⓜ Abbesses) Allow plenty of time to browse this super-stylish boutique-gallery, with a carefully selected collection of designer fashion put together by stylist Roberta Oprandi and artist Bruni Hadjadj. All the furniture – vintage 1950s to 1980s pieces by Eames et al – is also for sale, as is the contemporary artwork on the walls.

⊕ Le Marais, Ménilmontant & Belleville

Merci Gifts & Souvenirs
(Map p254; ☏01 42 77 00 33; www.merci-merci. com; 111 bd Beaumarchais, 3e; ⊙10am-7.30pm; Ⓜ St-Sébastien–Froissart) ✒ A Fiat Cinquecento marks the entrance to this unique store, which donates all its profits to a children's charity in Madagascar. Shop for fashion, accessories, linens, lamps and nifty designs for the home; and complete the experience with a coffee in its hybrid used-bookshop-cafe, a juice at its Cinéma Café (p178) or lunch in its stylish **La Cantine de Merci** (☏01 42 77 00 33; mains €16-21; ⊙10am-7.30pm).

Empreintes Design
(Map p254; www.empreintes-paris.com; 5 rue de Picardie, 3e; ⊙11am-7pm Mon-Sat; Ⓜ Temple) Spanning more than 600 sq metres over four floors, this design emporium has over 1000 items for sale at any one time from over 6000 emerging and established French artists and designers. Handcrafted jewellery, fashion and art are displayed alongside striking homewares (ceramics, cushions, furniture, lighting and more). Upstairs there's a cafe and a reference library.

Triangle d'Or

A stroll around the legendary **Triangle d'Or** (Golden Triangle; bordered by avs George V, Champs-Élysées and Montaigne, 8e) or on rue du Faubourg St-Honoré constitutes the walk of fame of top French fashion. Rubbing shoulders with the world's most renowned international designers are Paris' most influential French fashion houses:

Chanel (Map p246; ☏01 44 50 73 00; www. chanel.com; 42 av Montaigne, 8e; ⊙10am-7pm; Ⓜ George V)

Chloé (Map p246; ☏01 47 23 00 08; www. chloe.com; 50 av Montaigne, 8e; ⊙10.30am-7pm Mon-Sat; Ⓜ Franklin D Roosevelt)

Dior (Map p246; ☏01 45 63 12 51; www.dior. com; 30 av Montaigne, 8e; ⊙10am-7pm Mon-Sat, 1-9pm Sun; Ⓜ George V)

Givenchy (Map p246; ☏01 44 43 99 90; www.givenchy.com; 36 av Montaigne, 8e; ⊙10am-7pm Mon-Sat, 1-7pm Sun; Ⓜ George V)

Hermès (Map p246; ☏01 40 17 46 00; www. hermes.com; 24 rue du Faubourg St-Honoré, 8e; ⊙10.30am-6.30pm Mon-Sat; Ⓜ Concorde)

Lanvin (Map p246; ☏01 44 71 31 73; www. lanvin.com; 22 rue du Faubourg St-Honoré, 8e; ⊙10.30am-7pm Mon-Sat; Ⓜ Concorde)

Louis Vuitton (Map p246; ☏01 53 57 52 00; www.louisvuitton.com; 101 av des Champs-Élysées, 8e; ⊙10am-8pm Mon-Sat, 11am-7pm Sun; Ⓜ George V)

Saint Laurent (Map p246; ☏01 42 65 74 59; www.ysl.com; 38 rue du Faubourg St-Honoré, 8e; ⊙10.30am-7.30pm Mon-Sat; Ⓜ Concorde)

Kerzon Homewares, Cosmetics
(Map p254; www.kerzon.paris; 68 rue de Turenne, 3e; ⊙11.30am-8pm Tue-Sat; Ⓜ St-Sébastien–Froissart) Candles made from natural, biodegradable wax in Parisian scents such as Jardin du Luxembourg (with lilac and honey), Place des Vosges (rose and jasmine) and Parc des Buttes-Chaumont (cedar and sandalwood) make aromatic souvenirs of

Marché aux Puces d'Aligre (p83)

the city. The pretty white and sage-green boutique also stocks room fragrances, scented laundry liquids, and perfumes, soaps, bath oils and other toiletries.

Fromagerie Goncourt   Cheese
(Map p254; 📞01 43 57 91 28; 1 rue Abel Rabaud, 11e; ⏰9am-1pm & 4-8.30pm Tue-Fri, 9am-8pm Sat; Ⓜ Goncourt) Styled like a boutique, this contemporary *fromagerie* is a must-discover. Clément Brossault ditched a career in banking to become a *fromager* and his cheese selection – 70-plus types – is superb. Cheeses flagged with a bicycle symbol are varieties he discovered in situ during a two-month French cheese tour he embarked on as part of his training.

Paris Rendez-Vous   Gifts & Souvenirs
(Map p250; http://rendezvous.paris.fr; 29 rue de Rivoli, 4e; ⏰10am-7pm Mon-Sat; Ⓜ Hôtel de Ville) This chic city has its own designer line of souvenirs, from clothing and homewares to Paris-themed books, wooden toy sailing boats and signature Jardin du Luxembourg

Fermob chairs, sold in its own ubercool store inside the Hôtel de Ville. *Quel style!*

Andrea Crews   Fashion & Accessories
(Map p254; www.andreacrews.com; 83 rue de Turenne, 3e; ⏰1-7.30pm Wed-Fri, to 7pm Sat; Ⓜ St-Sébastien–Froissart) Using everything from discarded clothing to electrical fittings and household bric-a-brac, this bold art and fashion collective sews, recycles and reinvents to create the most extraordinary pieces. Watch out for 'happenings' in its Marais boutique.

Belleville Brûlerie   Coffee
(Map p254; 📞09 83 75 60 80; http://cafes belleville.com; 10 rue Pradier, 19e; ⏰11.30am-6.30pm Sat; Ⓜ Pyrénées) With its understated steel-grey façade, this ground-breaking roastery in Belleville is easy to miss. Don't! Belleville Brûlerie brought good coffee to Paris and its beans go into some of the best espressos in town. Taste the week's selection, compare tasting notes, and buy a bag to take home.

Candora
Perfume

(Map p254; 📞01 43 48 76 05; www.candora.fr; 1 rue du Pont Louis-Philippe, 4e; ⊙2-7pm Tue-Sat; MPont Marie) At this brother-and-sister-run *parfumerie* near the Seine, you can have bespoke scents made up in just 10 minutes. Or learn how to create fragrances yourself during a perfume-making workshop for adults and children. Workshops in English take place at 2.30pm on Tuesday and Friday and last 90 minutes (€79/54 per adult/child), and include a 15mL bottle.

Edwart
Chocolate

(Map p254; http://edwart.fr; 17 rue Vielle du Temple, 4e; ⊙11am-noon & 1-8pm Mon-Wed, 11am-8pm Thu-Sun; MHôtel de Ville) Wunderkind chocolatiers Edwin Yansané and Arthur Heinze (collectively 'Edwart') take their inspiration from Paris (and – as a global melting pot – by extension, the world). Feisty chocolates using unique ingredients such as Indian curry, Iranian saffron and Japanese whisky are sparingly displayed in their sleek Marais boutique.

Fleux
Design, Homewares

(Map p254; www.fleux.com; 39 & 52 rue Ste-Croix de la Bretonnerie, 4e; ⊙11am-8pm Mon-Fri, 10.30am-8pm Sat, 1-8pm Sun; MHôtel de Ville) Innovative homewares by European designers fill these neighbouring boutiques: textiles (curtains, cushions etc), vases, mirrors, sculptures, clocks, candles, travel and leather goods, kids' accessories, multimedia products and much more. Its e-boutique stocks about 10% of what you see on the shop floor, but Fleux can post most Paris purchases home for you (at a price, *bien sûr*).

Fromagerie Beaufils
Cheese

(Map p254; www.fromagerie-beaufils.com; 118 rue de Belleville, 20e; ⊙8.30am-8pm Tue-Sat, to 1pm Sun; MJourdain) The queue outside the door, especially at weekends, says it all. This family-run *fromagerie* (cheese shop) and *affineur* (ripener) in Belleville is among the

🗃 Flea Markets

Spanning nine hectares, vast flea market **Marché aux Puces de St-Ouen** (www.marcheauxpuces-saintouen.com; rue des Rosiers, St-Ouen; ⊙Sat-Mon; MPorte de Clignancourt) was founded in 1870 and is said to be Europe's largest. Over 2000 stalls are grouped into 15 *marchés* (markets) selling everything from 17th-century furniture to 21st-century clothing. Each market has different opening hours – check the website for details.

Close by, an abandoned Petite Ceinture train station has been repurposed as eco-hub **La REcyclerie** (www.larecyclerie.com; 83 bd Ornano, 18e; ⊙8am-midnight Mon-Thu, to 2am Fri & Sat, to 10pm Sun early Jan–mid-Dec; MPorte de Clignancourt) 🍴 with an urban farm along the old railway line featuring community vegetable and herb gardens and chickens. They provide ingredients for the mostly vegetarian cafe-canteen (tables stretch trackside in summer and the station houses a cavernous dining space). Look out for regular upcycling and repair workshops, flea markets and various other events.

Across town in the city's south, the **Marché aux Puces de la Porte de Vanves** (www.pucesdevanves.fr; av Georges Lafenestre & av Marc Sangnier, 14e; ⊙7am-2pm Sat & Sun; MPorte de Vanves) has over 380 stalls.

Paris' most central flea market is the small Marché aux Puces d'Aligre (p83).

best in Paris, with dozens of lesser-known French and international varieties.

L'Éclaireur
Fashion & Accessories

(Map p254; 📞01 48 87 10 22; www.leclaireur.com; 40 rue de Sévigné, 3e; ⊙11am-7pm Mon-Sat, 2-7pm Sun; MSt-Paul) Part art space, part lounge and part deconstructionist fashion

Top Paris Souvenirs

Art

At major museums, the Boutiques de Musées have painting-and-frame services: browse masterpieces, choose a frame and have replicas mailed to your home.

Perfume

Browse Parisian perfume at new innovators or department stores, or buy a bottle of Champs-Élysées on its namesake street at Guerlain (p150).

Chocolate

Exquisite chocolate boutiques throughout the city include star chef Alain Ducasse's bean-to-bar chocolate factory, La Manufacture de Chocolat (p158).

Candles

Candle-makers span from the world's oldest, Cire Trudon (p161), to scents of Parisian parks and gardens at Kerzon (p153).

Scarves

The ultimate Parisian accessory, whatever the season. Hermès (p162) creates timeless designs.

statement, this shop is known for having the next big thing first. Two tons of wooden planks, 147 TV screens and walls that move to reveal the men's and women's collection all form part of the stunning interior design by Belgian artist Arne Quinze.

La Cave Le Verre Volé   Wine

(Map p254; http://leverrevole.fr; 38 rue Oberkampf, 11e; ☺4-8.30pm Mon, 10am-1pm & 4-8.30pm Tue-Sat; ⒨Oberkampf) One of Paris' largest collections of natural wines is stocked at this wondrous wine shop. Its famous bistro (p126) is located by Canal St-Martin, and its **épicerie** (Map p254; specialist grocer; ✆01 48 05 36 55; 54 rue de la Folie Méricourt, 11e; 2-course lunch menus €9.90, sandwiches €4.90-6.90; ☺11am-2.30pm & 4.30-8pm Mon & Fri, 11am-8pm Tue-Thu & Sat; ☎; ⒨Oberkampf), where for €7 corkage you can drink bottles purchased here while dining on deli platters and gourmet sandwiches, is just around the corner.

Les Petits Bla-Blas   Children's Clothing

(Map p254; Atelier Pascaline Delcourt; www.facebook.com/atelierpascalinedelcourt; 7 rue de Crussol, 11e; ☺11am-7pm Mon-Fri; ⒨Filles du Calvaire) At her 11e *atelier* (workshop), Pascaline Delcourt makes children's clothing (up to six years), bibs, bags and onesies, and also stocks children's jewellery, toys, paper animal lanterns and soft cuddly toys. A personalisation service lets you add a name, date of birth or message to individual items.

Made by Moi   Fashion, Homewares

(Map p254; ✆01 58 30 95 78; www.madebymoi.fr; 86 rue Oberkampf, 11e; ☺2.30-8pm Mon, 10am-8pm Tue-Sat, 2.30-7pm Sun; ⒨Parmentier) 'Made by Me', aka handmade, is the driver of this appealing boutique on trendy rue Oberkampf – a perfect address to buy unusual gifts, from women's fashion to homewares such as 'Bobo brunch' scented candles by Bougies La Française and other beautiful objects such as coloured glass carafes, feathered headdresses, funky contact-lens boxes and retro dial telephones.

Maison Georges Larnicol   Chocolate

(Map p254; https://larnicol.com; 14 rue de Rivoli, 4e; ☺10am-10pm; ⒨St-Paul) Coco-ginger bites, caramels and chocolate sculptures are among the sweet treats created by this master chocolate maker from Brittany. But it's his syrupy, chewy *kouignettes* (Breton butter cakes unusually made in mini dimensions and different flavours) that steal the show. Oh, and the glass jars of *caramel au beurre salé* (butter caramel) sold with a small spoon...

Jamin Puech   Fashion & Accessories

(Map p254; www.jamin-puech.com; 68 rue Vieille du Temple, 4e; ☺10am-7.30pm Mon-Sat, 1-7pm Sun; ⒨Chemin Vert) Established by former theatre and opera costume designers Isabelle Puech and Benoît Jamin, who trained together in Paris, this design house creates beautiful handbags in all manner of bold colours, textures and textiles. For vintage pieces from the 1990s, head to the couple's first boutique at 61 rue d'Hauteville, 10e.

Finger in the Nose   Children's Clothing

(Map p254; www.fingerinthenose.com; 60 rue de Saintonge, 3e; ☺11am-7pm Tue-Sat; ⒨Filles du Calvaire) Homegrown Le Marais label Finger in the Nose creates edgy, urban clothing for kids at its nearby workshop and showcases its collections here at its flagship boutique. Look out for limited-edition lines, house-designed graphic prints and a great range of jeans.

Bring France Home   Gifts & Souvenirs

(Map p254; ✆09 81 64 91 09; http://bringfrancehome.com; 3 rue de Birague, 4e; ☺11am-7pm; ⒨Bastille) All of the quality items in this terrific little shop are made in France: jewellery, perfume, cards, tea towels, plates, posters, board games, *pétanque* sets, speciality foodstuffs such as foie gras, tinned sardines, Parisian honey, beer and absinthe kits, and much more. If you don't want to be laden down with shopping bags, purchases can be delivered to your hotel.

🅐 Bastille & Eastern Paris

La Manufacture de Chocolat Food
(Map p254; www.lechocolat-alainducasse.com;
40 rue de la Roquette, 11e; ⊗9.30am-6pm Mon-
Fri; Ⓜ Bastille) If you dine at superstar chef
Alain Ducasse's restaurants, the chocolate
will have been made here at Ducasse's
own chocolate factory (the first in Paris to
produce 'bean-to-bar' chocolate), which he
set up with his former executive pastry chef
Nicolas Berger. Deliberate over ganaches,
pralines and truffles and no fewer than
44 flavours of chocolate bar. You can also
buy Ducasse's chocolates at other outlets
including his Left Bank boutique, **Le Chocolat Alain Ducasse** (Map p246; ☑01 45 48
87 89; 26 rue St-Benoît, 6e; ⊗1.30-7.30pm Mon,
10.30am-7.30pm Tue-Sat; Ⓜ St-Germain des Prés).

La Cocotte Homewares
(Map p254; www.lacocotteparis.com; 5 rue
Paul Bert, 11e; ⊗noon-7pm Tue-Sat; Ⓜ Faidherbe-Chaligny) If the gourmet restaurants
along rue Paul Bert have inspired you to
get into the kitchen, stop by the boutique
of designers Andrea Wainer and Laetitia
Bertrand for stylish, often Paris- and/or
French-themed accoutrements such as tea
towels, oven mitts, aprons, mugs, shopping
bags and more, many incorporating La
Cocotte's signature hen motif.

Fermob Homewares
(Map p254; www.paris.fermob.com; 81-83 av
Ledru-Rollin, 12e; ⊗10am-7pm Mon-Sat; Ⓜ Ledru-Rollin) If you want to create the 'Jardin du
Luxembourg look' in your own garden, head
for Fermob. It makes French-park-style
benches and folding chairs in a range of
great colours – from carrot and lemon to
fuchsia and aubergine – along with lovely
cushions, rugs, throws, lamps and home
accessories. International shipping is available. There's a second, larger location in
St-Germain (Map p246; ☑01 45 44 10 28; www.
paris.fermob.com; 17 bd Raspail, 7e; ⊗10am-7pm
Tue-Sat; Ⓜ Rue du Bac).

*Paris' street markets are a
feast for the senses*

Marché aux Fleurs Reine Elizabeth II

ⓐ The Islands

Marché aux Fleurs
Reine Elizabeth II   Market

(Map p250; place Louis Lépin, 4e; ⊙8am-7.30pm Mon-Sat; Ⓜ Cité) Blooms have been sold at this flower market since 1808, making it the oldest market of any kind in Paris. On Sunday, it transforms into a cacophonous bird market, the **Marché aux Oiseaux** (Map p250; place Louis Lépin, 4e; ⊙8am-7pm Sun; Ⓜ Cité).

38 Saint Louis   Food & Drinks

(Map p252; 38 rue St-Louis en l'Île, 4e; ⊙8.30am-10pm Tue-Sat, 9.30am-4pm Sun; Ⓜ Pont Marie) Not only does this contemporary, creamy white-fronted *fromagerie* (cheese shop) run by young, dynamic, food-driven duo Didier Grosjean et Thibaut Lhirondelle have an absolutely superb selection of first-class French cheese; it also offers Saturday wine tastings, artisan fruit juices and prepared dishes to go such as sheep's-cheese salad with truffle oil, and wooden boxes filled with vacuum-packed cheese to take home.

ⓐ Latin Quarter

Shakespeare & Company   Books

(Map p252; ☎01 43 25 40 93; www.shakespeare andcompany.com; 37 rue de la Bûcherie, 5e; ⊙10am-10pm; Ⓜ St-Michel) Shake-speare's enchanting nooks and crannies overflow with new and secondhand English-language books. The original shop (12 rue l'Odéon, 6e; closed by the Nazis in 1941) was run by Sylvia Beach and became the meeting point for Hemingway's 'Lost Generation'. Readings by emerging and illustrious authors take place at 7pm most Mondays and there's a wonderful cafe (p181) next door.

Le Bonbon au Palais   Food

(Map p252; ☎01 78 56 15 72; www.bonbonsau palais.fr; 19 rue Monge, 5e; ⊙10.30am-7.30pm Tue-Sat; Ⓜ Cardinal Lemoine) Kids and kids-at-heart will adore this sugar-fuelled *tour*

Canal St-Martin

Bordered by shaded towpaths and criss-crossed with iron footbridges, **Canal St-Martin** (Ⓜ Jacques Bonsergent) wends through the city's northern neigh-bourhoods. Shopping streets home to offbeat boutiques include rue Beaure-paire: look out for rock 'n' roll fashion at **Liza Korn** (Map p254; www.liza-korn.com; 19 rue Beaurepaire, 10e; ⊙11am-7.30pm Mon-Sat) and colour-coded vintage cast-offs at **Frivoli** (Map p254; 26 rue Beaurepaire, 10e; ⊙1-7pm Mon, 11am-7pm Tue-Sat, 2-7pm Sun). Rue de Marseille is also lined with boutiques such as jewellery stu-dio-showroom **Medecine Douce** (Map p254; www.bijouxmedecinedouce.com; 10 rue de Marseille, 10e; ⊙11am-7pm Mon-Sat). Along the canal itself, check out design bookshop **Artazart** (Map p254; https://art azart.com; 83 quai de Valmy, 10e; ⊙10.30am-7.30pm Mon-Fri, 11am-7.30pm Sat, 1-7.30pm Sun), and the pastel-shaded **Antoine et Lili** (Map p254; www.antoineetlili.com; 95 quai de Valmy, 10e; ⊙11am-8pm Mon-Fri, 10am-8pm Sat, 11am-7pm Sun), stocking clothing for women (pink store) and children (green store), and eclectic homewares (yellow store).

de France. The school-geography-themed boutique stocks rainbows of artisan sweets from around the country. Glass jars brim with treats like *calissons* (diamond-shaped, icing-sugar-topped ground fruit and almonds from Aix-en-Provence), *rigolettes* (fruit-filled pillows from Nantes), *berlingots* (striped, triangular boiled sweets from Carpentras and elsewhere) and *papalines* (herbal liqueur-filled pink-chocolate balls from Avignon).

Fromagerie
Laurent Dubois   Cheese

(Map p252; ☎01 43 54 50 93; www.fromages laurentdubois.fr; 47ter bd St-Germain, 5e; ⊙8.30am-7.30pm Tue-Sat, 8.30am-1pm

Vintage Style

Scattered along one street, **Cherchem-inippes** (Map p246; www.chercheminippes.com; 102 rue du Cherche Midi, 6e; ⏱11am-7pm Mon-Sat; Ⓜ Vaneau) has a string of beautifully presented boutiques selling secondhand pieces by current designers. Each specialises in a different genre (haute couture, kids, menswear etc); items are perfectly ordered by size and designer. There are changing rooms.

Fans of Chanel and Hermès should visit **Catherine B** (Map p252; ☏01 43 54 74 18; http://les3marchesdecatherineb.com; 1 rue Guisarde, 6e; ⏱11am-7pm Mon-Sat; Ⓜ Mabillon), who specialises exclusively in authentic items from these two iconic French fashion houses.

Sun; Ⓜ Maubert-Mutualité) One of the best *fromageries* in Paris, this cheese-lover's nirvana is filled with to-die-for delicacies, such as St-Félicien with Périgord truffles. Rare, limited-production cheeses include blue Termignon and Tarentaise goat's cheese. All are appropriately cellared in warm, humid or cold environments. There's also a 15e branch (Map p246; ☏01 45 78 70 58; 2 rue de Lourmel, 15e; ⏱9am-1pm & 4-7.45pm Tue-Fri, 8.30am-7.45pm Sat, 9am-1pm Sun; Ⓜ Dupleix).

Fromagerie Maury
Cheese

(Map p252; ☏09 52 81 84 98; 1 rue des Feuillan-tines, 5e; ⏱2-9pm Tue-Thu, 10.30am-1.30pm & 3-8.30pm Fri & Sat; Ⓜ Censier Daubenton, RER Port Royal) ✎ This wonderful little *fromage-rie* feels more like a farm shop you'd find in the countryside than an inner-city Parisian boutique. Organic eggs sit in straw baskets (cartons are available) and owner Christo-phe Maury insists that you try his amazing range of carefully selected cheeses from small-scale producers in southwestern France, the Jura mountains, Corsica, Italy and Spain before you buy.

ⓐ St-Germain & Les Invalides

La Grande Épicerie de Paris
Food & Drinks

(Map p246; www.lagrandeepicerie.com; 36 rue de Sèvres, 7e; ⏱8.30am-9pm Mon-Sat, 10am-8pm Sun; Ⓜ Sèvres-Babylone) The magnificent food hall of department store Le Bon Marché sells 30,000 rare and/or luxury gourmet products, including 60 different types of bread baked on site and delica-cies such as caviar ravioli. Its fantastical displays of chocolates, pastries, biscuits, cheeses, fresh fruit and vegetables and deli goods are a Parisian sight in themselves. Wine tastings regularly take place in the basement.

Le Bon Marché
Department Store

(Map p246; ☏01 44 39 80 00; http://lebon marche.com; 24 rue de Sèvres, 7e; ⏱10am-8pm Mon-Wed, Fri & Sat, 10am-8.45pm Thu, 11am-8pm Sun; Ⓜ Sèvres-Babylone) Built by Gustave Eif-fel as Paris' first department store in 1852, this is the epitome of style, with a superb concentration of men's and women's fash-ions, homewares, stationery, books and toys. Break for a coffee, afternoon tea with cake or a light lunch at the Rose Bakery tea room on the 2nd floor.

Magasin Sennelier
Arts & Crafts

(Map p246; ☏01 42 60 72 15; www.magasinsen nelier.com; 3 quai Voltaire, 7e; ⏱2-6.30pm Mon, 10am-12.45pm & 2-6.30pm Tue-Sat; Ⓜ St-Germain des Prés) Cézanne and Picasso were among the artists who helped develop products for this venerable 1887-founded art supplier on the banks of the Seine, and it remains an exception-al place to pick up canvases, brushes, watercolours, oils, pastels, charcoals and more. The shop's forest-green façade with gold lettering, exquisite original timber cabinetry and glass display cases also fuel artistic inspiration.

Cantin
Cheese

(Map p246; ☏01 45 50 43 94; www.cantin.fr; 12 rue du Champs de Mars, 7e; ⏱2-7.30pm Mon,

La Grande Épicerie de Paris

8.30am-7.30pm Tue-Sat, 8.30am-1pm Sun; MÉcole Militaire) ✪ Opened in 1950 and still run by the same family today, this exceptional shop stocks cheeses only made in limited quantities on small rural farms. They're then painstakingly ripened in Cantin's own cellars (from two weeks up to two years) before being displayed for sale. Should you want to know how to concoct the perfect cheeseboard, Cantin runs informative tasting workshops.

Au Plat d'Étain
Toys

(Map p252; ☎01 43 54 32 06; www.soldats-plomb-au-plat-etain.fr; 16 rue Guisarde, 6e; ⊙10.30am-6.30pm Tue-Sat; MMabillon, St-Sulpice) Tiny tin *(étain)* and lead soldiers, snipers, cavaliers, military drummers and musicians (great for chessboard pieces) cram this fascinating boutique. In business since 1775, the shop itself is practically a collectable.

Bonton Surplus
Children's Clothing

(Map p246; ☎01 44 39 09 20; www.bonton.fr; 82 rue de Grenelle, 7e; ⊙10am-7pm Mon-Sat; MRue du Bac) What's left of previous seasons'

collections from one of Paris' most chic children's fashion shops is sold at reduced prices at this tiny boutique, a riot of colour and fun. The adjoining Bonton Store, also at No 82, stocks the current collection – or head to Bonton's flagship **concept store** (Map p254; 5 bd des Filles du Calvaire, 3e; ⊙10am-7pm Mon-Sat; MSt-Sébastien–Froissart) in Le Marais.

Cire Trudon
Gifts & Souvenirs

(Map p252; ☎01 43 26 46 50; https://trudon.com; 78 rue de Seine, 6e; ⊙11am-7pm Mon, 10am-7pm Tue-Sat; MOdéon) Claude Trudon began selling candles here in 1643, and the company – which officially supplied Versailles and Napoléon with light – is now the world's oldest candle-maker (look for the plaque to the left of the shop's royal-blue awning). A rainbow of candles and candlesticks fill the shelves inside.

Deyrolle
Antiques, Homewares

(Map p246; ☎01 42 22 30 07; www.deyrolle.com; 46 rue du Bac, 7e; ⊙10am-1pm & 2-7pm Mon, 10am-7pm Tue-Sat; MRue du Bac) Overrun with creatures including lions, tigers, zebras and

Hermès

storks, taxidermist Deyrolle opened in 1831. In addition to stuffed animals, it stocks minerals, shells, corals and crustaceans, stand-mounted ostrich eggs and pedagogical storyboards. There are also rare and unusual seeds (including many types of tomato), gardening tools and accessories.

Hermès   Fashion & Accessories
(Map p246; ☑01 42 22 80 83; www.hermes. com; 17 rue de Sèvres, 6e; ⊙10.30am-7pm Mon-Sat; Ⓜ Sèvres-Babylone) A stunning art deco swimming pool (originally belonging to neighbouring Hôtel Lutetia, no less) now houses luxury label Hermès' inaugural concept store. Retaining its original mosaic tiles and iron balustrades, the vast, tiered space showcases new directions in home furnishings, including fabrics and wallpaper, along with classic lines such as its signature scarves. Its cafe, Le Plongeoir (the Diving Board), is equally chic.

JB Guanti   Fashion & Accessories
(Map p246; www.jbguanti.com; 59 rue de Rennes, 6e; ⊙10am-7pm Mon-Sat; Ⓜ St-Sulpice) For the ultimate finishing touch, the men's and women's gloves at this boutique, which specialises solely in gloves, are the epitome of both style and comfort, whether unlined, silk lined, cashmere lined, lambskin lined or trimmed with rabbit fur. Buying for someone else? To get their glove size, measure the length in centimetres of their middle finger from the top to where it joins their palm – the number of centimetres equals the size (eg 5cm is a size 5).

La Dernière Goutte   Wine
(Map p250; ☑01 43 29 11 62; www.laderniere goutte.net; 6 rue du Bourbon le Château, 6e; ⊙3.30-8pm Mon, 10.30am-1.30pm & 3-8pm Tue-Fri, 10.30am-8pm Sat, 11am-7pm Sun; Ⓜ Mabillon) 'The Last Drop' is the brainchild of Cuban-American sommelier Juan Sánchez, whose tiny wine shop is packed with exciting, mostly organic French *vins de propriétaires* (estate-bottled wines) made by small independent producers. Wine classes lasting two hours (two white tastings, five red) regularly take place in English (per person €55); phone for schedules and

reservations. Free tastings with winemakers take place most Saturdays.

Pâtisserie Michalak — Food

(Map p246; ☎01 45 49 44 90; www.christophe michalak.com; 8 rue du Vieux Colombier, 6e; ◷10am-7pm; ⓂSt-Sulpice) At the bright, whitewashed Left Bank boutique of Christophe Michalak – one of Paris' most inventive pastry chefs – colourful displays include Michalak's signature deconstructed desserts in screw-capped glass jars, creative chocolates in shapes such as retro audio cassettes, flip-flops and electrical power boards, and his inspirational cookbooks.

Sabbia Rosa — Fashion & Accessories

(Map p246; ☎01 45 48 88 37; 73 rue des Sts-Pères, 6e; ◷10am-7pm Mon-Sat; ⓂSt-Germain des Prés) Only French-sourced fabrics (silk from Lyon, lace from Calais) are used by lingerie designer Sabbia Rosa for her ultra-luxe range at this upmarket boutique, open since 1976. Every piece is unique; items can be custom-made in 48 hours. The list of celebrity clients reads like a who's who: Serge Gainsbourg, Madonna, Naomi Campbell, Claudia Schiffer and George Clooney have all shopped here.

Alexandra Sojfer — Fashion & Accessories

(Map p246; ☎01 42 22 17 02; www.alexandra sojfer.com; 218 bd St-Germain, 7e; ◷10am-7pm Mon-Sat; ⓂRue du Bac) One-of-a-kind high-fashion *parapluies* (parasols) and *ombrelles* (umbrellas) as well as *cannes* (walking sticks) are handmade by Alexandra Sojfer, who bought this 1834-opened atelier in 2002, and whose family has been in the business for generations. If nothing on display catches your fancy, you can have one custom-made.

Atelier 144 — Fashion & Accessories

(Map p252; ☎01 43 26 45 83; www.atelier144.fr; 23 rue St-Sulpice, 6e; ◷11am-7pm Mon-Sat; ⓂSt-Sulpice) The height of elegance, Atelier 144 is a one-stop shop for beautiful *chapeaux* (hats) for men and women.

Bouquinistes Along the Seine

With some 3km of forest-green boxes lining the Seine – containing over 300,000 secondhand (and often out-of-print) books, rare magazines, postcards and old advertising posters – Paris' **bouquinistes** (Map p250; quai Voltaire, 7e, to quai de la Tournelle, 5e, & Pont Marie, 4e, to quai du Louvre, 1er; ◷11.30am-dusk), or used-book sellers, are as integral to the cityscape as Notre Dame. Many open only from spring to autumn (and many shut in August), but year-round you'll still find some to browse. The *bouquinistes* have been in business since the 16th century, when they were itinerant peddlers selling their wares on Parisian bridges.

⊙ Montparnasse & Southern Paris

Biérocratie — Drinks

(☎01 53 80 16 10; www.bierocratie.com; 32 rue de l'Espérance, 13e; ◷11am-8pm Tue & Thu-Sat, 4-8pm Wed; ⓂCorvisart) Craft beers from around the world (such as English Weird Beard and Canadian Dieu du Cieu) but especially France (including Île-de-France-brewed La Baleine, Distrikt and Parisis) fill this bottle-lined specialist shop run by fun-loving young husband-and-wife team Jaclyn and Pierre. Look out for Friday-evening tastings where you can meet the brewers.

Adam Montparnasse — Arts & Crafts

(Map p246; ☎01 43 20 68 53; www.adamparis.com; 11 bd Edgar Quinet, 14e; ◷9.30am-7pm Mon-Sat; ⓂEdgar Quinet) If Paris' art galleries have inspired you, pick up paintbrushes, charcoals, sketchpads, watercolours, oils, canvases and more at this historic shop. Picasso, Brancusi and Giacometti were among Édouard Adam's clients. Another seminal client was Yves Klein, with whom Adam developed the ultramarine 'Klein blue' – the VLB25 'Klein Blue' is sold exclusively here.

BAR OPEN

Coffee roasteries, cocktails, classic cafes
& cutting-edge wine bars

Bar Open

For the French, drinking and eating go together like wine and cheese, and the line between a cafe, salon de thé *(tearoom), bistro, brasserie, bar, and even* bar à vins *(wine bar) is blurred. The line between drinking and clubbing is often nonexistent – a cafe that's quiet midafternoon might have DJ sets in the evening and dancing later on. Many Parisians live in tiny apartments, and cafes and bars have traditionally served as the salon they don't have – a place to meet friends over* un verre *(glass of wine), read for hours over* un café *(coffee), debate politics while downing an espresso at a zinc counter, swill cocktails during* apéro *(aperitif; predinner drink) or get the party started aboard a floating club on the Seine.*

In This Section

Opening Hours

Many cafes and bars open first thing in the morning, around 7am. Closing time for cafes and bars tends to be 2am, though some have licences until dawn. Club hours vary depending on the venue, day and event.

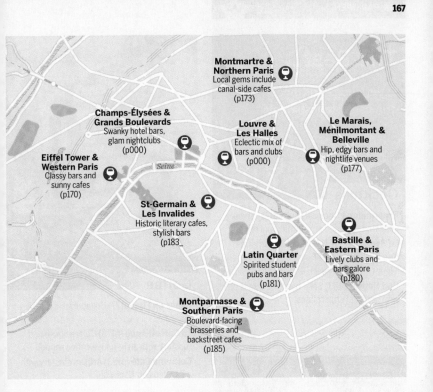

Montmartre & Northern Paris
Local gems include canal-side cafes
(p173)

Champs-Élysées & Grands Boulevards
Swanky hotel bars, glam nightclubs
(p000)

Louvre & Les Halles
Eclectic mix of bars and clubs
(p000)

Le Marais, Ménilmontant & Belleville
Hip, edgy bars and nightlife venues
(p177)

Eiffel Tower & Western Paris
Classy bars and sunny cafes
(p170)

Seine

St-Germain & Les Invalides
Historic literary cafes, stylish bars
(p183_

Latin Quarter
Spirited student pubs and bars
(p181)

Bastille & Eastern Paris
Lively clubs and bars galore
(p180)

Montparnasse & Southern Paris
Boulevard-facing brasseries and backstreet cafes
(p185)

Costs/Tipping

Costs An espresso/glass of wine/ cocktail starts at around €2/3.50/9; a *demi* (half-pint) of beer costs from €3.50. Club admission is free to around €20; it's often cheaper before 1am.

Tipping Not necessary at the bar. If drinks are brought to your table, tip as you would in a restaurant.

Useful Phrases

Un café Single shot of espresso.

Un café allongé Espresso with hot water.

Un café au lait Coffee with milk.

Un café crème Espresso with steamed milk.

Un double Double espresso.

Une noisette Espresso with a spot of milk.

The Best...

Experience Paris' finest drinking establishments

Cocktails

Experimental Cocktail Club (p171) Speakeasy that spawned an international empire.

Le Syndicat (p173) Cocktails incorporate rare French spirits.

Tiger (p185) Gin specialist with 130 varieties.

Cod House (p183) Sake-based cocktails pair with gourmet small plates.

Coffee

Beans on Fire (p177) Collaborative roastery and cafe.

La Caféothèque (p178) Coffee house and roastery with an in-house coffee school.

Coutume Café (p183) Artisan roastery with a flagship Left Bank cafe.

Wine Bars

Le Garde Robe (p171) Affordable natural wines and unpretentious vibe.

Le Baron Rouge (p180) Wonderfully convivial barrel-filled wine bar.

Au Sauvignon (p183) Original zinc bar and hand-painted ceiling.

Beer

Paname Brewing Company (p174) Craft-brewery taproom in a 19th-century waterside granary with a floating pontoon.

Outland (p180) Artisan beer bar serving Outland's own beers.

Clubs

Le Rex Club (p173) Renowned house and techno club with a phenomenal sound system.

Concrete (p180) Paris' first club with a 24-hour licence is aboard a barge by Gare de Lyon.

Le Batofar (p185) Iconic tugboat-housed club in the 13e.

Tearooms

Mariage Frères (p183) Paris' oldest and finest tearoom, founded in 1854.

La Mosquée (p108) Sip sweet mint tea and nibble delicious pastries at Paris' mosque.

Noglu (p185) Cakes, biscuits and savoury treats.

Angelina (p173) 1903 tearoom now frequented for its decadent hot chocolate.

Lonely Planet's Top Choices

Bar Hemingway (p171) Legendary cocktails inside the Ritz.

Pavillon Puebla (p174) Park-set pavilion.

Le Perchoir (p177) Hip rooftop bar best visited at sunset.

Les Deux Magots (p183) Famous St-Germain literary cafe.

Candelaria (p177) Clandestine cocktail bar.

Pavement Terraces

Chez Prune (p175) The boho cafe that put Canal St-Martin on the map.

Café des Anges (p180) The terrace of this 11e cafe buzzes night and day.

Shakespeare & Company Café (p181) Live the Parisian Left Bank literary dream.

🚇 Eiffel Tower & Western Paris

St James Paris   Bar

(Map p246; www.saint-james-paris.com; 43 av Bugeaud, 16e; ⏰7pm-1am; 📶; MPorte Dauphine) Hidden behind a stone wall, this historic mansion-turned-hotel opens its bar nightly to nonguests – and the setting redefines extraordinary. Winter drinks are in the wood-panelled library, in summer they're on the impossibly romantic 300-sq-metre garden terrace with giant balloon-shaped gazebos (the first hot-air balloons took flight here). There are over 70 cocktails and an adjoining Michelin-starred restaurant.

Yoyo   Club

(Map p246; http://yoyo-paris.com; 13 av du Président Wilson, 16e; ⏰hours vary; Mléna) Deep in the basement of the Palais de Tokyo, Yoyo has an edgy, raw-concrete Berlin-style vibe and a capacity of 800. Techno and house dominate, with diversions into hip-hop, electro, funk, disco, R&B and soul. Hours can vary; check the website to see what's on.

Bô Zinc Café   Bar

(📞01 42 24 69 05; 59 av Mozart, 16e; ⏰7am-2am; MRanelagh) With its soft sage-green façade and buzzing pavement terrace, Bô Zinc is one of those great hybrid addresses – perfect for hanging with locals over coffee, tea or after-work cocktails. Seating is a mix of wooden bistro chairs and 'flop-in' armchairs, while potted palm trees – inside and out – add a touch of chic. Top-notch nosh too, served until 11pm.

🚇 Champs-Élysées & Grands Boulevards

Honor   Coffee

(Map p246; www.honor-cafe.com; 54 rue du Faubourg St-Honoré, 8e; ⏰9am-6pm Mon-Sat; MMadeleine) Hidden off ritzy rue du Faubourg St-Honoré in a courtyard adjoining fashion house Comme des Garçons is Paris' 'first and only outdoor independent coffee shop', an opaque-plastic-sheltered black-and-white timber kiosk brewing coffee from small-scale producers around the globe. It also serves luscious cakes,

Bar Hemingway

ALAIN BENAINOUS/GETTY IMAGES ©

filled-to-bursting lunchtime sandwiches, quiches and salads (dishes €5 to €10.50), along with fresh juices, wine and beer.

Zig Zag Club
Club

(Map p246; http://zigzagclub.fr; 32 rue Marbeuf, 8e; ⊙11.30pm-7am Fri & Sat; Ⓜ Franklin D Roosevelt) With star DJs, a great sound and light system, and a spacious dance floor, Zig Zag has some of the hippest electro beats in western Paris. It can be pricey, but it still fills up quickly, so don't start the party too late.

❷ Louvres & Les Halles

Bar Hemingway
Cocktail Bar

(Map p246; www.ritzparis.com; Hôtel Ritz Paris, 15 place Vendôme, 1er; ⊙6pm-2am; ☎; Ⓜ Opéra) Black-and-white photos and memorabilia (hunting trophies, old typewriters and framed handwritten letters by the great writer) fill this snug bar inside the **Ritz** (☏01 43 16 30 30). Head bartender Colin Field mixes monumental cocktails, including three different Bloody Marys made with juice from freshly squeezed seasonal tomatoes. Legend has it that Hemingway himself, wielding a machine gun, helped liberate the bar during WWII.

Le Garde Robe
Wine Bar

(Map p250; ☏01 49 26 90 60; 41 rue de l'Arbre Sec, 1er; ⊙12.30-2.30pm & 6.30pm-midnight Tue-Fri, 4.30pm-midnight Mon-Sat; Ⓜ Louvre Rivoli) Le Garde Robe is possibly the world's only bar to serve alcohol alongside a detox menu. While you probably shouldn't come here for the full-on cleansing experience, you can definitely expect excellent, affordable natural wines, a casual atmosphere and a good selection of food, ranging from cheese and charcuterie plates to adventurous options (tuna gravlax with black quinoa and guacamole).

Experimental Cocktail Club
Cocktail Bar

(Map p250; ECC; www.experimentalevents.com; 37 rue St-Sauveur, 2e; ⊙7pm-2am; Ⓜ Réaumur Sébastopol) With a black curtain façade,

🍺 Craft Beer

Beer hasn't traditionally had a high profile in France and mass-produced varieties such as Kronenbourg 1664 (5.5%), brewed in Strasbourg, dominate. Paris' growing *bière artisanale* (craft beer) scene, however, is going from strength to strength, with an increasing number of city breweries, such as **Brasserie BapBap** (Map p254; ☏01 77 17 52 97; www.bapbap.paris; 79 rue St-Maur, 11e; guided tours €15; ⊙guided tours 11am Sat, shop 6-8pm Tue-Fri, 3-8pm Sat; Ⓜ Rue St-Maur) and **Brasserie la Goutte d'Or** (Map p249; ☏09 80 64 23 51; www.brasserielagouttedor.com; 28 rue de la Goutte d'Or, 18e; ⊙5-7pm Thu & Fri, 2-7pm Sat; Ⓜ Château Rouge, Barbès-Rochechouart) **FREE**, microbreweries and cafes offering limited-production brews on tap and by the bottle. An excellent resource for hopheads is www.hoppyparis.com.

this retro-chic speakeasy – with sister bars in London, Ibiza, New York and, *bien sûr*, Paris – is a sophisticated flashback to those *années folles* (crazy years) of Prohibition New York. Cocktails (€13 to €15) are individual and fabulous, and DJs keep the party going until dawn at weekends. It's not a large space, however, and fills to capacity quickly.

Danico
Cocktail Bar

(Map p250; www.facebook.com/danicoparis; 6 rue Vivienne, 2e; ⊙6pm-2am; Ⓜ Bourse) While not exactly a secret, Danico still feels like one – first you'll need to find the hidden, candlelit backroom in **Daroco** (Map p250; ☏01 42 21 93 71; www.daroco.fr; 6 rue Vivienne, 2e; mains €14-40; ⊙noon-2.30pm & 7-11.30pm; ☏; Ⓜ Bourse) before you get to treat yourself to one of Nico de Soto's extravagant cocktails. Chia seeds, kombucha tea, ghost peppers and pomegranate Champagne are some of the more unusual ingredients you'll find on the drink list.

French Wine

Wine is easily the most popular beverage in Paris and house wine can cost less than bottled water. Of France's dozens of wine-producing regions, the principal ones are Burgundy, Bordeaux, the Rhône and the Loire valleys, Champagne, Languedoc, Provence and Alsace. Wines are generally named after the location of the vineyard rather than the grape varietal. The best wines are Appellation d'Origine Contrôlée (AOC; currently being relabelled Appellation d'Origine Protégée, AOP), meaning they meet stringent regulations governing where, how and under what conditions they're grown, fermented and bottled.

Natural Wines

Les vins naturels (natural wines) have a fuzzy definition – no one really agrees on the details, but the general idea is that they are produced from organically grown grapes using few or no pesticides or additives. This means natural wines do not contain sulphites, which are added as a preservative in most wines. The good news is that this gives natural wines a much more distinct personality (or *terroir,* as the French say); the bad news is that these wines can also be more unpredictable. For more specifics, see the website www.morethanorganic.com.

Harry's New York Bar   Cocktail Bar

(Map p250; ☑01 42 61 71 14; http://harrysbar.fr; 5 rue Daunou, 2e; ☉noon-2am Mon-Sat, 4pm-1am Sun; Ⓜ Opéra) One of the most popular American-style bars in the pre-war years, Harry's once welcomed writers including F Scott Fitzgerald and Ernest Hemingway, who no doubt sampled the bar's unique cocktail and creation: the Bloody Mary. The Cuban mahogany interior dates from the mid-19th century and was brought over from a Manhattan bar in 1911.

There's a basement piano bar called Ivories where Gershwin supposedly composed *An American in Paris* and, for the peckish, old-school hot dogs and generous club sandwiches to snack on. Its enduring tagline is 'Tell the Taxi Driver Sank Roo Doe Noo'.

Frog & Underground   Pub

(Map p250; www.frogpubs.com; 173 rue Montmartre, 2e; ☉8am-1am Sun-Wed, to 3am Thu, to 5am Fri & Sat; 🛜; Ⓜ Grands Boulevards) FrogPubs has been brewing in Paris since 1993, and this central new rue Montmartre venue is its best yet. Spread over a cavernous ground floor and opening to a terrace, a vaulted cellar with a dance floor, and upstairs lounge (spanning 370 sq metre in all), its exciting beers include a wonderfully crisp dry-hopped Hopster pale ale.

Lockwood   Cocktail Bar

(Map p250; ☑01 77 32 97 21; www.lockwoodparis.com; 73 rue d'Aboukir, 2e; ☉6pm-2am Mon-Fri, 10am-4pm & 6pm-2am Sat, 10am-4pm Sun; Ⓜ Sentier) Cocktails incorporating premium spirits such as Hendrick's rose- and cucumber-infused gin and Pierre Ferrand Curaçao are served in Lockwood's stylish ground-floor lounge and subterranean candle-lit cellar. It's especially buzzing on weekends, when brunch stretches out between 10am and 4pm, with Bloody Marys, coffee brewed with Parisian-roasted Belleville Brûlerie (p154) beans and fare including eggs Benedict and Florentine (dishes €8.50 to €13).

Matamata   Coffee

(Map p250; ☑01 71 39 44 58; www.matamata coffee.com; 58 rue d'Argout, 2e; ☉8am-5pm Mon-Fri, 9am-5.30pm Sat & Sun; 🛜; Ⓜ Sentier) Beans from Parisian roastery Café Lomi are expertly brewed at this small, two-level space with tables and light fittings made from recycled timber and repurposed metal, and subtropical fern wallpaper. Homemade cakes, such as carrot or banana, go with its exceptional coffee, sandwiches, salads and house-toasted granola. In summer, cool down with a cold-drip coffee over ice.

Harry's New York Bar

The Bloody Mary was born in 1920s Paris at Harry's New York Bar

Le Rex Club Club

(Map p250; ☑01 42 36 10 96; www.rexclub.com; 5 bd Poissonnière, 2e; ☺midnight-7am Wed-Sat; ⓜBonne Nouvelle) Attached to the art deco Grand Rex cinema, this is Paris' premier house and techno venue where some of the world's hottest DJs strut their stuff on a 70-speaker, multidiffusion sound system.

Angelina Teahouse

(Map p246; ☑01 42 60 82 00; www.angelina-paris.fr; 226 rue de Rivoli, 1er; ☺7.30am-7pm Mon-Fri, 8.30am-7.30pm Sat & Sun; ⓜTuileries) Clink china with lunching ladies, their posturing poodles and half the students from Tokyo University at Angelina, a grande-dame tearoom dating from 1903. Decadent pastries are served here, but it's the super-thick 'African' hot chocolate (€8.20), which comes with a pot of whipped cream and a carafe of water, that prompts the constant queue for a table.

🌐 Montmartre & Northern Paris

Le Syndicat Cocktail Bar

(Map p250; http://syndicatcocktailclub.com; 51 rue du Faubourg St-Denis, 10e; ☺6pm-2am Mon-Sat, 7pm-2am Sun; ⓜChâteau d'Eau) Plastered top to bottom in peeling posters, an otherwise unmarked façade conceals one of Paris' hottest cocktail bars, but it's no fly-by-night. Le Syndicat's subtitle, Organisation de Défense des Spiritueux Français, reflects its impassioned commitment to French spirits. Ingeniously crafted (and named) cocktails include Saix en Provence (Armagnac, chilli syrup, lime and lavender).

Le Très Particulier Cocktail Bar

(Map p249; ☑01 53 41 81 40; www.hotel-particulier-montmartre.com; Pavillon D, 23 av Junot, 18e; ☺6pm-2am; ⓜLamarck–Caulaincourt) The clandestine cocktail bar of boutique Hôtel Particulier Montmartre is an entrancing spot for a summertime al fresco cocktail. Ring the buzzer at the unmarked black gated entrance and make a beeline for the

Tea and cake, Angelina (p173)

1871 mansion's flowery walled garden (or, if it's raining, the adjacent conservatory-style interior). DJs spin tunes from 9.30pm Wednesday to Saturday and from 7pm on Sunday.

Gravity Bar   Cocktail Bar
(Map p254; 44 rue des Vinaigriers, 10e; ⊙6pm-2am Tue-Sat; Ⓜ Jacques Bonsergent) Gravity's stunning wave-like interior, crafted from slats of plywood descending to the curved concrete bar, threatens to distract from the business at hand – serious cocktails, such as Back to My Roots (Provence herb-infused vodka, vermouth, raspberry purée and lemon juice), best partaken in the company of excellent and inventive tapas-style small plates like clam gnocchi.

Pavillon Puebla   Beer Garden
(Map p254; https://leperchoir.tv; Parc des Buttes Chaumont, 39 av Simon Bolivar, 19e; ⊙6pm-2am Wed-Fri, noon-2am Sat, noon-10pm Sun; 🛜; Ⓜ Buttes Chaumont) Strung with fairy lights, this rustic ivy-draped cottage's two rambling terraces in the Parc des Buttes Chaumont evoke a *guinguette*

(old-fashioned outdoor tavern/dance venue), with a 21st-century vibe provided by its Moroccan decor, contemporary furniture, and DJ beats from Thursdays to Saturdays. Alongside mostly French wines and craft beers, cocktails include its signature Spritz du Pavillon (Aperol, prosecco and soda).

Paname Brewing Company   Brewery
(www.panamebrewingcompany.com; 41bis quai de la Loire, 19e; ⊙11am-2am; 🛜; Ⓜ Crimée, Laumiere) Spectacularly situated in an industrial 1850s former granary on Bassin de la Villette, Paname's tap room has floor-to-ceiling windows and opens to a terrace shaded by an ancient cherry tree and a floating table-strewn pontoon. Its five seasonal beers typically include a pilsner, session, märzen, Berliner Weisse, pale ale or IPA (look out for them around Paris too).

Café Lomi   Coffee
(☏09 80 39 56 24; https://lomi.paris; 3ter rue Marcadet, 18e; ⊙8am-6pm Mon-Fri, 10am-7pm Sat & Sun; Ⓜ Marcadet–Poissonniers) Lomi's internationally sourced beans are roasted

here on site in the multiethnic La Goutte d'Or neighbourhood adjacent to its cafe. Brews include filter coffee (mug, Aeropress or Chemex) and wacky creations like Bleu d'Auvergne cheese dipped in espresso or tonic water with espresso. Three-hour coffee workshops in French or English (filter techniques, world coffee tours, latte art) start from €72.

Chez Prune Bar

(Map p254; 36 rue Beaurepaire, 10e, cnr quai de Valmy; ⏰8am-2am Mon-Sat, 10am-2am Sun; Ⓜ Jacques Bonsergent, République) This boho cafe put Canal St-Martin on the map and its good vibes, original mosaic-tiled interior and rough-around-the-edges look show no sign of disappearing in the near future. Chez Prune remains one of those timeless classic Paris addresses, fabulous for hanging out and people-watching any time of day. Weekend brunch buzzes.

La Fontaine de Belleville Coffee

(Map p254; http://lafontaine.cafesbelleville. com; 31-33 rue Juliette Dodu, 10e; ⏰8am-10pm; Ⓜ Colonel Fabien) Beans roasted by Belleville Brûlerie are the toast of Paris and the roastery has since opened its own cafe near Canal St-Martin, updating a long-standing local corner spot with gold lettering, woven sky-blue-and-cream bistro chairs and matching tables, and retaining its vintage fittings. Spectacular coffee is complemented by sandwiches, salads and small sharing plates.

CopperBay Cocktail Bar

(Map p254; www.copperbay.fr; 5 rue Bouchardon, 10e; ⏰6pm-2am Tue-Sat; Ⓜ Strasbourg–St-Denis) This sleek cocktail bar's floor-to-ceiling windows, polished pale-wood decor and glistening copper fixtures and fittings inject a generous dose of design flair into proceedings. The cocktail menu mixes classics with house specials such as L'Orangeraie (Japanese pepper-infused gin, ginger, lemon juice and orange blossom water) and Le Bouillon (coriander-infused vodka, red lentil purée, verjus, mezcal and zaatar syrup).

Nightlife: Clubbing & Live Music

Paris' residential make-up means nightclubs aren't ubiquitous. Lacking a mainstream scene, clubbing here tends to be underground and extremely mobile. The best DJs and their followings have short stints in a certain venue before moving on, and the scene's hippest *soirées clubbing* (clubbing events) float between venues – including the many dance-driven bars. In 2017 floating club Concrete (p180) became France's first to have a 24-hour licence. Dedicated clubbers may also want to check out the growing suburban scene – much more alternative and spontaneous in nature but also harder to reach.

Wherever you wind up, the beat is strong. Electronic music is of particularly high quality in Paris' clubs, with some excellent local house and techno. Funk and groove are also popular, and the Latin scene is huge; salsa-dancing and Latino-music nights pack out plenty of clubs. World music also has a following in Paris, where everything – from Algerian raï to Senegalese *mbalax* and West Indian *zouk* – goes at clubs. R&B and hip-hop pickings are decent, if not extensive.

Track tomorrow's hot 'n' happening soirée with these finger-on-the-pulse Parisian-nightlife links:

Paris DJs (www.parisdjs.com) Free downloads to get you in the groove.

Paris Bouge (www.parisbouge.com) Comprehensive listings site.

Sortir à Paris (www.sortiraparis.com) Click on 'Soirées & Bars', then 'Nuits Parisiennes'.

Tribu de Nuit (www.tribudenuit.com) Parties, club events and concerts galore.

Hardware Société Coffee

(Map p249; ☎01 42 51 69 03; 10 rue Lamarck, 18e; ⏰9am-4pm Mon-Fri, 9.30am-4.30pm Sat & Sun; 🛜; Ⓜ Château Rouge) With its Christian

Paris in a Glass

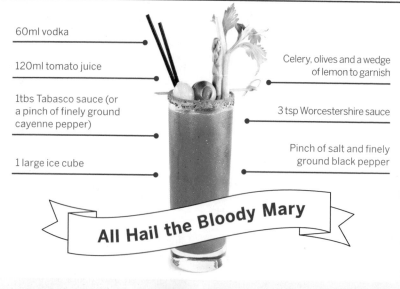

60ml vodka

120ml tomato juice

1tbs Tabasco sauce (or a pinch of finely ground cayenne pepper)

1 large ice cube

Celery, olives and a wedge of lemon to garnish

3 tsp Worcestershire sauce

Pinch of salt and finely ground black pepper

WOLLERTZ/SHUTTERSTOCK ©

All Hail the Bloody Mary

Best Bars for a Bloody Mary

Harry's New York Bar (p172)

Bar Hemingway (p171)

PasDeLoup (p177)

Tasting Notes

Sharp, piquant and refreshingly savoury, a Bloody Mary is ideal at any time of year, with the spicy heat balanced by the cooling tomato juice. Variations involve swapping vodka for gin or adding horseradish. Santé!

The Story Behind the Cocktail

The Bloody Mary was born in 1920s Paris at Harry's New York Bar, when Parisian barman Fernand 'Pete' Petiot experimented with newly available Russian vodka (distilled by immigrants who'd fled the Russian Revolution) and newly invented canned tomato juice.

It was christened by Harry's customer American singer/pianist Roy Barton after the Chicago nightclub Bucket of Blood and its waitress, Mary.

Lacroix butterflies fluttering across one wall, a black-and-white floor, and perfect love-heart-embossed cappuccinos, this is a fine spot around the Sacré-Cœur to linger over superb barista-crafted coffee (yes, that is a Slayer espresso machine). It's the Paris outpost of Melbourne's Hardware Société, with bountiful breakfasts and brunches served at marble-topped tables.

Lipstick
Cocktail Bar

(Map p249; www.lipstickparis.com; 5 rue Frochot, 9e; ☺6pm-5am Tue-Sat; ⓂPigalle) If the name isn't a clue, the decor certainly is: its bordello-like leopard-print lounges, red velour drapes and a pole in the centre of the bar reflect its former incarnation as a brothel in this gentrifying red-light district. Stupendous cocktails include Queen P (rose syrup, gin, Aperol, ginger ale and grapefruit juice).

Lulu White
Cocktail Bar

(Map p249; www.luluwhite.bar; 12 rue Frochot, 9e; ☺7pm-2am Mon, Wed, Thu & Sun, to 4am Fri & Sat; ⓂPigalle) Sip absinthe-based cocktails in Prohibition-era New Orleans surrounds at this elegant, serious and supremely busy cocktail bar named for an infamous early-20th-century brothel owner. It hosts regular live jazz and folk music.

❸ Le Marais, Ménilmontant & Belleville

Candelaria
Cocktail Bar

(Map p254; www.quixotic-projects.com; 52 rue de Saintonge, 3e; ☺bar 6pm-2am, taqueria noon-10.30pm Sun-Wed, noon-11.30pm Thu-Sat; ⓂFilles du Calvaire) A lime-green *taqueria* serving homemade tacos, quesadillas and tostadas conceals one of Paris' coolest cocktail bars through an unmarked internal door. Phenomenal cocktails made from agave spirits including mezcal are inspired by Central and South America, such as a Guatemalan El Sombrerón (tequila, vermouth, bitters, hibiscus syrup, pink-pepper-infused tonic and lime). Weekend evenings kick off with DJ sets.

Le Perchoir
Rooftop Bar

(Map p254; ☎01 48 06 18 48; http://leperchoir. tv; 14 rue Crespin du Gast, 11e; ☺6pm-2am Tue-Fri, 4pm-2am Sat; ☎; ⓂMénilmontant) Sunset is the best time to head up to this 7th-floor bar for a drink overlooking Paris' rooftops, where DJs spin on Saturday nights. Greenery provides shade in summer; in winter, it's covered by a sail-like canopy and warmed by fires burning in metal drums. It's accessed off an inner courtyard via a lift (or a spiralling staircase).

Beans on Fire
Coffee

(Map p254; https://thebeansonfire.com; 7 rue du Général Blaise, 11e; ☺8.30am-5pm Mon-Fri, 9.30am-6pm Sat & Sun; ☎; ⓂSt-Ambroise) Outstanding coffee is guaranteed at this innovative space. Not only a welcoming local cafe, it's also a collaborative roastery, where movers and shakers on Paris' reignited coffee scene come to roast their beans (ask about two-hour roasting workshops, available in English, if you're keen to roast your own). Overlooking a park, the terrace is a neighbourhood hotspot on sunny days.

PasDeLoup
Cocktail Bar

(Map p254; ☎09 54 74 16 36; www.pasdeloup paris.com; 108 rue Amelot, 11e; ☺6pm-1am Mon-Wed, to 2am Thu-Sat, to midnight Sun; ⓂFilles du Calvaire) Next to the Cirque d'Hiver Bouglione (Winter Circus), a small front bar with timber shelving gives way to a larger space out back where epicureans head for stunning cocktails such as Gardenia (absinthe, St-Germain elderflower liqueur, freshly squeezed OJ and lime) accompanied by superbly gourmet small plates and a loungey retro soundtrack. Happy hour runs from 6pm to 8pm.

The Hood
Cafe

(Map p254; www.thehoodparis.com; 80 rue Jean-Pierre Timbaud, 11e; ☺9.30am-5.30pm Mon & Wed-Fri, 10am-6pm Sat & Sun; ☎; ⓂParmentier) First and foremost this light-filled local hangout is about the coffee (Parisian-roasted Belleville Brûlerie beans are brewed to absolute perfection here), but it takes its music just as seriously with a great vinyl collection,

Gay & Lesbian Venues

Le Marais, especially the areas around the intersection of rue Ste-Croix de la Bretonnerie and rue des Archives, and eastwards to rue Vieille du Temple, has long been Paris' main centre of gay night-life and is still the epicentre of gay and lesbian life in Paris. Bars and clubs are generally all gay- and lesbian-friendly.

Top Choices:

Open Café (Map p254; www.opencafe.fr; 17 rue des Archives, 4e; ⊙11am-2am Sun-Thu, to 3am Fri & Sat; MHôtel de Ville) The wide terrace is prime for talent-watching.

Gibus Club (Map p254; ☑01 77 15 73 09; http://gibusclub.fr; 18 rue du Faubourg du Temple, 11e; admission €12-25; ⊙11pm-7am Thu-Sat; MRépublique) One of Paris' big-gest gay parties.

3w Kafé (Map p254; www.facebook.com/3wkafe; 8 rue des Écouffes, 4e; ⊙7pm-3am Wed & Sun, to 4am Thu, to 6.30am Fri & Sat; MSt-Paul) Flagship lesbian cocktail bar-pub.

spontaneous jam sessions and acoustic Sunday-afternoon 'folkoff' gigs. Fantastic lunches might include cinnamon-roasted chicken with red cabbage and soba noodles. Ask about English-language coffee-brewing workshops.

Boot Café   Coffee
(Map p254; 19 rue du Pont aux Choux, 3e; ⊙10am-6pm; ♠; MSt-Sébastien–Froissart) The charm of this three-table cafe is its façade. An old cobbler's shop, its original washed-blue exterior, 'Cordonnerie' lettering and fantastic red boot sign above are beautiful-ly preserved. Excellent coffee is roasted in Paris, to boot.

Café Charbon   Bar
(Map p254; www.lecafecharbon.fr; 109 rue Ober-kampf, 11e; ⊙8am-2am Mon-Wed, to 5am Thu, to 6am Fri & Sat; ♠; MParmentier) Canopied by a gold-stencilled navy-blue awning, Charbon

was the first of the hip bars to catch on in Ménilmontant and it remains one of the best. It's always crowded and worth heading to for the belle époque decor (high ceilings, chandeliers and leather booths) and sociable atmosphere. Happy hour is 5pm to 8pm; DJs and musicians play Friday and Saturday.

Cinéma Café Merci   Cafe
(Map p254; www.merci-merci.com; 111 bd Beaumarchais, 3e; ⊙11am-2pm Mon-Sat; MSt-Sébastien–Froissart) Dedicated to the seventh art, this street-level cafe inside concept store Merci (p153) is graced with retro film posters and projects vintage films on one wall. Its *citronnade maison* – extra tart and tongue-tickling, homemade lem-onade – and freshly squeezed fruit juices are worth every cent; alternatively you can get a glass of Champagne to accompany its excellent lunchtime salads and cheese/charcuterie platters.

La Belle Hortense   Bar
(Map p254; www.cafeine.com/belle-hortense; 31 rue Vieille du Temple, 4e; ⊙5pm-2am; MHôtel de Ville) Behind its charming chambray-blue-painted façade, this creative wine bar named after a Jacques Roubaud novel fuses shelf after shelf of lit-erary novels with an excellent wine list, rare varieties of armagnac, cognac, calvados and pastis, and an enriching weekly agenda of book readings, signings and art events.

La Caféothèque   Coffee
(Map p254; ☑01 53 01 83 84; www.lacafe otheque.com; 52 rue de l'Hôtel de Ville, 4e; ⊙8.30am-7.30pm Mon-Fri, noon-7.30pm Sat & Sun; ♠; MPont Marie, St-Paul) From the in-dustrial grinder to elaborate tasting notes, this coffee house and roastery is serious. Grab a seat, and pick your bean, filtration method (Aeropress, V60 filter, piston or drip) and preparation style. The in-house coffee school has tastings of different *crus* and various courses including two-hour Saturday-morning tasting initiations (five *terroirs*, five extraction methods) for €60 (English available).

Le Mary Céleste — Cocktail Bar

(Map p254; www.quixotic-projects.com/venue/mary-celeste; 1 rue Commines, 3e; ☺6pm-2am, kitchen 7-11.30pm; MFilles du Calvaire) Snag a stool at the central circular bar at this uber-popular brick-and-timber-floored cocktail bar or reserve one of a handful of tables in advance online. Innovative cocktails such as Ahha Kapehna (grappa, absinthe, beetroot, fennel and Champagne) are the perfect partner to tapas-style 'small plates' (grilled duck hearts, devilled eggs) to share.

Little Red Door — Cocktail Bar

(Map p254; ☎01 42 71 19 32; www.lrdparis.com; 60 rue Charlot, 3e; ☺6pm-2am Sun-Thu, to 3am Fri & Sat; MFilles du Calvaires) Behind an inconspicuous timber façade, a tiny crimson doorway is the illusionary portal to this low-lit, bare-brick drinking den filled with flickering candles. Ranked among the World's 50 Best Bars, it's a must for serious mixology fans. Its annual collection of 11 cocktails, in themes from 'art' to 'architecture', are intricately crafted from ingredients like glacier ice and paper syrup.

Ob-La-Di — Coffee

(Map p254; 54 rue de Saintonge, 3e; ☺8am-5pm Mon-Fri, 9am-6pm Sat & Sun; MFilles du Calvaire) Coffee roasted by Paris' Café Lomi is the big draw of this pocket-sized coffee shop, clad with large mirrors, geometric blue-and-white tiles and glass vases of fresh flowers. It's not designed for hanging out with your laptop, but the crowd is hip, and the *café*, cookies, cakes and dishes such as poached pear, ricotta and honey on toast are superb.

Sherry Butt — Cocktail Bar

(Map p254; www.sherrybuttparis.com; 20 rue Beautreillis, 4e; ☺6pm-2am Tue-Sat, 8pm-2am Sun & Mon; MBastille) Named for the sherry-seasoned oak casks used to age whisky, this dimly lit, stone-walled bar is one for serious cocktail connoisseurs. Seasonal menus might include Sherring is Caring (sweet and dry sherries, tonka bean syrup, lemon and soda) or Nux Aeterna (cognac, sweet sherry, red-wine-based Byrrh, dry vermouth and chocolate liqueur). It's standing room only on weekends when DJs play.

Café Charbon

PHOTO 12/ALAMY STOCK PHOTO ©

From left: Pastries, Les Deux Magots (p183); Café de Flore (p184); Le Baron Rouge

◉ Bastille & Eastern Paris

Concrete   Club
(www.concreteparis.fr; 69 Port de la Rapée, 12e; ⊙Thu-Sun; ⓜGare de Lyon) Moored by Gare de Lyon on a barge on the Seine, this wild-child club with two dance floors is famed for introducing an 'after-hours' element to Paris' somewhat staid clubbing scene, with the country's first 24-hour licence. Watch for world-class electro DJ appearances and all-weekend events on social media.

Le Baron Rouge   Wine Bar
(Map p254; ☎01 43 43 14 32; www.lebaronrouge. net; 1 rue Théophile Roussel, 12e; ⊙5-10pm Mon, 10am-2pm & 5-10pm Tue-Fri, 10am-10pm Sat, 10am-4pm Sun; ⓜLedru-Rollin) Just about the ultimate Parisian wine-bar experience, this wonderfully unpretentious local meeting place where everyone is welcome has barrels stacked against the bottle-lined walls and serves cheese, charcuterie and oysters in season. It's especially busy on Sunday after the Marché d'Aligre wraps up. For a small deposit, you can fill up 1L bottles straight from the barrel for under €5.

Outland   Craft Beer
(Map p254; https://outland-beer.com; 6 rue Emile Lepeu, 11e; ⊙6pm-2am Mon-Sat, to midnight Sun; ⓜCharonne) Of the 12 beers offered on tap at this artisanal beer bar, eight are Outland's own, brewed just east of central Paris in Fontenay-sous-Bois near the Bois de Vincennes. Among them are a double IPA, a session pale ale, a porter and a fabulously fermented plum göse. Soak up the beers with tapas including duck liver pâté, organic burrata and stuffed calamari.

Café des Anges   Cafe
(Map p254; ☎01 47 00 00 63; www.cafe desangesparis.com; 66 rue de la Roquette, 11e; ⊙7.30am-2am; ⓡ; ⓜBastille) With its pastel-shaded paintwork and locals sipping coffee beneath the terracotta-coloured awning on its busy pavement terrace, Angels Cafe lives up to the 'quintessential Paris cafe' dream. In winter wrap up beneath a blanket outside, or squeeze through the crowds at the zinc bar to snag a coveted table inside. Happy hour runs from 5pm to 9pm.

HEMIS/ALAMY STOCK PHOTO ©

Septime La Cave   Wine Bar

(Map p254; www.septime-charonne.fr; 3 rue
Basfroi, 11e; ⊙4-11pm; ⓜCharonne) Run by
Michelin-starred Septime (p134), this rustic
wine bar is an atmospheric spot to linger
over an *apéro* while waiting for a table at
one of the hip dining addresses around
the corner on foodie rue de Charonne. Sit
at the bar and enjoy exceptional, mostly
natural French wines paired with gourmet
nibbles. No reservations.

Bluebird   Cocktail Bar

(Map p254; 12 rue St-Bernard, 11e; ⊙6pm-2am;
ⓜFaidherbe-Chaligny) The ultimate neighbourhood hang-out, Bluebird is styled like
a 1950s apartment with retro decor, a giant
fish tank along one wall, and a soundtrack
of smooth lounge music. Cocktail recipes
date from the 1800s and early 1900s and
change seasonally, but the menu always
features six gin-based creations, six with
other spirits, and three low-alcohol wine-
and Champagne-based drinks.

Le Pure Café   Cafe

(Map p254; www.lepurecafe.fr; 14 rue Jean Macé,
11e; ⊙7am-1am Mon-Fri, 8am-1am Sat, 9am-mid-

night Sun; ⓜCharonne) A classic Parisian
corner cafe, Le Pure is a charming spot
to drop into for a morning coffee, aperitif, contemporary bistro meal or Sunday
brunch. Its selection of natural and organic
wines by the glass is particularly good. Film
buffs might recognise its cherry-red façade
and vintage-wood and zinc bar from the
Richard Linklater film *Before Sunset*.

🍷 Latin Quarter

Shakespeare &
Company Café   Cafe

(Map p252; ☑01 43 25 95 95; www.shakespeare
andcompany.com; 2 rue St-Julien le Pauvre, 5e;
⊙9.30am-7pm Mon-Fri, to 8pm Sat & Sun; 🛜;
ⓜSt-Michel) 🍃 Instant history was made
when this literary-inspired cafe opened in
2015 adjacent to magical bookshop Shakespeare & Company (p159), designed from
long-lost sketches to fulfil a dream of late
bookshop founder George Whitman from
the 1960s. Organic chai tea, turbo-power
juices and specialist coffee by Parisian
roaster Café Lomi (p174) marry with soups,

salads, bagels and pastries by Bob's Bake Shop of **Bob's Juice Bar** (Map p254; ☑09 50 06 36 18; www.bobsjuicebar.com; 15 rue Lucien Sampaix, 10e; dishes €3.50-6, pastries €1.75-3; ⊙8am-3pm Mon-Fri, 8.30am-4pm Sat; ☑; Ⓜ Jacques Bonsergent).

Little Bastards · Cocktail Bar

(Map p252; ☑01 43 54 28 33; www.facebook.com/lilbastards; 5 rue Blainville, 5e; ⊙6pm-2am Mon-Thu, 6pm-4am Fri & Sat; Ⓜ Place Monge) Only house-creation cocktails (€12) are listed on the menu at uberhip Little Bastards – among them Balance Ton Cochon (bacon-infused rum, egg white, lime juice, oak wood–smoked syrup and bitters) and Deep Throat (Absolut vodka, watermelon syrup and Pernod). The barmen will mix up classics too if you ask.

Nuage · Cafe

(Map p252; ☑09 82 39 80 69; www.nuagecafe.fr; 14 rue des Carmes, 5e; per hr/day €5/25; ⊙8.30am-7pm Mon-Fri, 11am-8pm Sat & Sun; ☜; Ⓜ Maubert-Mutualité) One of a crop of co-working cafes to mushroom in Paris, Nuage (Cloud) lures a loyal following of nomadic digital creatives with its cosy, home-like spaces in an old church (and subsequent school where Cyrano de Bergerac apparently studied). Payment for space is by the hour or day, craft coffee is by Parisian roaster Coutume and gourmet snacks stave off hunger pangs. Super-fast wi-fi, books to browse, games to play, music and a silent zone only add to the appeal.

Le Verre à Pied · Cafe

(Map p252; ☑01 43 31 15 72; 118bis rue Mouffetard, 5e; ⊙9am-9pm Tue-Sat, 9.30am-4pm Sun; Ⓜ Censier Daubenton) This *café-tabac* is a pearl of a place where little has changed since 1870. Its nicotine-hued mirrored wall, moulded cornices and original bar make it part of a dying breed, but it epitomises the charm, glamour and romance of an old Paris everyone loves, including stallholders from the rue Mouffetard market who yo-yo in and out.

Strada Café · Coffee

(Map p252; www.stradacafe.fr; 24 rue Monge, 5e; ⊙8am-6.30pm Mon-Fri, 10am-6.30pm Sat & Sun; ☜; Ⓜ Cardinal Lemoine) Beans from Parisian roastery L'Arbre à Café and Lyon's Mokxa

Les Deux Magots

roastery underpin the success of this sunlit corner cafe, strewn with an eclectic mix of armchairs and wooden-chair seating. Electrical sockets are plentiful (no laptops at weekends) and baristas are passionate about their brews. Breakfast, salad-and-soup lunch (€11.50 to €13.50), weekend brunch (€22) and gluten-free cakes.

⊕ St-Germain & Les Invalides

Les Deux Magots   Cafe

(Map p246; 📞01 45 48 55 25; www.lesdeux magots.fr; 170 bd St-Germain, 6e; ⊙7.30am-1am; Ⓜ St-Germain des Prés) If ever there was a cafe that summed up St-Germain des Prés' early-20th-century literary scene, it's this former hang-out of anyone who was anyone. You'll spend substantially more here than elsewhere to sip *un café* (€4.70) in a wicker-woven bistro chair on the pavement terrace shaded by dark-green awnings and geraniums spilling from window boxes, but it's an undeniable piece of Parisian history.

If you're feeling decadent, order its famous shop-made hot chocolate (without/with whipped cream €8/10), served in porcelain jugs. The name refers to the two *magots* (grotesque figurines) of Chinese dignitaries at the entrance.

Au Sauvignon   Wine Bar

(Map p246; 📞01 45 48 49 02; http://ausauvi gnon.com; 80 rue des Sts-Pères, 7e; ⊙8am-11pm Mon-Sat, 9am-10pm Sun; Ⓜ Sèvres-Babylone) Grab a table in the evening light at this wonderfully authentic wine bar or head to the quintessential bistro interior, with original zinc bar, tightly packed tables and hand-painted ceiling celebrating French viticultural tradition. A plate of *casse-croûtes au pain Poilâne* (toast with ham, pâté, terrine, smoked salmon and foie gras) is the perfect accompaniment.

Coutume Café   Coffee

(Map p246; 📞01 45 51 50 47; www.coutumecafe. com; 47 rue de Babylone, 7e; ⊙8.30am-5.30pm Mon-Fri, 9am-6pm Sat & Sun; 📶; Ⓜ St-François

Coffee & Tea

Coffee has always been Parisians' drink of choice to kick-start the day. So it's surprising, particularly given France's fixation on quality, that Parisian coffee long lagged behind world standards, with burnt, poor-quality beans and unrefined preparation methods. Recently, however, Paris' coffee revolution has seen local roasteries like Belleville Brûlerie and Coutume priming cafes citywide for outstanding brews made by professional baristas, often using cutting-edge extraction techniques. Caffeine fiends are now spoilt for choice and while there's still plenty of sub-standard coffee in Paris, you don't have to go far to avoid it.

Surprisingly, too, tea – more strongly associated with France's northwestern neighbours the UK and Ireland – is extremely popular in Paris. Tearooms offer copious varieties; learn about its history at the tea museum within the original Marais branch of **Mariage Frères** (www. mariagefreres.com; 30, 32 & 35 rue du Bourg Tibourg, 4e; ⊙10am-8pm; Ⓜ Hôtel de Ville).

Xavier) 🍃 The Parisian coffee revolution is thanks in no small part to Coutume, artisan roaster of premium beans for scores of establishments around town. Its flagship cafe – a bright, light-filled, postindustrial space – is ground zero for innovative preparation methods including cold extraction and siphon brews. Couple some of Paris' finest coffee with a tasty, seasonal cuisine and the place is always packed out.

Cod House   Cocktail Bar

(📞01 42 49 35 59; www.thecodhouse.fr; 1 rue de Condé, 6e; ⊙noon-3pm & 7.30-2am Mon-Sat; Ⓜ Odéon) 'Oh my cod!' screams the turquoise-neon 'tag' on the wall, and indeed, this achingly cool cocktail bar with a gold-and-blue, Scandinavian-style interior does excite. Sake-based cocktails

Café de Flore

play around with matcha-infused cachaça, cinnamon-infused pisco, homemade lemongrass syrup and fresh yuzu; while creative small plates (€5 to €16) titillate tastebuds with shrimp tempura, yellow-tail carpaccio with fresh chilli and a yuzu sauce, deep-fried chicken ravioli et al.

Le Bar des Prés — Cocktail Bar
(Map p246; ☑01 43 25 87 67; www.lebardespres. com; 25 rue du Dragon, 6e; ⊙noon-2.30pm & 7-11pm; MSt-Sulpice) Sake-based craft cocktails and tantalising shared plates (€18 to €24) by a Japanese chef create buzz at the chic cocktail-bar arm of Cyril Lignac's foodie empire. His glam, 1950s-styled bistro **Aux Prés** (Map p246; ☑01 45 48 29 68; www.restaurantauxpres.com; 27 rue du Dragon, 6e; 2-/3-course menu €38/49; ⊙noon-2.30pm & 7-11pm) is right next door. The scallops with caramelised miso, avocado and fresh coriander are heavenly, as is the yellow tail sashimi, jellied eel and other sushi.

Café de Flore — Cafe
(Map p246; ☑01 45 48 55 26; http://cafedeflore. fr; 172 bd St-Germain, 6e; ⊙7.30am-1.30am;

MSt-Germain des Prés) The red upholstered benches, mirrors and marble walls at this art deco landmark haven't changed much since the days when Jean-Paul Sartre and Simone de Beauvoir essentially set up office here, writing in its warmth during the Nazi occupation. Watch for monthly English-language *philocafé* (philosophy discussion) sessions.

Castor Club — Cocktail Bar
(Map p252; ☑09 50 64 99 38; 14 rue Hautefeuille, 6e; ⊙7pm-2am Tue & Wed, 7pm-4am Thu-Sat; MOdéon) Discreetly signed, this superb underground cocktail bar has an intimate English Gentleman's Club–style upstairs bar with vintage wall lamps and slinky, red velour stools. But it's downstairs, in the 18th-century stone cellar with hole-in-the-wall booths, that the real cocktail-sipping action happens. Smooth '50s, '60s and '70s tracks only add to the already cool vibe.

Frappé by Bloom — Cafe, Bar
(Map p250; ☑07 89 83 79 58; http://frappe. bloom-restaurant.fr; 2 rue Guénégaud, 6e,

Monnaie de Paris; ⊗8.30am-7pm Tue & Wed, 8.30am-midnight Thu & Fri, 10.30am-midnight Sat, 10.30am-7pm Sun; MPont Neuf) In keeping with Paris' penchant for stylish museum eateries, its 18th-century mint sports a super-stylish cafe-cum-cocktail bar with designer interior and one of the city's loveliest summertime terraces – in Cour de la Méridienne, one of the Monnaie de Paris' (p88) elegant neoclassical courtyards.

La Palette   Cafe

(Map p250; www.cafelapaletteparis.com; 43 rue de Seine, 6e; ⊗8am-2am; 🛜; MMabillon) In the heart of gallery land, this timeless *fin de siècle* cafe and erstwhile stomping ground of Paul Cézanne and Georges Braque attracts a grown-up set of fashion-industry professionals and local art dealers. Its summer terrace is beautiful.

Noglu   Cafe

(Map p246; ☑01 58 90 18 12; www.noglu.fr; 69 rue de Grenelle, 6e; ⊗8.30am-7pm Mon & Tue, 8.30am-10pm Wed-Fri, 9am-10pm Sat, 10am-6pm Sun; MRue du Bac) Put the kick back in your shopping stride with a coffee break at Noglu, a pretty-in-pink, mirrored cafe and *salon de thé* (tearoom) with – drumroll – almond, soya or rice milk only and strictly gluten-free cakes, cookies and savoury lunchtime fare. It also serves breakfast (the porridge, scones, croissants and sweet brioches are all gluten-free and organic).

Prescription Cocktail Club   Cocktail Bar

(Map p252; ☑09 50 35 72 87; www.prescription cocktailclub.com; 23 rue Mazarine, 6e; ⊗7pm-2am Mon-Thu, 7pm-4am Fri & Sat, 8pm-2am Sun; MOdéon) With bowler and flat-top hats as lampshades and a 1930s speakeasy New York air to the place, this cocktail club – run by the same mega-successful team as Experimental Cocktail Club (ECC; p171) – is very Parisian-cool. Getting past the doorman can be tough, but, once in, it's friendliness and old-fashioned cocktails all round.

Tiger   Cocktail Bar

(Map p252; www.tiger-paris.com; 13 rue Prin-cesse, 6e; ⊗6.30pm-2am Mon-Sat; MMabillon) Suspended bare-bulb lights and fretted timber make this split-level space a stylish spot for specialist gins (130 varieties). Signature cocktails include a Breakfast Martini (gin, triple sec, orange marma-lade and lemon juice) and Oh My Dog (white-pepper-infused gin, lime juice, raspberry and rose cordial and ginger ale). Dedicated G&T aficionados can work their way through a staggering 1040 combi-nations. Gin aside, Tiger serves Japanese sake, wine and craft beer.

❸ Montparnasse & Southern Paris

Le Batofar   Club

(☑01 53 60 37 85; www.batofar.fr; opposite 11 quai François Mauriac, 13e; ⊗6pm-7am Wed-Sat, to midnight Sun-Tue; MQuai de la Gare, Biblio-thèque) This much-loved, red-metal tugboat promises to be even more fabulous when it reopens post renovations. Its rooftop bar is a place to be seen in summer; it has a respected restaurant; and its club provides memorable underwater acoustics for edgy, experimental music and live performances (mostly electro-oriented but hip hop, new wave, rock, punk and jazz too).

Simone La Caves   Wine Bar

(☑01 43 37 82 70; www.simoneparis.com; 48 rue Pascal, 13e; ⊗5-11pm Tue-Sat; MLes Gobelins) Tucked away in the 13e, Simone La Cave lures a loyal wine-loving set keen to try its latest, outstanding natural and biodynamic wine selection. *Planches* (chopping boards, €10 to €15) stacked high with cured meats and boutique cheeses, oysters, pars-ley-marinated anchovies and homemade terrines provide the perfect accompani-ment. For more of the organic same, dine around the corner at **Simone Le Resto** (33 bd Arago, 13e; 2-/3-course lunch menu €18/22, tasting menu €49; ⊗noon-2.30pm & 7.30-10.30pm Tue-Fri, 7.30-10.30pm Sat).

SHOWTIME

Renowned ballet, opera, jazz clubs, street performers & buskers

Showtime

Catching a performance in Paris is a treat. French and international opera, ballet and theatre companies and cabaret dancers take to the stage in fabled venues, and a flurry of young, passionate, highly creative musicians, thespians and artists make the city's fascinating fringe art scene what it is. Paris became Europe's most important jazz centre after WWII and the city has some fantastic jazz clubs, as well as venues for stirring French chansons, dazzling cabarets including the iconic Moulin Rouge, cutting-edge cultural centres, wonderful independent cinemas, and dozens of orchestral, organ and chamber-music concerts each week.

In This Section

Tickets/Websites

The most convenient place to purchase concert, theatre and other cultural and sporting-event tickets is electronics and entertainment megashop Fnac (www.fnactickets.com), in person at the *billeteries* (ticket offices) or by phone or online. There are branches throughout Paris, including in the Forum des Halles. Tickets generally can't be refunded.

La Seine Musicale (p190)

Jazz Clubs

Café Universel (p194) Intimate club with unpretentious vibe and no cover.

New Morning (p192) Solid and varied line-up of everything from postbop and Latin to reggae.

Le Baiser Salé (p190) Reputable venue that focuses on Caribbean and Latin sounds.

Sunset & Sunside (p190) Blues, fusion and world sounds, as well as straight-up jazz.

Cave du 38 Riv' (p193) Rue de Rivoli jazz club with concerts and jam sessions.

Lonely Planet's Top Choices

Palais Garnier (p190) Paris' premier opera house is an artistic inspiration.

Point Éphémère (p192) Uber-cool cultural centre on the banks of Canal St-Martin.

Moulin Rouge (p191) The can-can creator razzle-dazzles with spectacular sets, costumes and choreography.

La Seine Musicale (p190) Magnificent 2017-opened concert venue on a Seine island.

✪ Eiffel Tower & Western Paris

La Seine Musicale   Concert Venue

(🖉01 74 34 54 00; www.laseinemusicale.com; Île Seguin, Boulogne-Billancourt; Ⓜ Pont de Sèvres) A landmark addition to Paris' cultural offerings, La Seine Musicale opened on the Seine island of Île Seguin in 2017. Constructed of steel and glass, the egg-shaped auditorium has a capacity of 1150, while the larger, modular concrete hall accommodates 6000. Ballets, musicals and concerts from classical to rock are all staged here, alongside exhibitions.

✪ Champs-Élysées & Grands Boulevards

Palais Garnier   Opera, Ballet

(Map p246; place de l'Opéra, 9e; Ⓜ Opéra) The city's original opera house (p100) is smaller than its Bastille counterpart, but has perfect acoustics. Due to its odd shape, some seats have limited or no visibility – book carefully. Ticket prices and conditions (including last-minute discounts) are available from the **box office** (Map p246; 🖉 international calls 01 71 25 24 23, within France 08 92 89 90 90; www.operadeparis.fr; cnr rues Scribe & Auber; ⊙10am-6.30pm Mon-Sat; Ⓜ Opéra). Online flash sales are held from noon on Wednesdays.

✪ Louvre & Les Halles

Le Baiser Salé   Live Music

(Map p250; 🖉01 42 33 37 71; www.lebaisersale. com; 58 rue des Lombards, 1er; ⊙daily, hours vary; Ⓜ Châtelet) Known for its Afro and Latin jazz, and jazz fusion concerts, the Salty Kiss combines big names and unknown artists. The place has a relaxed vibe, with sets usually starting at 7.30pm or 9.30pm.

La Place   Cultural Centre

(Map p250; 🖉01 70 22 45 48; http://laplace. paris; 10 passage de la Canopée, Forum des Halles, 1er; ⊙bar 1-7pm Tue-Sat, concert hours vary; Ⓜ Les Halles, RER Châtelet–Les Halles) The overhaul of the vast shopping mall Forum des Halles (p77) saw the launch of Paris' inaugural hip-hop cultural centre under its custard-yellow glass canopy, with a 400-capacity concert hall, a 100-capacity broadcast studio, several recording studios and street-art graffiti workrooms, along with a relaxed bar. Some concerts are free, while ticket prices vary for others – check the program online.

Le Grand Rex   Cinema

(Map p250; 🖉01 45 08 93 89; www.legrandrex. com; 1 bd Poissonnière, 2e; tours adult/child €11/9, cinema tickets adult/child €11/4.50; ⊙tours 10am-6pm Wed, Sat & Sun, extended hours during school holidays; Ⓜ Bonne Nouvelle) Blockbuster screenings and concerts aside, this 1932 art deco cinematic icon runs 50-minute behind-the-scenes tours (English soundtracks available) during which visitors – tracked by a sensor slung around their neck – are whisked up (via a lift) behind the giant screen, tour a sound-stage and experiment in a recording studio. Whizz-bang special effects along the way will stun adults and kids alike.

Sunset & Sunside   Live Music

(Map p250; 🖉01 40 26 46 60; www.sunset-sunside.com; 60 rue des Lombards, 1er; ⊙daily, hours vary; Ⓜ Châtelet) There are two venues in one at this well-respected club, which hosts electric jazz, fusion and occasional salsa at Sunset, in the vaulted cellar, and acoustics and concerts on the ground floor at Sunside.

✪ Montmartre & Northern Paris

La Cigale   Live Music

(Map p249; 🖉01 49 25 89 99; www.lacigale.fr; 120 bd de Rochechouart, 18e; Ⓜ Pigalle) Now classed as a historical monument, this music hall dates from 1887 but was redecorated a century later by Philippe Starck. Artists who have performed here include

Ryan Adams, Ibrahim Maalouf and the Dandy Warhols.

Le Divan du Monde — Live Music
(Map p249; ☎01 40 05 08 10; www.divandu monde.com; 75 rue des Martyrs, 18e; MPigalle) Take some cinematographic events and *nouvelles chansons françaises* (new French songs). Add in soul/funk fiestas, air-guitar face-offs and rock parties of the Arctic Monkeys/Killers/Libertines persuasion... You may now be getting some idea of the inventive, open-minded approach at this excellent cross-cultural venue in Pigalle.

Le Louxor — Cinema
(Map p249; ☎01 44 63 96 98; www.cinema louxor.fr; 170 bd de Magenta, 10e; tickets adult/ child €9.70/5; MBarbès-Rochechouart) Built in neo-Egyptian art deco style in 1921 and saved from demolition by a neighbourhood association seven decades later, this historical monument is a palatial place to catch a new release, classic, piano-accompanied 'ciné-concert', short-film festival, special workshop (such as singalongs) or live-music performance. Don't miss a drink at its bar, which opens to an elevated terrace overlooking Sacré-Cœur.

Moulin Rouge — Cabaret
(Map p249; ☎01 53 09 82 82; www.moulinrouge. fr; 82 bd de Clichy, 18e; show only from €87, lunch & show from €165, dinner & show from €190; ⏰show only 2.45pm, 9pm & 11pm, lunch & show 1.45pm, dinner & show 7pm; MBlanche) Immortalised in Toulouse-Lautrec's posters and later in Baz Luhrmann's film, Paris' legendary cabaret twinkles beneath a 1925 replica of its original red windmill. Yes, it's packed with bus-tour crowds. But from the opening bars of music to the last high cancan kick, it's a whirl of fantastical costumes, sets, choreography and Champagne. Book in advance and dress smartly (no trainers/sneakers). No entry for children under six.

Philharmonie de Paris — Concert Venue
(☎01 44 84 44 84; http://philharmoniedeparis.fr; 221 av Jean Jaurès, 19e; ⏰box office noon-6pm

💬 Buskers in Paris

Paris' gaggle of clowns, mime artists, living statues, acrobats, in-line skaters, buskers and other street entertainers can be loads of fun and cost substantially less than a theatre ticket (a few coins in the hat is appreciated). Some excellent musicians perform in the long, echo-filled corridors of the metro (artists audition for the privilege). Outside, you can be sure of a good show at the following:

Place Georges Pompidou, 4e The huge square in front of the Centre Pompidou.

Pont St-Louis, 4e The bridge linking Paris' two islands.

Pont au Double, 4e The pedestrian bridge linking Notre Dame with the Left Bank.

Place Joachim du Bellay, 1er Musicians and fire-eaters near the Fontaine des Innocents.

Parc de la Villette, 19e African drummers at the weekend.

Place du Tertre, Montmartre, 18e Montmartre's original main square is Paris' busiest busker stage.

Street artist playing a barrel organ, Montmartre
ELENA DIJOUR/SHUTTERSTOCK ©

Tue-Fri, 10am-6pm Sat & Sun, plus concerts; MPorte de Pantin) Major complex the Cité de la Musique – Philharmonie de Paris hosts an eclectic range of concerts – from classical to North African and Japanese – in the 2015-inaugurated Philharmonie building's Grande Salle Pierre Boulez, with

Moulin Rouge (p191)

an audience capacity of 2400 to 3600. The adjacent Cité de la Musique's Salle des Concerts has a capacity of 900 to 1600.

Point Éphémère
Live Music

(☑01 40 34 02 48; www.pointephemere.org; 200 quai de Valmy, 10e; ⊙12.30pm-2am Mon-Sat, to 11pm Sun; 🛜; Ⓜ Jaurès, Louis Blanc) On the banks of Canal St-Martin in a former fire station and later squat, this arts and music venue attracts an underground crowd for concerts, dance nights and art exhibitions. Its rockin' restaurant, Animal Kitchen, fuses gourmet cuisine with music from Animal Records (Sunday brunch from 1pm is a highlight). The rooftop bar, Le Top, opens in fine weather.

New Morning
Jazz, Blues

(Map p250; ☑01 45 23 51 41; www.newmorning. com; 7-9 rue des Petites Écuries, 10e; Ⓜ Château d'Eau) This highly regarded auditorium with excellent acoustics hosts big-name jazz concerts (Ravi Coltrane, Lake Street Dive) as well as a variety of blues, rock, funk, salsa, Afro-Cuban and Brazilian music.

✪ Le Marais, Ménilmontant & Belleville

La Bellevilloise
Cultural Centre

(☑01 46 36 07 07; www.labellevilloise.com; 19-21 rue Boyer, 20e; ⊙7pm-1am Wed & Thu, 7pm-2am Fri, 11am-2am Sat, 11.30am-midnight Sun; Ⓜ Gambetta) Gigs, concerts, theatrical performances, exhibitions, readings, dance classes and workshops: this arts centre is where it all happens after dark in Ménilmontant. The trendy cafe-restaurant, with its sunlit tables beneath 100-year-old olive trees, is packed during Sunday brunch's two sittings (11.30am or 2pm, adult/child €29/13), which is accompanied by live jazz. Advance reservations are recommended.

Le Bataclan
Live Music

(Map p254; ☑01 43 14 00 30; www.bataclan.fr; 50 bd Voltaire, 11e; Ⓜ Oberkampf, Filles du Calvaire) Built in 1864, intimate concert, theatre and dance hall Le Bataclan was Maurice Chevalier's debut venue in 1910. The 1497-capacity venue reopened with a concert by Sting on 12 November 2016, almost a year to the day following the tragic 13 November 2015 terrorist attacks that took place here, and once again hosts French and international rock and pop legends.

Le Carreau du Temple
Cultural Centre

(Map p254; ☎01 83 81 93 30; www.carreaudu temple.eu; 2 rue Perrée, 3e; ⏱box office 10am-9pm Mon-Fri, to 7pm Sat; Ⓜ Temple) The quarter's old covered market with gorgeous art nouveau ironwork has been transformed into a striking cultural centre and entertainment venue. The place where silks, lace, leather and other materials were sold in the 19th century is now a vast stage for exhibitions, concerts, sports classes and theatre.

Cave du 38 Riv'
Jazz

(Map p254; ☎01 48 87 56 30; www.38riv.com; 38 rue de Rivoli, 4e; concerts €15-30; ⏱concerts from 8.30pm Mon-Sat, from 5pm Sun; Ⓜ Hôtel de Ville) In the heart of Le Marais on busy rue de Rivoli, a tiny street frontage gives way to a fantastically atmospheric vaulted stone cellar with jazz concerts most nights; check the agenda online. Jam sessions with free admission typically take place on Mondays, Thursdays and Fridays.

Le Vieux Belleville
Live Music

(Map p254; ☎01 44 62 92 66; www.le-vieux-belleville.com; 12 rue des Envierges, 20e; ⏱concerts 8pm-2am Tue & Thu-Sat; Ⓜ Pyrénées) This old-fashioned bistro and *musette* at the top of Parc de Belleville is an atmospheric venue for performances of *chansons* featuring accordions and an organ grinder three times a week. It's a lively favourite with locals, so booking ahead is advised.

La Java
World Music

(Map p254; ☎01 42 02 20 52; www.la-java.fr; 105 rue du Faubourg du Temple, 11e; concerts free-€10; ⏱8pm-dawn Mon-Sat; Ⓜ Goncourt) Built in 1922, this is the dance hall where Édith Piaf got her first break, and it now reverberates to the sound of live salsa, rock and world music. Live concerts usually take place at 8pm or 9pm during the week. Afterwards a festive crowd gets dancing to electro, house, disco and Latino DJs.

Theatre Tips

Theatre in Paris (TIP; ☎01 85 08 66 89; www.theatreinparis.com; tickets €20-100; ⏱phone enquiries 10am-7pm Mon-Fri) lets non-French speakers access Paris' vibrant local theatre scene (and its resplendent venues). Bilingual hosts provide an English-language program and direct you to your seats, and performances are surtitled in English. Typically there are upwards of 10 shows on offer, from French classics to contemporary comedies and Broadway-style productions; book via its English online ticketing platform.

Pick up half-price tickets for same-day performances of ballet, opera and music at **Kiosque Théâtre Madeleine** (www.kiosqueculture.com; opposite 15 place de la Madeleine, 8e; ⏱12.30-7.30pm Tue-Sat, to 3.45pm Sun; Ⓜ Madeleine), a freestanding kiosk by place de la Madeleine.

✪ Bastille & Eastern Paris

Opéra Bastille
Opera

(Map p254; ☎international calls 01 71 25 24 23, within France 08 92 89 90 90; www.operade paris.fr; 2-6 place de la Bastille, 12e; ⏱box office 11.30am-6.30pm Mon-Sat, 1hr prior to performances Sun; Ⓜ Bastille) Paris' premier opera hall, Opéra Bastille's 2745-seat main auditorium also stages ballet and classical concerts. Online tickets go on sale up to three weeks before telephone or box-office sales (from noon on Wednesdays; online flash sales offer significant discounts). Standing-only tickets (*places débouts*; €5) are available 90 minutes before performances. French-language 90-minute **guided tours** take you backstage.

Significant discounts are available for those aged under 28.

Movie Houses

The film-lover's ultimate city, Paris has some wonderful movie houses to catch new flicks, avant-garde cinema and priceless classics.

Foreign films (including English-language films) screened in their original language with French subtitles are labelled 'VO' *(version originale)*. Films labelled 'VF' *(version française)* are dubbed in French.

L'Officiel des Spectacles lists the full crop of Paris' cinematic pickings and screening times; online, check out http://cinema.leparisien.fr.

The city's film archive, the **Forum des Images** (Map p250; ☑01 44 76 63 00; www.forumdesimages.fr; Forum des Halles, 2 rue du Cinéma, Porte St-Eustache, 1er; cinema tickets adult/child €6/4; ☉12.30-9pm Tue-Fri, 2-9pm Sat & Sun; MLes Halles, RER Châtelet–Les Halles), screens films set in Paris.

First-run tickets cost around €11.50 for adults (€13.50 for 3D). Students and over 60s get discounted tickets (usually around €8.50) from 7pm Sunday to 7pm Friday. Discounted tickets for children and teens have no restrictions. Most cinemas have across-the-board discounts before noon.

Le Champo
LOIC VENANCE/AFP/GETTY IMAGES ©

La Cinémathèque Française
Cinema

(☑01 71 19 33 33; www.cinematheque.fr; 51 rue de Bercy, 12e; tickets adult/child €6.50/4; ☉2.30-9pm or later Wed-Sun; MBercy) This **national institution** (☑01 71 19 33 33; www. cinematheque.fr; 51 rue de Bercy, 12e; adult/child €5/2.50, with film €8; ☉noon-7pm Wed-Mon; MBercy) is a temple to the 'seventh art' and always screens its foreign offerings in their original versions. Up to 10 films a day are shown, usually retrospectives (eg Spielberg, Altman, Eastwood) mixed in with related but more obscure films.

✪ Latin Quarter

Café Universel
Jazz, Blues

(Map p252; ☑01 43 25 74 20; www.facebook.com/cafeuniverseljazzbar; 267 rue St-Jacques, 5e; ☉8.30pm-1.30am Tue-Sat; ☏; MCensier Daubenton, RER Port Royal) Café Universel hosts a brilliant array of live concerts with everything from bebop and Latin sounds to vocal jazz sessions. Plenty of freedom is given to young producers and artists, and its convivial relaxed atmosphere attracts a mix of students and jazz lovers. Concerts are free, but tip the artists when they pass the hat around.

Le Champo
Cinema

(Map p252; www.cinema-lechampo.com; 51 rue des Écoles, 5e; tickets adult/child €9/4; MCluny–La Sorbonne) This is one of the most popular of the many Latin Quarter cinemas, featuring classics and retrospectives looking at the films of such actors and directors as Alfred Hitchcock, Jacques Tati, Alain Resnais, Frank Capra, Tim Burton and Woody Allen. One of the two *salles* (cinemas) has wheelchair access.

✪ St-Germain & Les Invalides

Le Lucernaire
Cultural Centre

(Map p246; ☑01 45 44 57 34; www.lucernaire.fr; 53 rue Notre Dame des Champs, 6e; ☉bar 9am-9pm Mon, 9am-12.30am Tue-Fri, 10am-12.30am Sat, 11am-9pm Sun; MNotre Dame des Champs) Sunday-evening concerts are a fixture on the impressive repertoire of the dynamic Centre National d'Art et d'Essai (National Arts Centre). Whether it's classical guitar,

La Cinémathèque Française

baroque, French *chansons* or East Asian music, these weekly concerts starting from 4pm (hours vary) are a real treat. Art and photography exhibitions, cinema, theatre, lectures, debates and guided walks round off the packed cultural agenda.

✪ Montparnasse & Southern Paris

EP7 — Arts Center
(📞 01 43 45 68 07; https://ep7.paris; 133 av de France, 13e; ⏰ 7.30am-2am; 📶; Ⓜ Bibliothèque)
It is impossible to miss the façade of this brand new cultural cafe and concert venue – the capital's first piece of 'interactive architecture', unveiled in early 2018. Contemporary works of pixel art prance across 12 giant screens covering the facade, creating a dazzling digital gallery. Inside the cultural cafe, named after the vintage vinyl format 'extended play', find art exhibitions and happenings, DJ sets, a trendy bistro serving local, fresh, seasonal cuisine (menu €26) and late-night bar with Seine view.

> *The film-lover's ultimate city*

Fondation Jérôme Seydoux-Pathé — Cinema
(📞 01 83 79 18 96; www.fondation-jerome seydoux-pathe.com; 77 ave des Gobelins, 13e; tickets adult/child €6.50/4.50; ⏰ 1-8pm Tue, 1-7pm Wed-Fri, 11.30am-7pm Sat; Ⓜ Place d'Italie)
This striking cinema with a small exhibition (€3) devoted to the history of cinema is a brilliant addition to the Paris flick scene. Where else can you watch silent B&W movies to the sound of a live pianist? The Pathé Foundation is hidden in a former theatre and cinema dating to 1869, but only the façade – sculpted by Rodin – remains. The rest of the building is an unbelievable, five-storey, contemporary 'slug' of a creation by world-class architect Renzo Piano.

Guided architecture tours (adult/child €7.50/4) take place Saturday at noon. The family-friendly *ciné-concerts* (films accompanied by live music) at weekends are particularly enchanting.

ACTIVE PARIS

Picturesque parks, sporting highlights
and unique local-led tours

Active

As Paris gears up to host the 2024 Summer Olympics and Summer Paralympics, you'll find increasing opportunities to watch spectator sports or take part yourself. To unwind with the Parisians, check out the city's glorious parks and two vast forests, the Bois de Boulogne and Bois de Vincennes, which act as its 'green lungs'. The city also has some stunning swimming pools, both historic and new, and a rapidly expanding network of cycling lanes.

As one of the world's most visited cities, Paris is well set up for visitors with a host of guided tours, from bike, boat, bus, scooter and walking tours (including some wonderful local-led options in off-the-beaten-track areas) to various themed options.

In This Section

What to Watch

From late May to mid-June, the French Open hits up at the Stade Roland Garros in the Bois de Boulogne. The Tour de France races up the Champs-Élysées at the end of July every year. The main football (soccer) season runs from August through to April.

Paris Saint-Germain football jersey

Spectator Sports

Local teams include football's Paris Saint-Germain (www.psg.fr) and rugby's sky-blue-and-white-dressed Racing 92 (www.racing92.fr) and pink-clad Stade Français Paris (www.stade.fr). Catch France's national football team, Les Bleus (www.fff.fr), at the Stade de France.

For upcoming events, click on Sports & Games (under the Going Out menu) at http://en.parisinfo.com.

Parks for Activities & Sports

Bois de Boulogne (p202) Sprawling western forest.

Bois de Vincennes (p202) Eastern forest home to a zoo and the kid-packed Parc Floral.

Jardin du Luxembourg (p68) Paris' most popular park.

Parc des Buttes Chaumont (p201) Hilly haven with t'ai chi vibes.

❸ Spectator Sports

Stade de France · Stadium
(☏01 55 93 00 45; www.stadefrance.com;
St-Denis La Plaine; stadium tours adult/child
€15/10; Ⓜ St-Denis-Porte de Paris) This
80,000-seat stadium was built for the
1998 FIFA World Cup, and hosts major
sports and music events. Stadium tours
lasting 90 minutes take you behind the
scenes, providing no event is under way.
Tours in English depart from Gate H;
confirm times and book tickets in advance
online.

Stade Roland Garros · Spectator Sport
(www.rolandgarros.com; 2 av Gordon Bennett,
16e, Bois de Boulogne; Ⓜ Porte d'Auteuil) The
French Open is held on clay at the Stade
Roland Garros late May to mid-June.
Much-needed renovations began in 2016
and will incorporate a new Court No 1
with 15,000 seats and a retractable roof,
among other changes. Legal challenges
have delayed construction and completion
won't be until 2020 at the earliest; the
tournament will continue during that time.

❸ Swimming Pools

Piscine de la Butte aux Cailles · Swimming
(☏01 45 89 60 05; http://equipement.paris.fr/
piscine-de-la-butte-aux-cailles-2927; 5 place Paul
Verlaine, 13e; adult/child €3.50/2, 10 entrances
€28/16; ☉hours vary; Ⓜ Place d'Italie) Built
in 1924, this art deco gem of a swimming
pool complex – a historical monument to
boot – takes advantage of the lovely warm
artesian well water nearby. It has a spectacular vaulted indoor pool and since, its 2017
renovation, is the only complex in Paris to
have a Nordic pool. In the depths of winter
this is where Parisians come to swim 25m
laps in a five-lane outdoor pool, heated to a
toasty 28°C.

Piscine Joséphine Baker · Swimming
(☏01 56 61 96 50; www.piscine-baker.fr; quai
François Mauriac, 13e; adult/child €6.20/3.10;
☉7-9am & 10am-11pm Mon-Fri, 10am-8pm Sat &

Parc des Buttes Chaumont

Sun Jun-Sep, shorter hours rest of year; MQuai de la Gare) Floating on the Seine, this striking swimming pool is named after the 1920s American singer. The 25m-by-10m, four-lane pool and large sun deck are especially popular in summer when the roof slides back. Also here is a children's paddling pool. In July and August, plus weekends from late May to September, admission is limited to two hours.

🛈 Parks

Parc de la Villette   Park
(https://lavillette.com; 211 av Jean Jaurès, 19e; ⊙6am-1am; MPorte de la Villette, Porte de Pantin) Spanning 55 hectares, this vast city park is a cultural centre, kids playground and landscaped urban space at the intersection of two canals, the Ourcq and the St-Denis. Its futuristic layout includes the colossal mirror-like sphere of the Géode cinema and the bright-red cubical pavilions known as *folies*. Among its themed gardens are the Jardin du Dragon (Dragon Garden), with a giant dragon's tongue slide for kids, the Jardin des Dunes (Dunes Garden) and Jardin des Miroirs (Mirror Garden).

Parc Monceau   Park
(35 bd de Courcelles, 8e; ⊙7am-10pm May-Aug, to 9pm Sep, to 8pm Oct-Apr; MMonceau) Marked by a neoclassical rotunda at its main bd Courcelles entrance, beautiful Parc Monceau sprawls over 8.2 lush hectares. It was laid out by Louis Carrogis Carmontelle in 1778–79 in English style with winding paths, ponds and flower beds. An Egyptian-style pyramid is the only original folly remaining today, but other distinctive features include a bridge modelled after Venice's Rialto, a Renaissance arch and a Corinthian colonnade. There are play areas, a carousel and scheduled puppet shows for kids.

Promenade Plantée   Park
(La Coulée Verte René-Dumont; Map p254; cnr rue de Lyon & av Daumesnil, 12e; ⊙8am-9.30pm Mon-Fri, from 9am Sat & Sun Mar-Oct,

---

> ### ⌖ Swimming Etiquette
>
> If you plan to go swimming at either your hotel or in a public pool, you'll need to don a *bonnet de bain* (bathing cap) – even if you don't have any hair. They are generally sold at most pools. Men are required to wear skin-tight trunks (Speedos); loose-fitting Bermuda shorts are not allowed.

8am-5.30pm Mon-Fri, from 9am Sat & Sun Nov-Feb; MBastille, Gare de Lyon, Daumesnil) The disued 19th-century Vincennes railway viaduct was reborn as the world's first elevated park, planted with a fragrant profusion of cherry trees, maples, rose trellises, bamboo corridors and lavender. Three storeys above ground, it provides a unique aerial vantage point on the city. Staircases provide access (lifts/elevators here invariably don't work). Along the first, northwestern section, above av Daumesnil, art-gallery workshops beneath the arches form the **Viaduc des Arts** (Map p254; www.leviaducdesarts.com; 1-129 av Daumesnil, 12e; ⊙hours vary; MBastille, Gare de Lyon).

Parc des Buttes Chaumont   Park
(Map p254; rue Manin & rue Botzaris, 19e; ⊙7am-10pm May-Sep, to 8pm Oct-Apr; MButtes Chaumont, Botzaris) One of the city's largest green spaces, Buttes Chaumont's landscaped slopes hide grottoes, waterfalls, a lake and even an island topped with a temple to Sibylle. Once a gypsum quarry and rubbish dump, it was given its present form by Baron Haussmann in time for the opening of the 1867 Exposition Universelle. The tracks of the abandoned 19th-century Petite Ceinture railway line, which once circled Paris, run through the park.

Parc Montsouris   Park
(http://equipement.paris.fr/parc-montsouris-1810; av Reille, 14e; ⊙8am-9.30pm Mon-Fri,

💬 Local Activities

Inline Skating

Rent a pair of in-line skates at **Nomadeshop** (Map p254; ☑01 44 54 07 44; www.nomadeshop.com; 37 bd Bourdon, 4e; half-/full-day skate rental from €5/8; ⊙11am-1.30pm & 2.30-7.30pm Tue-Fri, 10am-7pm Sat, noon-6pm Sun Apr-Oct, closed Sun Nov-Mar; Ⓜ Bastille) and join the Friday-evening skate, **Pari Roller** (Map p246; www.pari-roller.com; place Raoul Dautry, 14e; ⊙10pm-1am Fri, arrive 9.30pm; Ⓜ Montparnasse Bienvenüe) 𝐅𝐑𝐄𝐄, that zooms through the Paris streets, or join the more laid-back Sunday-afternoon skate, **Rollers & Coquillages** (Map p254; www.rollers-coquillages.org; place de la Bastille; ⊙2.30pm Sun; Ⓜ Bastille).

Boules

France's most popular traditional game, similar to lawn bowls, *boules* is played in parks and squares with suitably flat, shady patches of gravel. Absorb the scene at the **Arènes de Lutèce** (49 rue Monge, 5e; ⊙8am-9.30pm May-Aug, to 8.30pm Apr & Sep, shorter hours rest of year; Ⓜ Place Monge) 𝐅𝐑𝐄𝐄 *boulodrome* in a 2nd-century Roman amphitheatre.

9am-9.30pm Sat & Sun May-Aug, shorter hours rest of year; Ⓜ Porte d'Orléans, RER Cité-Universitaire) The name of this sprawling lakeside park – planted with horse-chestnut, yew, cedar, weeping beech and buttonwood trees – derives from *moque souris* (mice mockery) because the area was once overrun with the critters. Today it's a delightful picnic spot and has endearing playground areas, such as a concrete 'road system' where littlies can trundle matchbox cars (BYO cars). On Wednesday, Saturday and Sunday from 3pm to 6pm there are marionette shows and pony rides.

❻ Forests

Bois de Vincennes   Park

(bd Poniatowski, 12e; Ⓜ Porte de Charenton, Porte Dorée) In the southeastern corner of Paris, Bois de Vincennes encompasses some 995 hectares. Originally royal hunting grounds, the woodland was annexed by the army following the Revolution and then donated to the city in 1860 by Napoléon III. A fabulous place to escape the Parisian concrete, Bois de Vincennes also contains a handful of notable sights including a bona fide royal château, **Château de Vincennes** (☑01 48 08 31 20; www.chateau-de-vincennes.fr; 1 av de Paris, Vincennes; adult/child €9/free; ⊙10am-6pm mid-May–mid-Sep, to 5pm mid-Sep–mid-May; Ⓜ Château de Vincennes), with massive fortifications and a moat.

Paris' largest, state-of-the-art zoo, the **Parc Zoologique de Paris** (Zoo de Vincennes; ☑08 11 22 41 22; www.parczoologique deparis.fr; cnr av Daumesnil & rte de Ceinture du Lac Daumesnil, 12e; adult/child €22/16.50; ⊙9.30am-8.30pm May-Aug, shorter hours Sep-Apr; Ⓜ Porte Dorée), is also here, as is the magnificent botanical park **Parc Floral de Paris** (☑01 49 57 24 81; www.parcfloraldeparis jeux.com; Esplanade du Chateau de Vincennes or rte de la Pyramide; adult/child €2.50/1.50; ⊙9.30am-8pm Apr-Sep, to 6.30pm Oct, to 5pm Nov-Feb, to 6.30pm Mar; Ⓜ Château de Vincennes), with exciting playgrounds for older children. The wood also has a lovely lake, with boats to rent and ample green lawns to picnic on.

Bois de Boulogne   Park

(bd Maillot, 16e; Ⓜ Porte Maillot) On the western edge of Paris just beyond the 16e, the 845-hectare Bois de Boulogne owes its informal layout to Baron Haussmann, who was inspired by Hyde Park in London. Be warned that the Bois de Boulogne becomes a distinctly adult playground after dark, especially along the allée de Longchamp, where sex workers cruise for clients.

In the south are two horse-racing tracks, the **Hippodrome de Longchamp** (☑01 44 30 75 00; www.parislongchamp.com; 2 rte des Trib-

Cycling tour in front of the Eiffel Tower (p36)

unes, 16e, Bois de Boulogne; Ⓜ Porte Maillot, Porte d'Auteuil) for flat races and the **Hippodrome d'Auteuil** (🖉 01 40 71 47 47; www.france-galop. com; Champ de Courses d'Auteuil, 16e, Bois de Boulogne; adult from €5, child free; Ⓜ Porte d'Auteuil) for steeplechases.

Guided Tours

Parisien d'un Jour – Paris Greeters   Walking
(https://greeters.paris; by donation) See Paris through local eyes with these two- to three-hour city tours. Volunteers – mainly knowledgable Parisians passionate about their city – lead groups (maximum six people) to their favourite spots. Minimum two weeks' notice is needed.

Paris Walks   Walking
(🖉 01 48 09 21 40; www.paris-walks.com; 2hr tours adult/child €15/10) Long established and well respected, Paris Walks offers two-hour thematic walking tours (art, fashion, chocolate, the French Revolution etc).

Paris à Vélo, C'est Sympa!   Cycling
(Map p254; 🖉 01 48 87 60 01; https://parisvelo-sympa.com; 22 rue Alphonse Baudin, 11e; Ⓜ Richard Lenoir) Runs three guided bike tours (adult/child €35/29, three hours): a Heart of Paris tour, Unusual Paris (taking in artist studios and mansions) and the Contrast tour, combining nature and modern architecture. Tours depart from its bike rental shop (p237).

Set in Paris   Walking
(🖉 09 84 42 35 79; http://setinparis.com; 3 rue Maître Albert, 5e; 2hr tours €25; ⊘ tours 10am & 3pm; Ⓜ Maubert-Mutualité) From its cinema-style 'box office' HQ in the Latin Quarter, Set in Paris offers themed walking tours (Hemingway, Coco Chanel, French markets...). Its two-hour 'Paris Movie Tour' covers locations throughout Paris where films including *The Devil Wears Prada, The Bourne Identity, The Three Musketeers, The Hunchback of Notre Dame, Ratatouille, Before Sunset,* several James Bond instalments and many others were shot.

REST YOUR HEAD

Top tips for the best accommodation

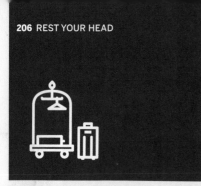

Rest Your Head

As one of the world's most visited cities, Paris has a wealth of accommodation for all budgets, from a recently reinvigorated hostel scene that now includes purpose-built, state-of-the-art flashpacker pads to charming old-school hotels, intimate boutique gems, hipster hang-outs, eye-popping designer havens, sleep-drink-dine-dance lifestyle hotels, and deluxe hotels and palaces, some of which rank among the finest in the world. Be sure to reserve as far ahead as possible, especially at busy times including weekends, public and school holidays and the summer months.

Apartment rentals are also very popular in Paris and give you the opportunity to live like a Parisian, shopping at the local markets and visiting neighbourhood bars. Choosing a central option with good transport links will allow you to maximise your time.

In This Section

Prices/Tipping

A 'budget hotel' in Paris generally costs up to €130 for a double room with en suite bathroom in high season (breakfast not included). For a midrange option, plan on spending €130 to €250. Luxury options run €250 and higher.

Bellhops usually expect €1 to €2 per bag; it's not necessary to tip the concierge, cleaners or front-desk staff.

Room at the Sofitel Paris Le Faubourg hotel, interior design by Didier Gomez

Reservations

Reservations are almost always essential – walk-ins are practically impossible and rack rates are unfavourable relative to online deals (usually best directly via hotels' official websites). Reserve your room as early as possible and make sure you understand the cancellation policy. Check-in is generally in the middle of the afternoon and check-out in the late morning.

Useful Websites

Lonely Planet (www.lonelyplanet.com/france/paris/hotels) Reviews of Lonely Planet's top choices.

Paris Attitude (www.parisattitude.com) Thousands of apartment rentals, professional service, reasonable fees.

Haven In (https://havenin.com) Charming Parisian apartments for rent.

Apartment Rentals

Families – and anyone wanting to self-cater – should consider renting a short-stay apartment. Paris has a number of excellent apartment hotels, including the international chain Citadines (www.citadines.com).

For an even more authentic Parisian experience, home-sharing options are also available, whether a room in someone's apartment or the entire property. Rental agencies (eg Paris Attitude) are among the organisations that list furnished residential apartments for short stays. Apartments often include facilities such as washing machines, and can be good value. The cheapest rates are usually in local neighbourhoods in outer (higher-numbered) *arrondissements*. Many older Parisian buildings don't have lifts/elevators; check the *étage* (floor). Parisian apartments are often tiny (in studios, the sofa often doubles as the only bed); confirm the size beforehand. Also establish whether prices include electricity.

Beware of direct-rental scams whereby scammers compile fake apartment advertisements at too-good-to-be-true prices from photos and descriptions on legitimate sites. Book only with reputable companies. Above all, never send money via an untraceable money transfer.

Accommodation Types

Hotels

Hotels in Paris are inspected by government authorities and classified into six categories, from no star to five stars. The vast majority are two- and three-star hotels, which are generally well-equipped. All hotels must display their rates, including TVA (*taxe sur la valeur ajoutée*; valued-added tax), though you'll often get *much* cheaper prices online, especially on the hotels' own websites, which invariably offer the best deals.

Parisian hotel rooms tend to be small by international standards. Families will probably need connecting rooms, but if children are too young to stay in their own room, it's possible to make do with triples, quads or suites in some places.

Cheaper hotels may not have lifts/elevators and/or air-conditioning. Some don't accept credit cards.

Breakfast is rarely included in hotel rates; heading to a cafe often works out to be better value (and more atmospheric).

Hostels

Paris is awash with hostels, and standards are consistently improving. A wave of state-of-the-art hostels include the design-savvy 950-bed 'megahostel' by leading hostel chain Generator near Canal St-Martin, 10e, and, close by, two by the switched-on St Christopher's group.

The more traditional (ie institutional) hostels can have daytime lock-outs and curfews; some have a maximum three-night stay. Places that have upper age limits tend not to enforce them, except at the busiest of times. Only the official *auberges de jeunesse* (youth hostels) require guests to present Hostelling International (HI) cards or their equivalent.

Not all hostels have self-catering kitchens, but rates generally include a basic continental breakfast.

Lobby of the Sofitel Paris Le Faubourg

B&Bs & Homestays

Bed-and-breakfast (B&B) accommodation (*chambres d'hôte* in French) offers an immersive way to experience the city. Paris' tourist office maintains a list of B&Bs in Paris; visit https://en.parisinfo.com/where-to-sleep-in-paris.

🖴 Need to Know

Taxe de Séjour

The city of Paris levies a *taxe de séjour* (tourist tax) per person per night on all accommodation. The rate depends on the type of accommodation, as outlined below:

Palaces (and similar) €4.40
5 stars €3.30
4 stars €2.53
3 stars €1.65
2 stars €0.99
1 star & B&Bs €0.88
Unrated/unclassified €0.88
3- to 5-star campgrounds €0.66
1- and 2-star campgrounds and marinas €0.22

Internet Access

Wi-fi (pronounced *wee*-fee in French) is virtually always free of charge at hotels and hostels. You may find that in some hotels, especially older ones, the higher the floor, the less reliable the wi-fi connection.

Smoking

Smoking is officially banned in all Paris hotels.

Price Ranges

The following price ranges are an indication of accommodation costs in Paris (prices refer to a double room with en-suite bathroom in high season, breakfast not included).

Budget Less than €130
Midrange €130–€250
Top End More than €250

Where to Stay

Neighbourhood	Atmosphere
Eiffel Tower & Western Paris	Close to Paris' iconic sights. Upmarket area with quiet streets. Short on budget and midrange options. Limited nightlife.
Champs-Élysées & Grands Boulevards	Luxury hotels, boutiques and department stores, gastronomic restaurants, great nightlife. Some areas pricey. Can be noisy.
Louvre & Les Halles	Epicentral location, excellent transport links, major museums, shopping galore. Not many bargains. Noise can be an issue.
Montmartre & Northern Paris	Village atmosphere. Hilly streets, some parts very touristy. Pigalle's red-light district won't appeal to all travellers.
Le Marais, Ménilmontant & Belleville	Buzzing nightlife, hip shopping, fantastic eating options. Lively gay and lesbian scene. Very central. Can be noisy.
Bastille & Eastern Paris	Few tourists, allowing you to see the 'real' Paris. Excellent markets, loads of nightlife. Some areas slightly out-of-the-way.
The Islands	As geographically central as it gets. No metro station on the Île St-Louis. Limited self-catering shops, minimal nightlife.
Latin Quarter	Energetic student area, stacks of eating and drinking options, late-opening bookshops.
St-Germain & Les Invalides	Stylish, central location, superb shopping, sophisticated dining, proximity to the Jardin du Luxembourg.
Montparnasse & Southern Paris	Good value, few tourists, excellent links to both major airports. Some areas out of the way and/or not well served by metro.

Left: The luxurious Ritz Paris

Jardin des Tuileries (p90)

In Focus

Champs-Élysées (p150)

AUGUSTIN LAZAROIU/SHUTTERSTOCK ©

Paris Today

Paris has bounced back in a big way since the turbulent
events of 2015: visitor numbers are at a record high,
energetic president Emmanuel Macron is revitalising
France's economy, and a raft of infrastructure projects
are underway, as are green initiatives including more
car-free and reduced-traffic areas. And the capital is
gearing up to host the 2023 Rugby World Cup, 2024
Summer Olympics and 2024 Summer Paralympics.

Grand Plans

The gargantuan Grand Paris (Greater Paris) redevelopment project will ultimately connect the outer suburbs beyond the bd Périphérique ring road with the city proper. This is a significant break in the physical and conceptual barrier that the *périphérique* has imposed until now but, due to the steadily growing suburban population, a real need to redefine Paris has arisen.

The crux of Grand Paris is a massive decentralised metro expansion, with four new metro lines, the extension of several existing lines, and a total of 68 new stations, with a target completion date of 2030. The principal goal is to connect the suburbs with one another, instead of relying on a central inner-city hub from which all lines radiate outwards. Ultimately, the surrounding suburbs – Vincennes, St-Denis etc – will lose their autonomy and become part of a much larger Grand Paris governed by the Hôtel de Ville.

Evolving Architecture

Architectural change doesn't come easy in Paris, given the need to balance the city's heritage with demands on space. But new projects continue to gather steam. At Porte de Versailles, 2019's Tour Triangle, a glittering glass triangular tower designed by Jacques Herzog and Pierre de Meuron, will be the first skyscraper in Paris since 1973's Tour Montparnasse (itself set to get a new reflective façade and green rooftop; the tower will close from late 2019 until mid-2023). Other high-rise projects include Duo, two Jean Nouvel–designed towers (180m and 122m) in the 13e, due in 2020.

Nouvel is among the architects working on the 74-hectare Île Seguin-Rives de Seine development of the former Renault plant on a Seine island in Boulogne-Billancourt. Another Nouvel project is Gare d'Austerlitz' multimillion euro renovation with hotels and a 20,000 sq m shopping area, wrapping up in 2021.

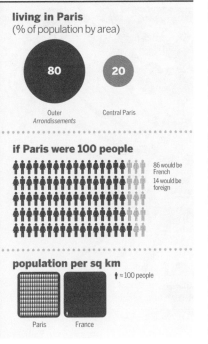

living in Paris
(% of population by area)

80 — Outer *Arrondissements*
20 — Central Paris

if Paris were 100 people

86 would be French
14 would be foreign

population per sq km

♦ ≈ 100 people

Paris   France

Greener Living

Mayor of Paris Anne Hidalgo is focused on greening the city and reducing car traffic and pollution. Ongoing projects include investing €150 million in cycling infrastructure (including an av des Champs-Élysées cycling lane), reducing parking spaces by 55,000 per year, instigating a city-wide maximum speed limit of 30km per hour (except major arteries) by 2020 to minimise noise pollution, and banning diesel cars by 2024 and petrol cars by 2030.

Green initiatives also include a goal of 100 hectares of green roofs, façades and vertical walls, a third of which will be devoted to urban agriculture. Green walkways and gardens will connect two of Paris' busiest mainline stations – Gare du Nord and Gare de l'Est – from 2019. A 'pedestrian peninsula' linking place de la Bastille with the Port de l'Arsenal marina is also scheduled to open in 2019.

Economic Advancement

To compete with other key European cities to attract tourism and investment, Paris has established ZTIs (international tourist zones) that allow late-night and Sunday trading for shops.

The world's biggest start-up campus, Station F, in the 13e, was inaugurated by President Macron, who is seeking to bring more businesses to the city and country. Unemployment is now at its lowest level since 2009, with a series of labour reforms expected to reduce it even further. The City of Light's future is bright.

Emblem of the Sun King (Louis XIV) on the entrance gates to Château de Versailles (p84)

History

With its cobbled streets, terraced cafes and iconic landmarks, Paris evokes a sense of timelessness, yet the city has changed and evolved dramatically over the centuries. And Paris' epic history – from Roman battles to revolution and beyond – is not just consigned to museums and archives: reminders of the city's past can be glimpsed around every corner.

3rd century BC
Celtic Gauls called Parisii arrive in the Paris area and set up wattle-and-daub huts on the Seine.

52 BC
Roman legions under Titus Labienus crush a Celtic revolt on Mons Lutetius and establish the town of Lutetia.

AD 509
Clovis I becomes the first king of the Franks and declares Paris the seat of his new kingdom.

View over Paris from the Galerie des Chimères (Gargoyles Gallery; p47), Notre Dame

The Beginnings to the Renaissance

Paris was born in the 3rd century BC, when a tribe of Celtic Gauls known as the Parisii set-tled on what is now the Île de la Cité. Centuries of conflict between the Gauls and Romans ended in 52 BC, when Julius Caesar's legions crushed a Celtic revolt. Christianity was introduced in the 2nd century AD, and Roman rule ended in the 5th century with the arrival of the Germanic Franks. In 508 Frankish king Clovis I united Gaul and made Paris his seat.

France's west coast was beset in the 9th century by Scandinavian Vikings (also known as Norsemen and, later, as Normans). Three centuries later, the Normans started pushing toward Paris, which had risen rapidly in importance: construction had begun on the cathe-dral of Notre Dame in the 12th century, the Louvre began life as a riverside fortress around 1200, Sainte-Chapelle was consecrated in 1248 and the Sorbonne opened in 1253.

The Vikings' incursions heralded the Hundred Years' War between Norman England and Paris' Capetian dynasty, bringing French defeat in 1415 and English control of the capital in

1643
'Sun King' Louis XIV ascends the throne aged five but only assumes absolute power in 1661.

14 July 1789
The French Revolution begins when a mob arms itself with stolen weapons and storms the prison at Bastille.

1793
Louis XVI is tried, con-victed and executed; Marie-Antoinette's turn comes nine months later.

Conciergerie

1420. In 1429 the 17-year-old Jeanne d'Arc (Joan of Arc) rallied the French troops to defeat the English at Orléans. With the exception of Calais, the English were eventually expelled from France in 1453.

The Renaissance helped Paris get back on its feet in the late 15th century. Less than a century later, however, turmoil ensued as clashes between Huguenot (Protestant) and Catholic groups culminated in the St Bartholomew's Day massacre in 1572.

The Revolution to a New Republic

A five-year-old Louis XIV (later known as the Sun King) ascended the throne in 1643 and ruled until 1715, virtually emptying the national coffers with his ambitious battling and building, including the construction of his extravagant palace at Versailles. The excesses of this grandiose king and his heirs, including Louis XVI and his Vienna-born queen Marie-Antoinette, eventually led to an uprising of Parisians on 14 July 1789, kick-starting the French Revolution. Within four years, the Reign of Terror was in full swing.

The unstable post-revolutionary government was consolidated in 1799 under Napoléon Bonaparte, who declared himself First Consul. In 1804 he had the Pope crown him emperor of the French, and went on to conquer most of Europe before his eventual defeat at Waterloo in present-day Belgium in 1815. He was exiled to St Helena, and died in 1821.

France struggled under a string of mostly inept rulers until a coup d'état in 1851 brought Emperor Napoléon III to power. At his behest, Baron Haussmann razed whole tracts of the city, replacing them with sculptured parks, a hygienic sewer system and – strategically – boulevards too broad for rebels to barricade. Napoléon III embroiled France in a costly war with Prussia in 1870, which ended within months with the French army's defeat and the capture of the emperor. When the masses in Paris heard the news, they took to the streets, demanding a republic.

1799
Napoléon Bonaparte overthrows the Directory and seizes control of the government in a coup d'état.

1852–70
During the Second Empire of Napoléon III much of the city is redesigned or rebuilt by Baron Haussmann as the Paris we know today.

1940
Germany launches the battle for France, and the four-year occupation of Paris under direct German rule begins.

Twentieth-Century History

Out of the conflict of WWI, in which 1.3 million French soldiers lost their lives, came increased industrialisation that confirmed Paris' place as a major commercial, as well as artistic, centre and established its reputation among freethinking intellectuals.

This was halted by WWII and the Nazi occupation of 1940. During Paris' occupation, almost half the population evacuated, including General Charles de Gaulle, France's under-secretary of war, who fled to London and set up a government-in-exile. In a radio broadcast he appealed to French patriots to continue resisting the Germans, and established the Forces Françaises Libres (Free French Forces) to fight the Germans alongside the Allies. Following Paris' liberation, de Gaulle set up a provisional government, but resigned in 1946; he formed his own party (Rassemblement du Peuple Français) and remained in opposition until 1958, when he was returned to power. He was succeeded as president in 1969 by Gaullist leader Georges Pompidou.

After the war, Paris regained its position as a creative nucleus and nurtured a revitalised liberalism that peaked with the student-led uprisings of May 1968 – the Sorbonne was occupied, the Latin Quarter blockaded and a general strike paralysed the country.

Under centre-right President Jacques Chirac's watch, the late 1990s saw Paris seize the international spotlight with the rumour-plagued death of Princess Diana in 1997, and France's first-ever World Cup victory in July 1998.

The New Millennium

In May 2001 Socialist Bertrand Delanoë was elected mayor, becoming widely popular for making Paris more liveable through improved infrastructure and green spaces.

Chirac's second presidential term, starting in 2002, was marred in 2005 by the deaths of two teenagers who were electrocuted while allegedly hiding from police in an electricity substation, which sparked riots that quickly spread across Paris, and then across France.

Against the backdrop of the global recession, Chirac's successor, Nicolas Sarkozy, struggled to keep the French economy buoyant. His popularity plummeted, paving the way for Socialist François Hollande's victory in the 2012 presidential elections. Hollande's own economic policies proved ineffectual, and his popularity plunged even faster and further than Sarkozy's, resulting in a near total wipeout for French Socialists in the 2014 municipal elections. The 2014 election of Socialist Anne Hidalgo, Paris' first female mayor, meant the capital was one of the few cities to remain on the political left.

Turbulent Times

The year 2015 was bookended by tragedy. On 7 January the offices of magazine *Charlie Hebdo* were attacked in response to satirical images it published of the prophet Muham-mad. Eleven staff and one police officer were killed and a further 22 people injured.

25 August 1944	**1968**	**2005**
Spearheaded by Free French units, Allied forces liberate Paris and the city escapes destruction.	Paris is rocked by student-led riots; de Gaulle is forced to resign the following year.	The suburbs surrounding Paris are wracked by rioting youths.

View of the Hôtel des Invalides from the Pont Alexandre III

★ **Best WWII-Era History**

Hôtel des Invalides (p104)

Bronze plaque, Arc de Triomphe (p45)

Bar Hemingway (p171)

Worse still, on the night of 13 November 2015, a series of coordinated terrorist attacks occurred in Paris and St-Denis – the deadliest on French soil since WWII. Explosions shook the Stade de France; neighbourhood restaurants and their outdoor terraces in the 10e and 11e *arrondissements* were attacked by gunmen and suicide bombers; and gunmen fired into the audience of Le Bataclan, where American band Eagles of Death Metal were performing. Over the course of the evening, 130 people lost their lives (89 in Le Bataclan alone) and 368 were injured. Paris was in lockdown, the army was mobilised and a state of emergency declared.

Residents established memorials at the fatality sites and place de la République, which became the focal point for the city's outpouring of grief, and by taking to cafe terraces and other public spaces. The hashtag #jesuisenterrasse ('I am on the terrace') represented Parisians' refusal to live in fear.

The long-planned United Nations Climate Change Conference (COP21) went ahead from 30 November to 12 December 2015, during which world leaders reached an agreement to limit global warming to less than 2°C by the end of the century. Le Bataclan reopened in November 2016, and again hosts local and international artists.

France's New President

France's most recent presidential elections took place in 2017. The traditional parties were eliminated in the first round, with Emmanuel Macron, who launched his centrist, pro-EU movement En Marche! in 2016 – now the party La République en Marche – defeating far-right Front National candidate Marine Le Pen 66.1% to 33.9% in the second-round run-off. At age 39, Macron became the youngest-ever French president.

La République en Marche went on to field candidates in 2017's legislative elections and secured an absolute majority (308 seats) in the Assemblée Nationale, allowing Macron to forge ahead with economic reforms.

2014	2015	2017
Spanish-born Anne Hidalgo becomes the first female mayor of Paris.	Deadly terrorist attacks take place at the offices of *Charlie Hebdo* on 7 January, and in multiple locations on 13 November.	Without the support of an established party, Emmanuel Macron makes history by being elected France's first centrist president.

Philharmonie de Paris (p191)

© WILLIAM BEAUCARDET / PHILHARMONIE DE PARIS

Architecture

It took disease, clogged streets and Baron Georges-Eugène Haussmann to drag architectural Paris out of the Middle Ages and into the modern world – yet ever since Haussmann's radical transformation of the city in the 19th century, Paris has never looked back. Its contemporary skyline shimmers with the whole gamut of architectural styles, from Roman arenas to futuristic skyscrapers.

Gallo-Roman

Traces of Roman Paris can be seen in the residential foundations in the Crypte Archéologique in front of Notre Dame; in the Arènes de Lutèce; and in the *frigidarium* (cooling room) and other remains of Roman baths dating from around AD 200 at the Musée National du Moyen Âge.

The latter museum also contains the *Pillier des Nautes* (Boatsmen's Pillar), one of the most valuable legacies of the Gallo-Roman period. It is a 2.5m-high monument dedicated to Jupiter and was erected by the boatmen's guild during the reign of Tiberius (AD 14–37) on the Île de la Cité. The boat has become the symbol of Paris, and the city's Latin motto is '*Fluctuat Nec Mergitur*' (Tossed by Waves but Does Not Sink).

⭐ **Best Medieval Treasures**

Notre Dame (p46)

Sainte-Chapelle (p92)

Musée du Louvre (p52)

Stained-glass window, Sainte-Chapelle

PHOTOGOLFER/SHUTTERSTOCK ©

Romanesque

A religious revival in the 11th century led to the construction of many *roman* (Romanesque) churches, typically with round arches, heavy walls, few (and small) windows, and a lack of ornamentation that bordered on the austere.

No remaining building in Paris is entirely Romanesque, but several have important representative elements, including Église St-Germain des Prés, the Romanesque bell tower of which, above the west entrance, has changed little since AD 1000.

Gothic

In the 14th century, the Rayonnant – or Radiant – Gothic style, named after the radiating tracery of the rose windows, developed. Interiors became even lighter thanks to broader windows and more translucent stained glass. One of the most influential Rayonnant buildings was Sainte-Chapelle, the stained glass of which forms a curtain of glazing on the 1st floor. The two transept façades of Cathédrale de Notre Dame de Paris and the vaulted Salle des Gens d'Armes (Cavalrymen's Hall) in the Conciergerie, the largest surviving medieval hall in Europe, are other fine examples of Rayonnant Gothic style. By the 15th century, decorative extravagance led to Flamboyant Gothic, so named because the wavy stone carving made the towers appear to be blazing or flaming *(flamboyant)*. Several *hôtels particuliers* (private mansions) were built in this style, including Hôtel de Cluny, now the Musée National du Moyen Âge.

Renaissance

The Renaissance set out to realise a 'rebirth' of classical Greek and Roman culture and first affected France at the end of the 15th century, when Charles VIII began a series of invasions of Italy, returning with new ideas. The Early Renaissance style blends a variety of classical components and decorative motifs (columns, tunnel vaults, round arches, domes etc) with the rich decoration of Flamboyant Gothic. Mannerism was introduced around 1530; in 1546 Pierre Lescot designed the richly decorated southwestern corner of the Cour Carrée at the Musée du Louvre. The Right Bank district of Le Marais remains the best area for Renaissance reminders in Paris proper, with some fine *hôtels particuliers,* such as Hôtel Carnavalet, housing part of the Musée Carnavalet (the museum itself is closed for renovations until 2020).

Baroque

During the baroque period (tail end of the 16th to late 18th centuries), painting, sculpture and classical architecture were integrated to create structures and interiors of great subtlety, refinement and elegance. With the advent of the baroque, architecture became more pictorial, with painted church ceilings illustrating the Passion of Christ to the faithful, and palaces invoking the power and order of the state. Salomon de Brosse designed the Palais du Luxembourg in the Jardin du Luxembourg in 1615.

Neoclassicism

Neoclassical architecture emerged about 1740 and had its roots in the renewed interest in classical forms – a search for order,

Baron Haussmann

The iconic apartment buildings that line the boulevards of central Paris, with their cream-coloured stone and curvy wrought-iron balconies, are the work of Baron Haussmann (1809–91), prefect of the Seine *département* between 1853 and 1870.

reason and serenity through the adoption of forms and conventions of Graeco-Roman antiquity: columns, geometric forms and traditional ornamentation.

Among the earliest examples of this style are the Petit Trianon at Versailles, designed by Jacques-Ange Gabriel for Louis XV in 1761. France's greatest neoclassical architect of the 18th century was Jacques-Germain Soufflot, creator of the Panthéon in the Latin Quarter.

Neoclassicism came into its own under Napoléon, who used it to embody the grandeur of imperial France and its capital: examples include the Arc de Triomphe and the Arc de Triomphe du Carrousel. The climax to this great 19th-century movement was Palais Garnier, the city's opera house designed by Charles Garnier.

Art Nouveau

Art nouveau, which emerged in Europe and the USA in the second half of the 19th century under various names (Jugendstil, Sezessionstil, Stile Liberty), caught on quickly in Paris, and its influence lasted until about 1910. It was characterised by sinuous curves and flowing, asymmetrical forms reminiscent of creeping vines, water lilies, the patterns on insect wings and the flowering boughs of trees. Influenced by the arrival of exotic objets d'art from Japan, art nouveau's French name came from a Paris gallery that featured works in the 'new art' style.

It's expressed to perfection in Paris by Hector Guimard's graceful metro entrances, the Musée d'Orsay and the city's main department stores, Le Bon Marché and Galeries Lafayette.

20th Century

Until 1968, French architects almost exclusively trained at the conformist École de Beaux-Arts, reflected in most of the early impersonal and forgettable 'lipstick tubes' and 'upended shoebox' structures erected in the skyscraper district of La Défense and the 210m-tall Tour Montparnasse (1973).

Paris' most notable 20th-century additions were at the behest of the French presidents' *'grands projets'* ('great works'). Georges Pompidou commissioned the once reviled, now much-loved Centre Pompidou. His successor, Valéry Giscard d'Estaing, was instrumental in transforming the derelict Gare d'Orsay train station into the glorious Musée d'Orsay (1986).

François Mitterrand surpassed all of the postwar presidents with monumental projects. Jean Nouvel's Institut du Monde Arabe (1987), built during this time, mixes modern Arab and Western elements and is arguably one of the city's most beautiful late-20th-century buildings. Mitterrand also oversaw the city's second opera house, tile-clad Opéra Bastille, designed by Carlos Ott in 1989; the monumental Grande Arche de la Défense by Johan-Otto von Sprekelsen (1989); IM Pei's glass-pyramid entrance at the hitherto

Institute du Monde Arabe

sacrosanct and untouchable Musée du Louvre (1989); and the four open book-shaped glass towers of the €2 billion Bibliothèque Nationale de France (Dominique Perrault, 1995).

Jacques Chirac orchestrated the magnificent Musée du Quai Branly, a glass, wood and sod structure with 3-hectare experimental garden, also by Jean Nouvel.

Contemporary

IM Pei's Louvre pyramid paved the way for Mario Bellini and Rudy Ricciotti's magnificent 'flying carpet' roof atop the museum's Cour Visconti in 2012.

Drawing on the city's longstanding tradition of metalwork and glass in its architecture, Frank Gehry used 12 enormous glass 'sails' to design the Fondation Louis Vuitton, which opened in the Bois de Boulogne in late 2014.

Jean Nouvel's Philharmonie de Paris, a state-of-the-art creation with a dazzling metallic façade that took three years to build and cost €381 million, opened in 2015.

Glass is a big feature of the 1970s Forum des Halles shopping centre in the 1er – a curvaceous, curvilinear and glass-topped construction by architects Patrick Berger and Jacques Anziutti, completed in 2016.

Clad in a pixelated matrix of glass embedded with LED lights, the new headquarters of national media group Le Monde, designed by Norwegian architectural firm Snøhetta, will be unveiled in 2019.

Looking ahead, the massive Gare d'Austerlitz renovation, headed by Jean Nouvel is expected to finish in 2021. Porte Maillot will be transformed by Mille Arbres (Thousand Trees), a spectacular tree-topped glass structure by Japanese architect Sou Fujimoto and French architect Manal Rachdi. It will provide a pivotal link between central Paris and Grand Paris (Greater Paris) when it opens in 2022,

Art Deco Renaissance

Recent years have seen a renaissance of some of Paris' loveliest art deco buildings. Neo-Egyptian cinema Le Louxor reopened in 2013. The following year, a five-star hotel and spa opened in the Molitor swimming pool complex in western Paris, where the bikini made its first appearance in the 1930s. In Le Marais, thermal-baths-turned-1980s-nightclub Les Bain Douches – another legendary address – opened as luxury hotel Les Bains.

Art deco swimming complexes Piscine de la Butte aux Cailles and Piscine des Amiraux reopened in 2017; the latter was built in 1930 by La Samaritaine architect Henri Sauvage.

Founded in 1870 by Ernest Cognacq and Louise Jaÿ, department store La Samaritaine is finally reopening in 2019. The project, awarded to the Pritzker Prize–winning Japanese firm Sanaa, will preserve an estimated 75% of the original art nouveau and art deco exterior.

Statue, Notre Dame (p46)

ANA CANDIDA/SHUTTERSTOCK ©

Arts

*While art in Paris today means anything and
everything – bold installations in the metro,
monumental wall frescoes, Space Invader tags and other
gregarious street art – the city's rich art heritage has
its roots firmly embedded in the traditional genres of
painting and sculpture. Then there are the literary arts,
music and film in which Paris plays a starring role.*

Baroque to Neoclassicism

According to philosopher Voltaire, French painting proper began with baroque painter
Nicolas Poussin (1594–1665), the greatest representative of 17th-century classicism, who
frequently set scenes from ancient Rome, classical mythology and the Bible in ordered
landscapes bathed in golden light.

Jean-Baptiste Chardin (1699–1779) brought the humbler domesticity of the
Dutch masters to French art, while in 1785, neoclassical artist Jacques Louis David
(1748–1825) wooed the public with his vast portraits with clear republican messages.
Jean-Auguste-Dominique Ingres (1780–1867), David's most gifted pupil in Paris, continued
the neoclassical tradition.

Romanticism

One of the Louvre's most gripping paintings, *The Raft of the Medusa* by Théodore Géricault (1791–1824), hovers on the threshold of romanticism; his friend Eugène Delacroix (1798–1863), best known for his masterpiece commemorating the July Revolution of 1830, *Liberty Leading the People*, was a leader of the movement.

In sculpture, the work of Paris-born Auguste Rodin (1840–1917) overcame the conflict between neoclassicism and romanticism. One of Rodin's most gifted pupils was his lover Camille Claudel (1864–1943), whose work can be seen with Rodin's in the Musée Rodin.

Realism

The realists were all about social comment. Édouard Manet (1832–83) used realism to depict Parisian middle classes, yet he included in his pictures numerous references to the Old Masters.

One of the best sculptors of this period was François Rude (1784–1855), creator of the relief on the Arc de Triomphe and several pieces in the Musée d'Orsay. By the mid-19th century, memorial statues in public places had replaced sculpted tombs, making such statues all the rage.

Sculptor Jean-Baptiste Carpeaux (1827–75) began as a romantic, but his work in Paris – such as *The Dance* on the Palais Garnier and his fountain in the Jardin du Luxembourg – recalls the gaiety and flamboyance of the baroque era.

Impressionism

Paris' Musée d'Orsay is the crown jewel of impressionism. Initially a term of derision, 'impressionism' was taken from the title of an 1874 experimental painting, *Impression: Soleil Levant* (Impression: Sunrise) by Claude Monet (1840–1926). Monet was the leading figure of the school, and a visit to the Musée d'Orsay unveils a host of other members, among them Alfred Sisley (1839–99), Camille Pissarro (1830–1903), Pierre-Auguste Renoir (1841–1919) and Berthe Morisot (1841–95). The impressionists' main aim was to capture the effects of fleeting light, painting almost universally in the open air – and light came to dominate the content of their painting.

Edgar Degas (1834–1917) was a fellow traveller of the impressionists, but he preferred painting cafe life *(Absinthe)* and in ballet studios *(The Dance Class)* than the great outdoors – several beautiful examples hang in the Musée d'Orsay.

Henri de Toulouse-Lautrec (1864–1901) chose subjects one or two notches below: people in the bistros, brothels and music halls of Montmartre (eg *Au Moulin Rouge*). He is best known for his posters and lithographs, in which the distortion of the figures is both satirical and decorative.

Paul Cézanne (1839–1906) is celebrated for his still lifes and landscapes depicting southern France, though he spent many years in Paris after breaking with the impressionists. Paul Gauguin (1848–1903) is famed for his studies of Tahitian and Breton women. Both Cézanne and Gauguin were post-impressionists, a catch-all term for the diverse styles that flowed from impressionism.

Pointillism & Symbolism

Pointillism was a technique developed by Georges Seurat (1859–91), who applied paint in small dots or uniform brush strokes of unmixed colour to produce fine 'mosaics' of warm and cool tones. His tableaux *Une Baignade, Asnières* (Bathers at Asnières) is a perfect example.

Henri Rousseau (1844–1910) was a contemporary of the post-impressionists, but his 'naive' art was unaffected by them. His dreamlike pictures of the Paris suburbs and of jungle and desert scenes (eg *The Snake Charmer*) – again in Musée d'Orsay – have influenced art right up to this century.

20th-Century Art

Twentieth-century French painting styles included fauvism, named after the slur of a critic who compared the exhibitors at the 1905 Salon d'Automne (Autumn Salon) in Paris with *fauves* (wild animals) because of their wild brush strokes and radical use of intensely bright colours. Among these 'beastly' painters was Henri Matisse (1869–1954).

Cubism was launched in 1907 with *Les Demoiselles d'Avignon* by Spanish prodigy Pablo Picasso (1881–1973). Cubism, as developed by Picasso, Georges Braque (1882–1963) and Juan Gris (1887–1927), deconstructed the subject into a system of intersecting planes and presented various aspects simultaneously.

Marcel Duchamp (1887–1968) captured the rebellious, iconoclastic spirit of Dadaism – a Swiss-born literary and artistic movement of revolt – in his *Mona Lisa,* complete with moustache and goatee. In 1922 German Dadaist Max Ernst (1891–1976) moved to Paris and worked on surrealism, a Dada offshoot that flourished between the wars. The most influential of this style in Paris was Spanish-born artist Salvador Dalí (1904–89), who arrived in the French capital in 1929 and painted some of his most seminal works while residing here. To see his work, visit the Dalí Espace Montmartre.

Contemporary Art

Street art took off in Paris thanks to Blek le Rat (Xavier Prou; b 1951), whose pioneering stencilled black rats across the city inspired artists such as Banksy, as well French artist Levalet (Charles Leval; b 1988), who pastes lifelike, site-specific images in Indian ink on craft paper on walls.

Metro Art

Art adorns many of the 300-plus stations of Paris' world-famous Métropolitain. Themes often relate to the *quartier* (neighbourhood) or name of the station. The following is just a sample of the most interesting from an artistic perspective.

Abbesses (line 12 metro entrance) The noodle-like pale-green metalwork and glass canopy of the station entrance is one of the finest examples of the work of Hector Guimard (1867–1942), the celebrated French art nouveau architect whose signature style once graced most metro stations. For a complete list of the metro stations that retain *édicules* (shrine-like entranceways) designed by Guimard, see www.parisinconnu.com.

Bastille (line 5 platform) A 180-sq-metre ceramic fresco features scenes taken from newspaper engravings published during the Revolution, with illustrations of the infamous prison's destruction.

Chaussée d'Antin-Lafayette (line 7 platform) Large allegorical painting on the vaulted ceiling recalls the Marquis de Lafayette (1757–1834) and his role as general in the American Revolution.

Cluny–La Sorbonne (line 10 platform) A large mosaic replicates the signatures of intellectuals, artists and scientists from the Latin Quarter through history, including Molière (1622–73), Rabelais (c 1483–1553) and Robespierre (1758–96).

Concorde (line 12 platform) What look like children's building blocks in white-and-blue ceramic on the walls of the station are 45,000 tiles that spell out the text of the *Déclaration des Droits de l'Homme et du Citoyen* (Declaration of the Rights of Man and of the Citizen), which set forth the principles of the Revolution.

Palais Royal–Musée du Louvre (line 1 metro entrance) The zany entrance on place du Palais by Jean-Michel Othoniel (b 1964) is composed of two crown-shaped cupolas (one represents day, the other night) consisting of 800 glass balls.

★ **Best Literary Pilgrimages**

Cimetière du Père Lachaise (p78)

Shakespeare & Company (p159)

Bar Hemingway (p171)

Shakespeare & Company

Today, street art remains huge; in addition to tiled Space Invader tags and vast murals covering entire high-rise buildings, graffitied streets such as Belleville's rue Dénoyez and art-collective canvases including rue Oberkampf's Le MUR, there are now two street art museums in the city and companies running dedicated guided tours.

Digital art is also gaining ground: 2018 saw the opening of arts centre EP7, which screens projections, and L'Atelier des Lumières, Paris' first digital art museum.

Literary Arts

Flicking through a street directory reveals just how much Paris honours its literary history, with listings including places Colette and Victor Hugo, avs Marcel Proust and Émile Zola, and rue Balzac. The city has nurtured countless French authors over the centuries who, together with expat writers from Dickens onwards – including the Lost Generation's Hemingway, Fitzgerald and Joyce – have sealed Paris' literary reputation.

Contemporary French writers include Jean Echenoz, Erik Orsenna, Marc Levy, Christine Angot and comedian/dramatist Nelly Alard, whose second novel *Moment d'un couple* (Moment of a Couple), published in 2013, was translated into English as Couple Mechanics in 2016.

Delving into the mood and politics of the capital's notable ethnic population is Faïza Guène (b 1985), a French literary sensation who writes in an 'urban slang' style.

Ex–French border guard turned author Romain Puértolas (b 1975) had an instant hit with his surreal, partly Paris-set 2013 novel *L'Extraordinaire Voyage du Fakir Qui Était Resté Coincé Dans une Armoire Ikea* (The Extraordinary Journey of the Fakir Who Got Trapped in an Ikea Wardrobe). Follow-ups include 2015's *La Petite Fille Qui Avait Avalé un Nuage Grand Comme la Tour Eiffel* (The Little Girl Who Swallowed a Cloud as Big as the Eiffel Tower) and 2017's *Tout un Été Sans Facebook* (A Summer Without Facebook) centred on a reading club.

Music

From organ recitals and classical concerts in Gothic architectural splendour to a legendary jazz scene, stirring *chansons,* groundbreaking electronica, award-winning world music and some of the world's best rap, music is embedded deep in the Parisian soul – this is a city where talented musicians have to audition even to perform in the metro.

Pop

French pop has come a long way since the *yéyé* (imitative rock) days of the 1960s as sung by Johnny Hallyday. Nosfell is one of France's most creative and intense musicians, who sings in his own invented language called 'le klokobetz'. His third album, *Massif Armour* (2014), opens and closes in 'le klokobetz' but otherwise woos listeners with powerful French love lyrics.

In 2011 Sylvie Hoarau and Aurélie Saada formed the indie folk duo Brigitte; their debut album *Et vous, tu m'aimes?* went platinum in France. Their 2014 album *A bouche que veux-tu* also achieved widespread success.

Internationally successful modern pop stars include singer-songwriters Christine and the Queens (aka Héloïse Letissier; b 1988), who released her first album *Chaleur Humaine* in 2014, and Jain (Jeanne Galice; b 1992), whose debut album, *Zanaka,* was released in 2015.

Jazz

Jazz hit Paris in the 1920s with Josephine Baker, an African American cabaret dancer. In 1934 a chance meeting between Parisian jazz violinist Stéphane Grappelli (1908–97) and three-fingered Roma guitarist Django Reinhardt (1910–53) in a Montparnasse nightclub led to the formation of the Hot Club of France quintet. Claude Luter and his Dixieland band were hip in the 1950s. Today there are jazz clubs throughout the city, both hallowed and new.

Electronica

Paris' electronic dance music is renowned; internationally successful bands such as Daft Punk and Justice head up the scene. David Guetta, Laurent Garnier, Martin Solveig and Bob Sinclair (aka Christophe Le Friant, originally nicknamed 'Chris the French Kiss') are top Parisian electronica producers and DJs who travel the international circuit. Breakbot (Thibaut Berland; b 1981) released his first album in 2012 and gained a rapid following for his remixes. His 2016-released album *Still Waters* includes the track Star Tripper, included in Disney's *Star Wars*–themed music album *Star Wars Headspace*.

Film

Paris is one of the world's most cinematic cities. The world's first paying-public film screening was held in Paris' Grand Café on blvd des Capucines, 9e, in December 1895 by the Lumière brothers, inventors of 'moving pictures'. Since that time, the French capital has produced a bevy of blockbuster film-makers and stars and is the filming location of countless box-office hits by both home-grown and foreign directors. Fabulous experiences for film buffs range from exploring behind the scenes at an art deco cinema to catching a classic retrospective in one of the Latin Quarter's many cinemas, or following in the footsteps of iconic screen heroine Amélie Poulain through the streets of Montmartre.

French cinema hasn't looked back since 2012 when *The Artist* (2011), a silent black-and-white romantic comedy set in 1920s Hollywood, won seven BAFTAs and five Oscars to become the most awarded film in French cinema history. The awards included Best Director for Parisian Michel Hazanavicius (b 1967), and Best Actor for Jean Dujardin (b 1972), whose later roles have included a WWII French soldier in George Clooney's *The Monuments Men* (2014).

France's leading lady is Parisian Marion Cotillard (b 1975), the first French woman since 1959 to win an Oscar for her role as Édith Piaf in Olivier Dahan's *La Môme* (*La Vie en Rose*; 2007). The versatile actress went on to play an amputee in art film *De Rouille et d'Os* (Rust and Bone; 2012) directed by Parisian Jacques Audiard (b 1952). In *Deux Jours, Une Nuit* (Two Days, One Night; 2014), Cotillard plays an employee in a solar-panel factory who learns she will lose her job if her co-workers don't each sacrifice €1000 bonuses offered to them. Her latest roles are 2017's *Rock'n Roll,* as the partner of Guillaume Canet (her real-life partner), who plays an actor told by his young co-star that he's no longer 'Rock'n' Roll' enough to sell films any more; and *Les Fantômes d'Ismaël* (Ismael's Ghosts), as a wife who returns from a 20-year disappearance.

For an overview of French films, including upcoming films, visit www.filmsdefrance.com.

Checking the map outside the Cité metro station

Survival Guide

Directory A–Z

Discount Cards

Almost all museums and monuments in Paris have discounted tickets (*tarif réduit*) for students and seniors (generally over 60 years), provided they have valid ID. Children often get in free; the cut-off age for a child is anywhere between six and 18 years. EU citizens under 26 years get in for free at national monuments and museums.

○ **Paris Museum Pass** (www.parismuseum pass.com; 2/4/6 days €48/62/74) Gets you into 50-odd venues in and around Paris; a huge advantage is that pass holders usually enter larger sights at a different entrance meaning you bypass (or substantially reduce) ridiculously long ticket queues.

○ **Paris Passlib'** (www. parisinfo.com; 2/3/5 days €109/129/155) Sold on its website and at the **Paris Convention & Visitors Bureau** (Paris Office de Tourisme; www.parisinfo.com; 25 rue des Pyramides, 1er; ⏱9am-7pm May-Oct, 10am-7pm Nov-Apr; 🛜; Ⓜ Pyramides), this handy city pass covers unlimited public transport in zones 1

to 3, admission to some 50 museums in the Paris region, a one-hour boat cruise along the Seine, and a one-day hop-on hop-off open-top bus service around central Paris' key sights with **L'Open Tour** (📞01 42 66 56 56; www.paris. opentour.com; 1-day pass adult/ child €33/17, night tour €27/17; 🛜). An extra €20 buys a skip-the-line ticket to levels one and two of the Eiffel Tower.

⚠ Electricity

Type E
230V/50Hz

⚠ Emergency

Ambulance (SAMU)	📞15
Fire	📞18
Police	📞17
EU-wide emergency	📞112

Book Your Stay Online

For more accommodation reviews by Lonely Planet authors, check out http://hotels. lonelyplanet.com/paris. You'll find independent reviews, as well as recommendations on the best places to stay. Best of all, you can book online.

Health

Hospitals

Paris has some 50 hospitals including the epicentral **Hôpital Hôtel Dieu** (📞01 42 34 88 19; www.aphp.fr; 1 Parvis Notre Dame – place Jean-Paul-II, 4e; Ⓜ Cité). It is one of the city's main government-run public hospitals; after 8pm use the emergency entrance on rue de la Cité.

Pharmacies

Pharmacies (chemists) are marked by a large illuminated green cross outside. At least one in each neighbourhood is open for extended hours; see www.parisinfo. com for listings.

Insurance

Comprehensive travel insurance to cover theft, loss and medical problems is highly

Practicalities

Smoking Smoking is illegal in indoor public spaces, including restaurants and bars (hence the crowds of smokers in doorways and on pavement terraces outside).

Weights & Measures France uses the metric system.

recommended. Worldwide travel insurance is available at www.lonelyplanet.com/travel-insurance. You can buy, extend and claim online anytime – even if you're already on the road.

Internet Access

◦ Free wi-fi is available in hundreds of public places, including parks, libraries and municipal buildings. For complete details and a map of hotspots, see www.paris.fr/wifi.

◦ Expect to pay around €4 per hour in internet cafes; Milk (www.milklub.com) has a central branch near Les Halles.

◦ Co-working cafes have sprung up across Paris; you typically pay for a set amount of time, with wi-fi, drinks and snacks included.

Money

◦ ATMs (*distributeur automatique de billets* in French) are widespread.

◦ Visa and MasterCard are accepted in most hotels, shops and restaurants; fewer accept American Express. France uses cards with an embedded microchip and PIN – few places accept swipe-and-signature. Ask your bank for advice before you leave.

Opening Hours

The following are *approximate* standard opening hours. Many businesses close in August for summer holidays.

Banks 9am to 1pm and 2pm to 5pm Monday to Friday, some Saturday morning

Bars & cafes 7am to 2am

Museums 10am to 6pm, closed Monday or Tuesday

Post offices 8am to 7pm Monday to Friday, and until noon Saturday

Restaurants noon to 2pm and 7.30pm to 10.30pm

Shops 10am to 7pm Monday to Saturday (later and on Sunday in tourist zones), occasionally close in the early afternoon for lunch and sometimes all day Monday

Public Holidays

In France a *jour férié* (public holiday) is celebrated strictly on the day on which it falls – if it's a Saturday or Sunday, no provision is made for an extra day off.

The following holidays are observed in Paris:

New Year's Day (Jour de l'An) 1 January

Easter Sunday & Monday (Pâques & Lundi de Pâques) Late March/April

May Day (Fête du Travail) 1 May

Victory in Europe Day (Victoire 1945) 8 May

Ascension Thursday (L'Ascension) May; celebrated on the 40th day after Easter

Whit Monday (Lundi de Pentecôte) Mid-May to mid-June (seventh Monday after Easter)

Bastille Day/National Day (Fête Nationale) 14 July

Assumption Day (L'Assomption) 15 August

All Saints' Day (La Toussaint) 1 November

Armistice Day/Remembrance Day (Le Onze Novembre) 11 November

Christmas (Noël) 25 December

Safe Travel

In general, Paris is well lit and safe, and random street assaults are rare.

Stay alert for pickpockets and take precautions: don't carry more money than you need, and keep your credit cards and passport in a concealed pouch.

Metro stations best avoided late at night include Châtelet–Les Halles, Château Rouge, Gare du Nord, Strasbourg St-Denis, Réaumur Sébastopol, Stalingrad and Montparnasse Bienvenüe. Marx Dormoy, Porte de la Chapelle and Marcadet–Poissonniers can be sketchy day and night.

Telephone

Check with your provider about roaming costs before you leave home, or ensure your phone's unlocked to use a French SIM card (available cheaply in Paris).

- There are no area codes in France – you always dial the 10-digit number.
- France's country code is ☎33 and the international access code is ☎00.

Time

- France is on Central European Time, one hour ahead of GMT.
- Daylight-saving time (two hours ahead of GMT) runs from the last Sunday in March to the last Sunday in October.

Toilets

- Public toilets in Paris are signposted *toilettes* or *WC*. On main roads, *sanisettes* (self-cleaning cylindrical toilets) are open 24 hours and are free of charge. Look for the words libre ('available'; green-coloured) or occupé ('occupied'; red-coloured).
- Cafe owners do not appreciate you using their facilities if you are not a paying customer (a coffee can be a good investment). Other good bets are major department stores and big hotels.

Tourist Information

Paris Convention & Visitors Bureau (Paris Office de Tourisme; www.parisinfo.com; 25 rue des Pyramides, 1er; ⏲9am-7pm May-Oct, 10am-7pm Nov-Apr; 📶; Ⓜ Pyramides) The main branch is 500m northwest of the Louvre.

Travellers with Disabilities

- For information about which cultural venues in Paris are accessible to people with disabilities, check Accès Culture (www.accesculture.org).
- Download Lonely Planet's free *Accessible Travel* guide from http://lptravel.to/AccessibleTravel.

Visas

- Generally no restrictions for EU citizens. Usually not required for most other nationalities for stays of up to 90 days.
- Check www.france.diplomatie.fr for the latest visa regulations and the closest French embassy to your current residence.

Transport

Arriving in Paris

Practically every major airline flies though one of Paris' three airports, and most European train and bus routes cross it.

Flights, tours and rail tickets can be booked online at www.lonelyplanet.com.

Air

Charles de Gaulle Airport

Most international airlines fly to **Aéroport de Charles de Gaulle** (CDG; ☎01 70 36 39 50; www.parisaeroport.fr), 28km northeast of central

Paris. In French the airport is commonly called 'Roissy' after the suburb in which it is located.

Bus

There are six main bus lines.

Le Bus Direct line 2 (€17; one hour; every 30 minutes, 5.45am to 11pm) Links the airport with the Arc de Triomphe via the Eiffel Tower and Trocadéro. Children under four years travel free.

Le Bus Direct line 4 (€17; 50 to 80 minutes; every 30 minutes, 6am to 10.30pm from the airport, 5.30am to 10.30pm from Montparnasse) Links the airport with Gare Montparnasse (80 minutes) in southern Paris via Gare de Lyon (50 minutes) in eastern Paris. Under fours travel free.

Noctilien bus 140 & 143 (€8 or four metro tickets) Part of the RATP night service, Noctilien has two buses that link CDG with Gare de l'Est via nearby Gare du Nord: bus 140 (1am to 4am; from Gare de l'Est 1am to 3.40am), taking 80 minutes, and bus 143 (12.32am to 4.32am; from Gare de l'Est 12.55am to 5.08am), taking 55 minutes.

RATP bus 350 (€6 or three metro tickets; 70 minutes; every 30 minutes, 5.30am to 11pm) Links the airport with Gare de l'Est in northern Paris.

RATP bus 351 (€6 or three metro tickets; 70 minutes; every 30 minutes, 5.30am to 11pm) Links the airport with place de la Nation in eastern Paris.

Roissybus (€12.50; one hour; from CDG every 15 to 20 minutes, 6am to 12.30am; from Paris every 15 minutes, 5.15am to 12.30am) Links the airport with Opéra.

Taxi

⊙ A taxi to the city centre takes 40 minutes. Since 2016, fares have been standardised to a flat rate: €50 to the Right Bank and €55 to the Left Bank. The fare increases by 15% between 7pm and 7am and on Sundays.

⊙ Only take taxis at a clearly marked rank. Never follow anyone who approaches you at the airport and claims to be a driver.

Train

CDG is served by the RER B line (€11.40, child four to nine €7.90), approximately 50 minutes, every 10 to 20 minutes), which connects with central Paris stations including Gare du Nord, Châtelet–Les Halles and St-Michel–Notre Dame. Trains run from 4.50am to 11.50pm (from Gare du Nord 4.53am to 12.15am) every six to 15 minutes.

Orly Airport

Aéroport d'Orly (ORY; ✆01 70 36 39 50; www.parisaeroport.fr) is 19km south of central Paris but, despite being closer than CDG, it is not as frequently used by international airlines, and public transport options aren't quite as straightforward.

Bus

Two bus lines serve Orly:

Le Bus Direct line 1 (€12; one hour, every 20 minutes 5.50am to 11.30pm from Orly, 4.50am to 10.30pm from the Arc de Triomphe) Runs to/from the Arc de Triomphe (one hour) via Gare Montparnasse (40 minutes), La Motte-Picquet and Trocadéro. Under fours travel free.

Orlybus (€8.70, 30 minutes, every 15 to 20 minutes, 6am to 12.30am from Orly, 5.35am to midnight from

Climate Change & Travel

Every form of transport that relies on carbon-based fuel generates CO_2, the main cause of human-induced climate change. Modern travel is dependent on aeroplanes, which might use less fuel per kilometre per person than most cars but travel much greater distances. The altitude at which aircraft emit gases (including CO_2) and particles also contributes to their climate change impact. Many websites offer 'carbon calculators' that allow people to estimate the carbon emissions generated by their journey and, for those who wish to do so, to offset the impact of the greenhouse gases emitted with contributions to portfolios of climate-friendly initiatives throughout the world. Lonely Planet offsets the carbon footprint of all staff and author travel.

Paris) Runs to/from place Denfert-Rochereau in southern Paris.

Taxi

A taxi to the city centre takes roughly 30 minutes. Standardised flat-rate fares since 2016 mean a taxi costs €30 to the Left Bank and €35 to the Right Bank. The fare increases by 15% between 7pm and 7am and on Sundays.

Train

There is currently no direct train to/from Orly; you'll need to change halfway. Note that while it is possible to take a shuttle to the RER C line, this service is quite long and not recommended.

RER B (€13.25, children four to nine €6.60, 35 minutes, every four to 12 minutes) This line connects Orly with the St-Michel–Notre Dame, Châtelet–Les Halles and Gare du Nord stations in the city centre. In order to get from Orly to the RER station (Antony), you must first take the Orlyval automatic train. The service runs from 6am to 11.35pm. You only need one ticket to take the two trains.

Tram

Tramway T7 (€1.90, every six minutes, 40 minutes, 5.30am to 12.30am) links Orly with Villejuif-Louis Aragon metro station in southern Paris; buy tickets from the machine at the tram stop as no tickets are sold on board.

Beauvais Airport

Aéroport de Beauvais (BVA; ✆08 92 68 20 66; www.aeroportbeauvais.com) is 75km north of Paris and is served by a few low-cost flights. Before you snap up that bargain, consider if the postarrival journey is worth it.

The Beauvais *navette* (shuttle bus; €17, 1¼ hours) links the airport with **Parking Pershing** (16-24 bd Pershing, 17e; ⓂPorte Maillot) on central Paris' western edge; services are coordinated with flight times.

Train

Gare du Nord

Gare du Nord (www.gares-sncf.com; rue de Dunkerque, 10e; ⓂGare du Nord) is the terminus for northbound domestic trains as well as several international services. Located in northern Paris.

Eurostar (www.eurostar.com) The London–Paris line runs from St Pancras International to Gare du Nord. Voyages take 2¼ hours.

Thalys (www.thalys.com) Trains pull into Paris' Gare du Nord from Brussels, Amsterdam and Cologne.

Other Mainline Train Stations

Paris has five other stations for long-distance trains, each with its own metro station: Gare d'Austerlitz, Gare de l'Est, Gare de Lyon, Gare Montparnasse and Gare St-Lazare; the station used

depends on the direction from Paris.

Contact Oui.SNCF (www.oui.sncf) for connections throughout France and continental Europe.

Bus

Eurolines (www.eurolines.fr) connects all major European capitals to Paris' eastern **Gare Routiére Internationale de Paris-Galliéni** (28 av du Général de Gaulle, Bagnolet; ⓂGalliéni). Major European bus company Flixbus (www.flixbus.com) and the Beauvais airport shuttle both use western **Parking Pershing** (16-24 bd Pershing, 17e; ⓂPorte Maillot).

Getting Around

Paris' metro and RER trains, trams, buses and night buses are run by RATP (www.ratp.fr), which has an online journey planner. Free transport maps are available at metro ticket windows and can be downloaded from the website.

Train

Paris' underground network consists of two separate but linked systems: the metro and the Réseau Express Régional (RER) suburban train line. The metro has 14 numbered lines; the RER has five main lines (but you'll probably only need to use A, B and C). When buying tickets consider how many zones your journey

Tourist Transport Passes

The Mobilis and Paris Visite passes are valid on the metro, RER, SNCF's suburban lines, buses, night buses, trams and Montmartre funicular railway. No photo is needed, but write your card number on the ticket.

Passes are sold at metro and RER stations, SNCF offices in Paris, and the airports. Children aged four to 11 years pay roughly half price. Passes operate by date (rather than 24-hour periods), so activate them early in the day for the best value.

o The **Mobilis** card allows unlimited travel for one day and costs €7.50 (two zones) to €17.80 (five zones). Depending on how many times you plan to hop on/off the metro in a day, a *carnet* might work out cheaper.

o **Paris Visite** allows unlimited travel as well as discounted entry to certain museums and other discounts and bonuses. The 'Paris+Suburbs+Airports' pass includes transport to/from the airports and costs €25.25/38.35/53.75/65.80 for one/two/three/five days. The cheaper 'Paris Centre' pass, valid for zones 1 to 3, costs €12/19.50/26.65/38.35 for one/two/three/five days.

will cover; there are five concentric transportation zones rippling out from Paris (5 being the furthest); if you travel from Charles de Gaulle airport to Paris, for instance, you will have to buy a zone 1–5 ticket.

Metro

o Metro lines are identified by both their number (eg *ligne* 1; line 1) and their colour, listed on official metro signs and maps.

o Signs in metro and RER stations indicate the way to the correct platform for your line. The *direction* signs on each platform indicate the terminus. On lines that split into several branches (such as lines 7 and 13), the terminus of each train is indicated on the cars and on signs on each platform giving the number of minutes until the next and subsequent train.

o Signs marked *correspondance* (transfer) show how to reach connecting trains. At stations with many intersecting lines, like Châtelet and Montparnasse Bienvenüe, walking from one platform to the next can take a very long time.

o Different station exits are indicated by white-on-blue *sortie* (exit) signs. You can get your bearings by checking the *plan du quartier* (neighbourhood maps) posted at exits.

o Each line has its own schedule, but trains usually start at around 5.30am, with the last train beginning its run between 12.35am and 1.15am (2.15am on Friday and Saturday).

RER

o The RER is faster than the metro, but the stops are much further apart.

o If you're going out to the suburbs (eg Versailles, Disneyland), make sure your ticket is for the correct zone.

Tickets & Fares

o The same RATP tickets are valid on the metro, the RER (for travel within the city limits), buses, trams and the Montmartre funicular.

o A ticket – white in colour and called *Le Ticket t+* – costs €1.90 (half price for children aged four to nine years) if bought individually and €14.90 for adults for a *carnet* (book) of 10.

o Tickets are sold at all metro stations. Ticket windows accept most credit cards; however automated machines do not accept credit cards without embedded chips (and even then, not all foreign chip-embedded cards).

o One ticket lets you travel between any two metro stations (no return journeys) for a period of 1½ hours, no matter how many transfers are required. You can also use it on the RER for travel within zone 1, which encompasses all of central Paris.

○ Transfers from the metro to bus or vice versa are not possible.

○ Always keep your ticket until you exit from your station or risk a fine.

Bicycle

Vélib'

The **Vélib'** (☐01 76 49 12 34; www.velib-metropole.fr; day/week subscription for up to 5 people €5/15, standard bike hire up to 30/60min free/€1, electric bike €1/2) bike-share scheme changed operators in 2018; check the website for the latest information. Tens of thousands of bikes (30% electric) at some 1400 stations throughout Paris will be accessible around the clock.

○ To get a bike, you first need to purchase a one- or seven-day subscription, either at the terminals found at docking stations or online. The terminals require a chip-and-PIN credit card (even then, not all foreign chip-embedded cards will work). Alternatively, you can pre-purchase a subscription online.

○ After you authorise a deposit (€300) to pay for the bike should it go missing, you'll receive an ID number and PIN code and you're ready to go.

○ Bikes are rented in 30-minute intervals. If you return a standard bike before a half-hour is up and

then take a new one, you will not be charged (electric bikes incur a charge).

○ Bikes are geared to cyclists aged 14 and over. Bring your own helmet (they are not required by law).

○ **Cityscoot** (www.cityscoot. eu; per 1/100min €0.28/25; ⊙7am-11pm) is a similar share scheme for electric scooters. Any driver's licence (including a foreign-issued licence) is valid for those born before 1 January 1988; anyone born after that date requires a current French or EU driver's licence.

Rentals

Most rental places will require a deposit. Take ID and bank card/credit card.

Freescoot (☐01 44 07 06 72; www.freescoot.com; 63 quai de la Tournelle, 5e; 50/125cc scooters per 24hr from €65/75, bicycle/tandem/electric-bike rental per 24hr from €25/40/50; ⊙9am-1pm & 2-7pm mid-Apr–mid-Sep, closed Sun & Wed mid-Sep–mid-Apr; Ⓜ Maubert-Mutualité)

Gepetto et Vélos (☐01 43 54 19 95; www.gepetto-velos.com; 28 rue des Fossées St-Bernard, 5e; bike rental per hour/day/weekend €4/16/20, tandem €8/30/45; ⊙9am-7pm Tue-Sat; Ⓜ Cardinal Lemoine)

Paris à Vélo, C'est Sympa (☐01 48 87 60 01; https://parisvelosympa.fr; 22 rue Alphonse Baudin, 11e; half-day/full day/24hr bike from €12/15/20, electric bike €20/30/40; ⊙9.30am-1pm & 2-6pm Mon-Fri, 9am-7pm Sat & Sun Apr-Oct, shorter hours Nov-Mar; Ⓜ Richard Lenoir)

Boat

Glassed-in trimarans that dock every 20 to 25 minutes at small piers along the

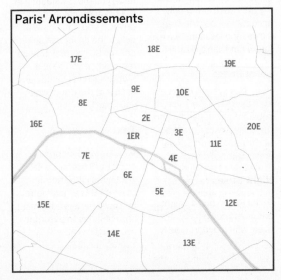

Paris' Arrondissements

17E
18E
19E
9E
10E
8E
2E
16E
1ER
3E
20E
11E
7E
4E
6E
5E
15E
12E
14E
13E

Seine are run by **Batobus** (www.batobus.com; adult/child 1-day pass €17/8, 2-day pass €19/10; ⏱10am-9.30pm late Apr-Aug, shorter hours Sep-late Apr). Key stops include the Eiffel Tower, Musée d'Orsay, St-Germain des Prés, Notre Dame, Jardin des Plantes/Cité de la Mode et du Design, Hôtel de Ville, Musée du Louvre and Champs-Élysées.

Buy tickets online, at ferry stops or tourist offices. You can also buy a Pass+ that includes **L'Open Tour** (☎01 42 66 56 56; www.paris. opentour.com; 1-day pass adult/ child €33/17, night tour €27/17; 🛜) buses, to be used on consecutive days. A two-day pass per adult/child costs €46/21; a three day-pass is €50/21.

Bus

Buses can be a scenic way to get around – and there are no stairs to climb, meaning they are more widely accessible – but they're slower and less intuitive to figure out than the metro.

Local Buses

Paris' bus system is operated by RATP. Hours vary substantially depending on the line. Services are drastically reduced on Sunday and public holidays.

Night Buses

o The RATP runs 47 night bus lines known as Noctilien, which depart hourly

from 11.45pm to 6am. Look for navy-blue N or Noctilien signs at bus stops.

o Noctilien services are included on your Mobilis or Paris Visite pass for the zones in which you are travelling. Otherwise you pay a certain number of standard €1.90 metro/bus tickets, depending on the length of your journey.

Tickets & Fares

o Normal bus rides embracing one or two bus zones cost one metro ticket; longer rides require two or even three tickets. Transfers to other buses – but not the metro – are allowed on the same ticket as long as the change takes place 1½ hours between the first and last validation. This does not apply to Noctilien services.

o Whatever kind of single-journey ticket you have, you must validate it in the ticket machine near the driver. If you don't have a ticket, the driver can sell you one for €2 (correct change required). If you have a Mobilis or Paris Visite pass, flash it at the driver when you board.

Taxi

o The maximum *prise en charge* (flagfall) is €4. Within the city limits, it costs €1.07 per kilometre for travel between 10am and 5pm Monday to Saturday

(*Tarif A;* white light on taxi roof and meter).

o At night (5pm to 10am), on Sunday from 7am to midnight, and in the inner suburbs the rate is €1.29 per kilometre (*Tarif B;* orange light).

o Travel in the city limits and inner suburbs on Sunday night (midnight to 7am Monday) and in the outer suburbs is at *Tarif C,* €1.56 per kilometre (blue light).

o The minimum taxi fare for a short trip is €7.10.

o There's no additional charge for luggage.

o Flagging down a taxi in Paris can be difficult; it's best to find an official taxi stand.

o To order a taxi, call or reserve online with **Taxis G7** (☎3607, 01 41 27 66 99; www. g7.fr), **Taxis Bleus** (☎3607, 01 41 27 66 99; www.g7.fr) or **Alpha Taxis** (☎01 45 85 85 85; www.alpha-taxis-paris.fr).

Car & Motorcycle

Driving in Paris is defined by the triple hassle of navigation, heavy traffic and limited parking. Petrol stations are also difficult to locate and access. It doesn't make sense to use a car to get around, but if you're heading out of the city on an excursion, then your own wheels can certainly be useful. If you plan on hiring a car, it's best to do so online and in advance.

Language

The sounds used in spoken French can almost all be found in English. There are a couple of exceptions: nasal vowels (represented in our pronunciation guides by 'o' or 'u' followed by an almost inaudible nasal consonant sound 'm', 'n' or 'ng'), the 'funny' *u* sound ('ew' in our guides) and the deep-in-the-throat *r*. Bearing these few points in mind and reading our pronunciation guides below as if they were English, you'll be understood just fine. The markers (m) and (f) indicate the forms for male and female speakers respectively.

To enhance your trip with a phrasebook, visit **lonelyplanet.com**. Lonely Planet iPhone phrasebooks are available through the Apple App store.

Basics

Hello.
Bonjour. — bon·zhoor
Goodbye.
Au revoir. — o·rer·vwa
How are you?
Comment allez-vous? — ko·mon ta·lay·voo
I'm fine, thanks.
Bien, merci. — byun mair·see
Please.
S'il vous plaît. — seel voo play
Thank you.
Merci. — mair·see
Excuse me.
Excusez-moi. — ek·skew·zay·mwa
Sorry.
Pardon. — par·don
Yes./No.
Oui./Non. — wee/non
I don't understand.
Je ne comprends pas. — zher ner kom·pron pa
Do you speak English?
Parlez-vous anglais? — par·lay·voo ong·glay

Shopping

I'd like to buy ...
Je voudrais acheter ... — zher voo·dray ash·tay ...

I'm just looking.
Je regarde. — zher rer·gard
How much is it?
C'est combien? — say kom·byun
It's too expensive.
C'est trop cher. — say tro shair
Can you lower the price?
Vous pouvez baisser le prix? — voo poo·vay bay·say ler pree

Eating & Drinking

..., please.
..., s'il vous plaît. — ... seel voo play
  A coffee — *un café* — un ka·fay
  A table for two — *une table pour deux* — ewn ta·bler poor der
  Two beers — *deux bières* — der bee·yair

I'm a vegetarian.
Je suis végétarien/ végétarienne. (m/f) — zher swee vay·zhay·ta·ryun/ vay·zhay·ta·ryen
Cheers!
Santé! — son·tay
That was delicious!
C'était délicieux! — say·tay day·lee·syer
The bill, please.
L'addition, s'il vous plaît. — la·dee·syon seel voo play

Emergencies

Help!
Au secours! — o skoor
Call the police!
Appelez la police! — a·play la po·lees
Call a doctor!
Appelez un médecin! — a·play un mayd·sun
I'm sick.
Je suis malade. — zher swee ma·lad
I'm lost.
Je suis perdu/ perdue. (m/f) — zhe swee pair·dew
Where are the toilets?
Où sont les toilettes? — oo son lay twa·let

Transport & Directions

Where's ...?
Où est ...? — oo ay ...
What's the address?
Quelle est l'adresse? — kel ay la·dres
I want to go to ...
Je voudrais aller à ... — zher voo·dray a·lay a ...

Behind the Scenes

Curator Thanks

Catherine Le Nevez

Merci mille fois first and foremost to Julian and to the innumerable Parisians who provided insights, inspiration and great times. Huge thanks too to my Paris co-writers Chris and Nicola, Destination Editor Daniel Fahey and everyone at Lonely Planet. As ever, a heartfelt *merci encore* to my parents, brother, *belle-sœur, neveu* and *nièce* for sustaining my lifelong love of Paris and France.

Acknowledgements

Climate map data adapted from Peel MC, Finlayson BL & McMahon TA (2007) 'Updated World Map of the Köppen-Geiger Climate Classification', *Hydrology and Earth System Sciences*, 11, 1633–44.

Illustrations pp50–1, pp56–7, pp80–81 and pp86–7 by Javier Zarracina.

This Book

This book was curated by Catherine Le Nevez, who researched and wrote the content along with Christopher Pitts and Nicola Williams. Damian Harper researched and wrote the Giverny content. Catherine Le Nevez also curated, researched and wrote the previous edition. This guidebook was produced by the following:

Destination Editor Daniel Fahey

Product Editor Kate Mathews

Book Designer Virginia Moreno

Senior Cartographer Mark Griffiths

Assisting Editors Sarah Bailey, Judith Bamber, Katie Connolly, Lucy Cowie, Andrea Dobbin, Bruce Evans, Kristin Odijk, Fionnuala Twomey

Cover Researcher Naomi Parker

Thanks to Will Allen, Andi Jones, Genna Patterson, Carly Plumridge, Jessica Ross, Tony Wheeler, Amanda Williamson

Send Us Your Feedback

We love to hear from travellers – your comments keep us on our toes and help make our books better. Our well-travelled team reads every word on what you loved or loathed about this book. Although we cannot reply individually to postal submissions, we always guarantee that your feedback goes straight to the appropriate authors, in time for the next edition. Each person who sends us information is thanked in the next edition, the most useful submissions are rewarded with a selection of digital PDF chapters.

Visit lonelyplanet.com/contact to submit your updates and suggestions or to ask for help. Our award-winning website also features inspirational travel stories, news and discussions.

Note: We may edit, reproduce and incorporate your comments in Lonely Planet products such as guidebooks, websites and digital products, so let us know if you don't want your comments reproduced or your name acknowledged. For a copy of our privacy policy visit lonelyplanet.com/privacy.

Index

A

accessible travel 233

accommodation 19, 205-11, 231, **211**

activities 28, 197-203, *see also individual activities*

for children 70-1

air travel 233-5

apartment rentals 208

apiaries 71

Arabic culture 109

Arc de Triomphe 42-5

Arc de Triomphe du Carrousel 91

architects, *see also* architecture

Garnier, Charles 100

Hardouin-Mansart, Jules 84-5, 88

Le Vau, Louis 84-5

Nouvel, Jean 109, 215, 223, 224

Pei, IM 55

Piano, Renzo 74, 159

architecture 40, 215, 221-4, *see also* architects

area codes 233

arrondissements 19, **237**

art 29, 30, 225-8, *see also individual artists*

impressionism 65, 226

street art 112-13

art deco 224

art galleries, *see individual galleries, museums*

art nouveau 28, 223

Atelier Brancusi 76

ATMs 232

B

baguettes 135

bakeries 135, 139

Basilique du Sacré-Cœur 58-61

Bastille Day 12

bathrooms 233

beaches 12

beer 11, 168, 171

Belleville

drinking 177-9

entertainment 192-3

food 129-33

shopping 153-7

bicycle travel, *see* cycling

bistros 120

Bloody Mary 176

boat travel 72-3, 237-8

Bois de Boulogne 202-3

Bois de Vincennes 202

boules 202

bouquinistes 163

Bourse de Commerce 30, 77

Brancusi, Constantin 76, 109

breweries 171

budget 31

bus travel 238

business hours 146, 166, 232

buskers 191

C

Canal St-Martin 159

car travel 238

Catacombes, Les 94-5

cell phones 18, 233

cemeteries 78-81, 94-5

Centre Pompidou 74-7

Cézanne, Paul 65, 160, 226

Champs-Élysées **246-7**

accommodation 211

drinking 170-1

entertainment 190

food 122-3

shopping 150

Château de Versailles 84-7

Château de Vincennes 202

cheese 132

chemists 231

children, travel with 32-3

activities 70-1

museums 107

shopping 148

workshops 77, 97

chocolate 16, 156

Cimetière du Montparnasse 95

Cimetière du Père Lachaise 78-81, **80-1**

cinemas 194, 195, *see also* film

Cité de l'Architecture et du Patrimoine 40

climate 4-17, 19

Clos Montmartre 61

clubs 169, 175, 189

cocktails 6, 168, 176

coffee 168, 183

Conciergerie 93

cooking courses 96-7

costs 18, 118, 167, 206

courses 96-7

crêpes 120

cruises 72-3

culture 225-9

currency 18

cycling 203, 237

events 12

D

da Vinci, Leonardo 55

Dalí, Salvador 60-1, 227

dangers, *see* safety

Degas, Edgar 65, 226

Delacroix, Eugène 79, 89, 226

demographics 215

disabilities, travellers with 233

discount cards 231

districts 19, **237**

drinking 165-85, **167**, *see also* drinks, *individual neighbourhoods*

costs 167

festivals 6, 11, 16

highlights 168-9

opening hours 166

phrases 167

Basilique du Sacré-Cœur (p58), Montmartre

Paris Maps

Champs-Élysées, St-Germain, Les Invalides & Montparnasse

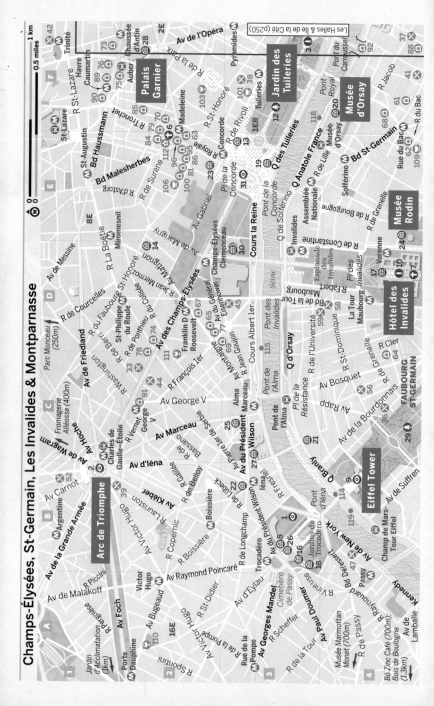

Les Halles & Île de la Cité (p250)

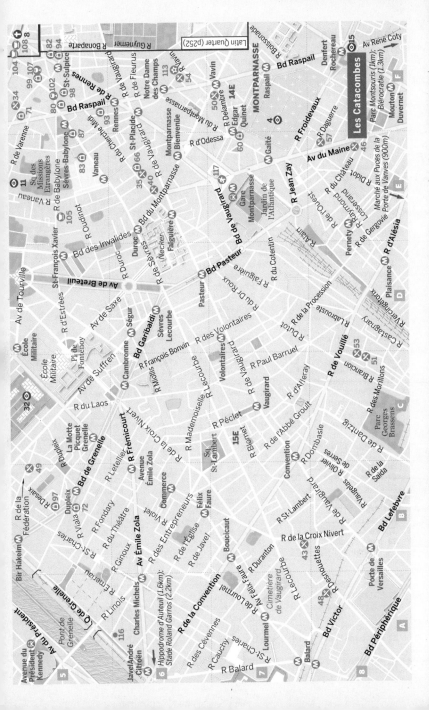

Champs-Élysées, St-Germain, Les Invalides & Montparnasse

Montmartre

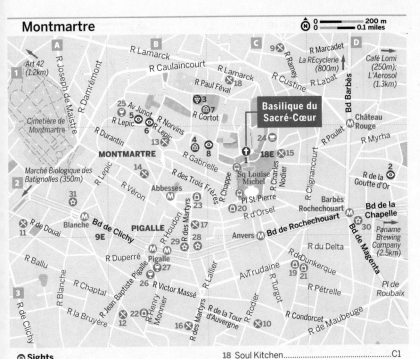

Sights
1 Basilique du Sacré-Cœur C2
2 Brasserie la Goutte d'Or D2
3 Clos Montmartre B1
4 Espace Dalí B2
5 Moulin Blute Fin B1
6 Moulin Radet B1
7 Musée de Montmartre B1
8 Place du Tertre C2

Eating
9 Abattoir Végétal C1
10 Aspic C3
11 Crêperie Pen-Ty A2
12 L'affineur Affiné B3
13 Le Bistrot de la Galette B2
14 Le Grenier à Pain B2
15 L'Été en Pente Douce C2
16 Mesdemoiselles Madeleines B3
17 Pain Pain B2

18 Soul Kitchen C1

Shopping
19 Balades Sonores C3
20 Belle du Jour C2
21 La Binouze C3
22 Pigalle B3
23 Spree B2

Drinking & Nightlife
24 Hardware Société C2
25 Le Très Particulier B1
26 Lipstick B3
27 Lulu White B3

Entertainment
28 La Cigale B3
29 Le Divan du Monde B3
30 Le Louxor D2
31 Moulin Rouge A2

Les Halles & Île de la Cité

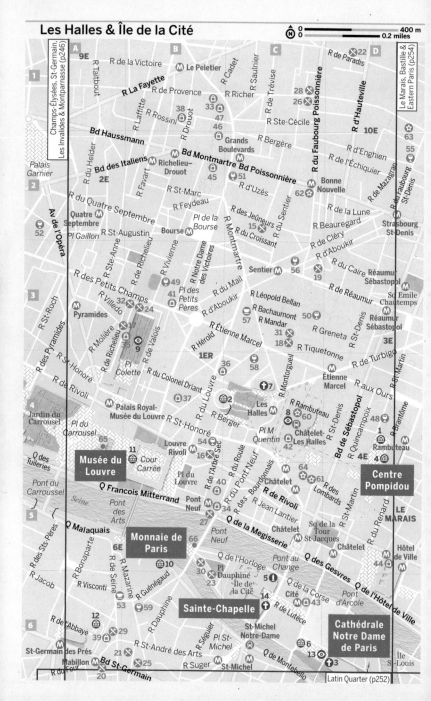

Champs-Élysées, St-Germain, Les Invalides & Montparnasse (p246)

Le Marais, Bastille & Eastern Paris (p254)

9E

R Taitbout

R de la Victoire

Le Peletier

R Cadet

R Saulnier

R de Trévise

R de Paradis

R d'Hauteville

10E

D

R de Provence

R Richer

R La Fayette

R Laffitte

R Rossini

38

33

47

46

Grands Boulevards

R Ste-Cécile

28

26

R du Faubourg Poissonnière

R d'Enghien

R de l'Échiquier

63

55

Bd Haussmann

R du Helder

Bd des Italiens

Richelieu-Drouot

Bd Montmartre Bd Poissonnière

R Bergère

2E

R Favart

45

51

R d'Uzès

Bonne Nouvelle

62

R de la Lune

Strasbourg St-Denis

Palais Garnier

R du Quatre Septembre

R St-Marc

R Feydeau

Pl de la Bourse

R des Jeûneurs

R Beauregard

R de Mazagran

R du Faubourg St-Denis

52

Quatre Septembre

Pl Gaillon

R St-Augustin

Bourse

15

R du Croissant

R de Cléry

R d'Aboukir

R de la Lune

Av de l'Opéra

R Ste-Anne

R de Richelieu

R Vivienne

R Notre Dame des Victoires

R Montmartre

Sentier

56

R du Caire

19

Réaumur Sébastopol

R des Petits Champs

49

Pl des Petits Pères

R du Mail

R Léopold Bellan

R de Réaumur

Sq Émile Chautemps

41

R d'Aboukir

R Bachaumont

50

Réaumur Sébastopol

Pyramides

R Villedo

32

24

57

R Mandar

31

R Greneta

R St-Denis

3E

R Molière

35

9

R de Valois

R Hérold

R Étienne Marcel

18

R Tiquetonne

R de Turbigo

R des Pyramides

R de Richelieu

Pl Colette

36

58

Étienne Marcel

R aux Ours

R St-Martin

R St-Honoré

R du Colonel Driant

1ER

7

37

2

R du Louvre

R Berger

Les Halles

8

60

R Rambuteau

Bd de Sébastopol

48

1

Pôterne

4E

Palais Royal-Musée du Louvre

R St-Honoré

42

Châtelet-Les Halles

R Quincampoix

Rambuteau

4

Centre Pompidou

Jardin du Carrousel

Pl du Carrousel

65

11

Cour Carrée

54

Louvre Rivoli

16

Pl M Quentin

64

61

R des Lombards

LE MARAIS

Musée du Louvre

R de l'Arbre Sec

Pl du Louvre

40

Châtelet

R de Rivoli

R du Renard

Q des Tuileries

Pont du Carrousel

R du Pont Neuf

R des Bourdonnais

R Jean Lantier

4E

Hôtel de Ville

Seine

Pont des Arts

Q François Mitterrand

Pont Neuf

34

R de Rivoli

Châtelet

44

Q Malaquais

Monnaie de Paris

66

27

Pont Neuf

Q de la Mégisserie

Sq de la Tour St-Jacques

Châtelet

R des Sts-Pères

R Bonaparte

R de Seine

6E

10

R Mazarine

Q de l'Horloge

Pont au Change

Q de la Corse

Q des Gesvres

Q de l'Hôtel de Ville

R Jacob

R Guénégaud

30

23

Pl Dauphine

5

Cité

43

Pont d'Arcole

R Visconti

53

59

Île de la Cité

14

R de Lutèce

Cathédrale Notre Dame de Paris

Île St-Louis

12

Sainte-Chapelle

39

29

R Dauphine

R Séguier

Pl St-Michel

St-Michel Notre-Dame

6

13

3

St-Germain des Prés

21

R St-André des Arts

Mabillon

25

Bd St-Germain

R Suger

St-Michel

Q de Montebello

R du Four

20

Latin Quarter (p252)

Les Halles & Île de la Cité

Latin Quarter

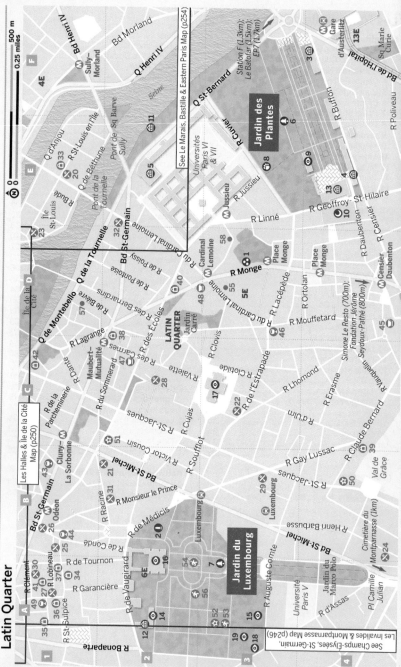

See Le Marais, Bastille & Eastern Paris Map (p254)

Les Halles & Île de la Cité Map (p250)

See Champs-Élysées, St-Germain, Les Invalides & Montparnasse Map (p246)

Jardin des Plantes

Jardin du Luxembourg

LATIN QUARTER

Jardin Carré

0   500 m
0   0.25 miles

R St-Sulpice
R Bonaparte
Bd St-Germain
Odeon
R Clément
R Lobineau
R Garancière
R de Tournon
R de Condé
R de Vaugirard
R de Médicis
R Monsieur le Prince
R Racine
Bd St-Michel
Cluny–La Sorbonne
R de la Parcheminerie
R Dante
Maubert-Mutualité
R des Carmes
R du Sommerard
R Lagrange
Q de Montebello
Île de la Cité
R de Bièvre
R des Bernardins
R de Pontoise
R de Poissy
Bd St-Germain
Q de la Tournelle
Pont de la Tournelle
Île St-Louis
Q de Béthune
R St-Louis en l'Île
Q d'Anjou
Sully-Morland
Bd Henri IV
Q Henri IV
Bd Morland
Seine
Pont de Sully
Sq Barye
Q St-Bernard
Universités Paris VI & VII
Jussieu
R Jussieu
R Linné
R Cuvier
Q St-Bernard
R Buffon
Gare d'Austerlitz
Sq Marie Curie
Bd de l'Hôpital
13E
R Poliveau
R Censier
Censier-Daubenton
R Daubenton
R Geoffroy- St-Hilaire
R Ortolan
R Mouffetard
R Lacépède
Place Monge
Place Monge
Cardinal Lemoine
R Monge
R du Cardinal Lemoine
Bd St-Germain
5E
R Clovis
R Valette
R Clotilde
R de l'Estrapade
R Lhomond
R d'Ulm
R Erasme
R Cujas
R St-Jacques
R Soufflot
R Victor Cousin
R Gay Lussac
R St-Jacques
R Claude Bernard
Val de Grâce
Luxembourg
Luxembourg
R Henri Barbusse
Bd St-Michel
Cimetière du Montparnasse (1km)
Jardin du Marco Polo
Université Paris V
R d'Assas
Pl Camille Julian
R Auguste Comte
6E

Station F (1.3km);
Le Batofar (1.5km);
EP7 (1.7km)

Simone Le Resto (700m);
Fondation Jérôme
Seydoux-Pathé (800m)

Latin Quarter

Le Marais, Bastille & Eastern Paris

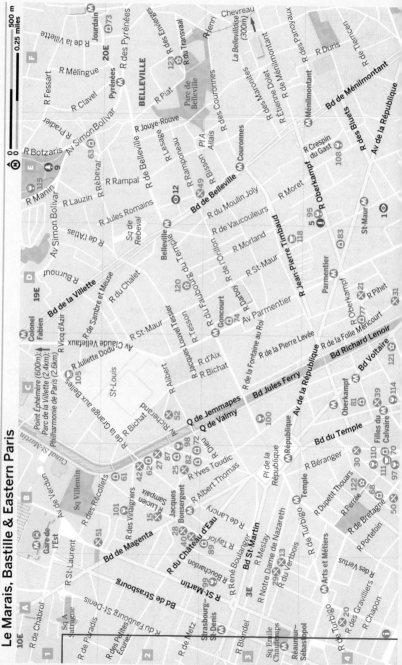

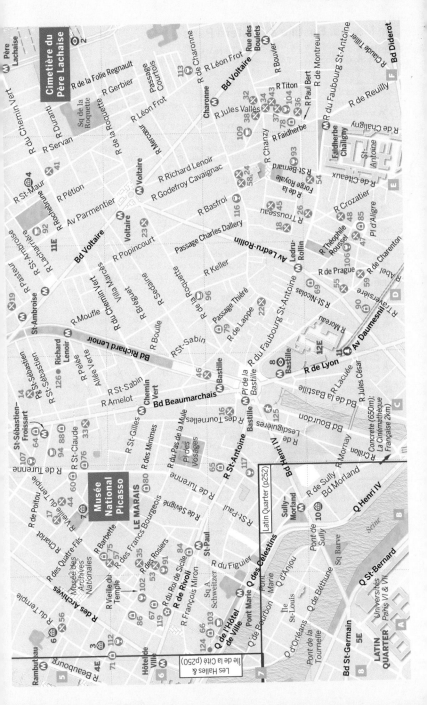

Cimetière du Père Lachaise

Musée National Picasso

LE MARAIS

Latin Quarter (p252)

Les Halles & Île de la Cité (p250)

LATIN QUARTER

11E

12E

4E

5E

Le Marais, Bastille & Eastern Paris

Symbols & Map Key

Look for these symbols to quickly identify listings:

- ◉ Sights
- ❸ Activities
- ❺ Courses
- ❼ Tours
- ❸ Festivals & Events
- ❌ Eating
- ❾ Drinking
- ❸ Entertainment
- ❻ Shopping
- ❶ Information & Transport

These symbols and abbreviations give vital information for each listing:

🌿 Sustainable or green recommendation

FREE No payment required

- 📞 Telephone number
- 🕑 Opening hours
- Ⓟ Parking
- 🚭 Nonsmoking
- ❄ Air-conditioning
- @ Internet access
- 📶 Wi-fi access
- 🏊 Swimming pool
- 🚌 Bus
- ⛴ Ferry
- 🚊 Tram
- 🚆 Train
- 📖 English-language menu
- 🥗 Vegetarian selection
- 👪 Family-friendly

Find your best experiences with these Great For... icons.

- 🖼 Art & Culture
- 🏖 Beaches
- 💰 Budget
- ☕ Cafe/Coffee
- 🚲 Cycling
- 🧭 Detour
- 🍷 Drinking
- 🎟 Entertainment
- 🎆 Events
- 👨‍👩‍👧 Family Travel
- 🍴 Food & Drink
- 📖 History
- 💬 Local Life
- 🐿 Nature & Wildlife
- 📷 Photo Op
- 🔭 Scenery
- 🛍 Shopping
- 🎿 Short Trip
- 🏀 Sport
- 🚶 Walking
- ❄ Winter Travel

Sights

- 🏖 Beach
- 🐦 Bird Sanctuary
- ☸ Buddhist
- 🏰 Castle/Palace
- ✝ Christian
- ☯ Confucian
- 🕉 Hindu
- ☪ Islamic
- 卍 Jain
- ✡ Jewish
- 🗿 Monument
- 🏛 Museum/Gallery/Historic Building
- 🏚 Ruin
- ⛩ Shinto
- 🪯 Sikh
- ☯ Taoist
- 🍷 Winery/Vineyard
- 🐾 Zoo/Wildlife Sanctuary
- ◉ Other Sight

Points of Interest

- 🏄 Bodysurfing
- ⛺ Camping
- ☕ Cafe
- 🛶 Canoeing/Kayaking
- • Course/Tour
- 🤿 Diving
- 🍷 Drinking & Nightlife
- ❌ Eating
- 🎭 Entertainment
- ♨ Sento Hot Baths/Onsen
- 🛍 Shopping
- ⛷ Skiing
- 🛏 Sleeping
- 🤿 Snorkelling
- 🏄 Surfing
- 🏊 Swimming/Pool
- 🚶 Walking
- 🏄 Windsurfing
- ❸ Other Activity

Information

- 💲 Bank
- 🏛 Embassy/Consulate
- ➕ Hospital/Medical
- @ Internet
- 👮 Police
- ✉ Post Office
- 📞 Telephone
- 🚻 Toilet
- ❶ Tourist Information
- • Other Information

Geographic

- 🏖 Beach
- ⊢ Gate
- 🏠 Hut/Shelter
- 🗼 Lighthouse
- 🔭 Lookout
- ▲ Mountain/Volcano
- 🌴 Oasis
- 🌳 Park
-)(Pass
- 🍴 Picnic Area
- 💧 Waterfall

Transport

- ✈ Airport
- Ⓑ BART station
- ⊗ Border crossing
- Ⓣ Boston T station
- 🚌 Bus
- 🚠 Cable car/Funicular
- 🚲 Cycling
- ⛴ Ferry
- Ⓜ Metro/MRT station
- 🚝 Monorail
- Ⓟ Parking
- ⛽ Petrol station
- 💲 Subway/S-Bahn/Skytrain station
- 🚕 Taxi
- 🚂 Train station/Railway
- 🚊 Tram
- Ⓣ Tube Station
- Ⓤ Underground/U-Bahn station
- • Other Transport

Our Story

A beat-up old car, a few dollars in the pocket and a sense of adventure, In 1972 that's all Tony and Maureen Wheeler needed for the trip of a lifetime – across Europe and Asia overland to Australia. It took several months, and at the end – broke but inspired – they sat at their kitchen table writing and stapling together their first travel guide, *Across Asia on the Cheap*. Within a week they'd sold 1500 copies. Lonely Planet was born.

Today, Lonely Planet has offices in Franklin, London, Melbourne, Oakland, Dublin, Beijing, and Delhi, with more than 600 staff and writers. We share Tony's belief that 'a great guidebook should do three things: inform, educate and amuse'.

Our Writers

Catherine Le Nevez

Catherine's wanderlust kicked in when she roadtripped across Europe from her Parisian base aged four, and she's been hitting the road at every opportunity since, travelling to around 60 countries and completing her Doctorate of Creative Arts in Writing, Masters in Professional Writing, and postgraduate qualifications in editing and publishing along the way. Over the past dozen-plus years she's written scores of Lonely Planet guides and articles covering Paris, France, Europe and far beyond. Her work has also appeared in numerous online and print publications. Topping Catherine's list of travel tips is to travel without any expectations.

Christopher Pitts

Born in the year of the Tiger, Chris' first expedition in life ended in failure when he tried to dig from Pennsylvania to China at the age of six. Hardened by reality but still infinitely curious about the other side of the world, he went on to study Chinese in university, living for several years in Kunming, Taiwan and Shanghai. A chance encounter led to a Paris relocation, where he lived with his wife and two children for over a decade before the lure of Colorado's sunny skies and outdoor adventure proved too great to resist.

Nicola Williams

Border-hopping is a way of life for British writer, runner, foodie, art aficionado and mum-of-three Nicola Williams. Nicola has authored more than 50 guidebooks on Paris, Provence, Rome, Tuscany, France, Italy and Switzerland for Lonely Planet and covers France as a destination expert for the *Telegraph*. She also writes for the *Independent*, the *Guardian*, lonelyplanet.com, *Lonely Planet Magazine, French Magazine, Cool Camping France* and others. Catch her on the road on Twitter and Instagram @tripalong.

Contributing Writer

Damian Harper researched and wrote the Giverny content. Damian has been writing for Lonely Planet for over two decades, covering destinations including China, Vietnam, Thailand, Ireland and London.

STAY.IN TOUCH LONELYPLANET.COM/CONTACT

AUSTRALIA The Malt Store, Level 3, 551 Swanston St, Carlton, Victoria 3053 ☎03 8379 8000, fax 03 8379 8111

IRELAND Digital Depot, Roe Lane (off Thomas St), Digital Hub, Dublin 8, D08 TCV4, Ireland

USA 124 Linden Street, Oakland, CA 94607 ☎510 250 6400, toll free 800 275 8555, fax 510 893 8572

UK 240 Blackfriars Road, London SE1 8NW ☎020 3771 5100, fax 020 3771 5101

 twitter.com/lonelyplanet   facebook.com/lonelyplanet   instagram.com/lonelyplanet   youtube.com/lonelyplanet   lonelyplanet.com/newsletter